THE POLITICS OF JESÚS

Religion in the Modern World

Series Advisors

Kwok Pui-lan, Episcopal Divinity School Joerg Rieger, Southern Methodist University

This series explores how various religious traditions wrestle with the dynamic and changing role of religion in the modern world and examines how past changes reflect on today's critical issues. Accessibly and engagingly written, books in this series will look at secularization, global society, gender, race, class, sexuality and their relation to religious life and religious movements.

Titles in the Series

THE POLITICS OF JESÚS

A Hispanic Political Theology

Miguel A. De La Torre

ROWMAN & LITTLEFIELD
Lanham • Boulder • New York • London

Published by Rowman & Littlefield
A wholly owned subsidary of The Rowman & Littlefield Publishing Group,
Inc.
4501 Forbes Boulevard, Suite 200, Lanham, Maryland 20706
www.rowman.com

Unit A, Whitacre Mews, 26-34 Stannary Street, London SE11 4AB

British Library Cataloguing in Publication Information Available

Library of Congress Cataloging-in-Publication Data

De La Torre, Miguel A.
The politics of Jesús : a hispanic political theology / Miguel A. De La Torre.
pages cm. — (Religion in the modern world)
Includes bibliographical references and index.
ISBN 978-1-4422-5035-2 (cloth : alk. paper) — ISBN 978-1-4422-5036-9 (pbk. : alk. paper) —
ISBN 978-1-4422-5037-6 (electronic)
1. Jesus Christ—Hispanic American interpretations. 2. Liberation theology. 3. Marginality, Social—Religious aspects—Christianity. I. Title.
BT304.918.D4 2015
232.089'68073—dc23
2015017834

Printed in the United States of America

To: The Ethicists Responsible for my
Early Formation

Glenn Stassen, my first ethics professor who stressed the importance of faith

John Raines, the chair of my dissertation committee who introduced me to the intersection of postmodern and postcolonial thought with ethics

Katie Cannon, dissertation member who expanded my understanding of liberationist ethical thought to include those on my margins

Allen Verhey, who pushed a reluctant institution to hire me at my first teaching post

CONTENTS

ACKNOWLEDGMENTS

I am deeply grateful to the honor students and faculty of the Religion Department at the University of Johannesburg in South Africa. During the fall of 2014, they invited me to be a visiting professor and provided a comfortable house where I could write. While there, I wrote the bulk of this book. Free from distractions, I had time to think deeply about who and what Jesus is to the Hispanic community and to me personally. The hospitality shown to me while in South Africa made this book possible. A special thanks is offered to the department chair, Farid Esack, and faculty members Lily Nortje-Meyer, Hennie Viviers, Shahid Mathee, and Maria Fraham-Arp. They gave generously of their time, taking me to different parts of the city and teaching me what it meant to live in the "new South Africa." They proved to be excellent conversation partners, providing valuable feedback after reading early rough drafts of this manuscript. I am also grateful to the AbuBakr Karolia family for opening their home to me, and to Maurice Jacquesson, Mohamed Ismael, and K. Ashraf, who were kind enough to spend much time showing me around the country.

This trip was also made possible thanks to the Iliff School of Theology, who provided me with the funds to travel and the release time to teach abroad. Specifically, I want to thank the president, Thomas V. Wolfe, and the dean of academic affairs, Albert Hernández for their vision to make Iliff a truly international institution. And finally, I need to thank my family, especially my wife from whom I was separated for several months while I was teaching abroad. I am deeply grateful for her belief in the work I do.

FOREWORD

In 1992 I dissolved my thirteen-year-old real estate company and moved to Louisville, Kentucky, to begin a seminary education at "the" Southern Baptist Theological Seminary. An avowed capitalist, a conservative Christian, and an activist in rightwing Republican politics in Miami (who ran in 1988 for the Florida House of Representatives), I now wanted to become a pastor, hoping to make a difference in the world for the cause of Jesus Christ. I wanted to embody the Good News of Jesus within society by making a political move toward what I, at the time, defined as a fairer and more equitable society. In short, I wanted to claim the United States for Jesus! While at Southern, I took the required ethics class that was then taught by Glen Stassen. Prior to entering his classroom, I erroneously equated ethics with a review of a pastoral code of behavior focused on personal piety; a do's and don'ts list for future ministers. If I'm honest, I was not looking forward to such a discussion, but it was, after all, required for graduation. To my pleasant surprise, the class Stassen taught instead challenged me to think deeper on the role of humans, specifically Christians, within society. What is our responsibility, our duty, as people of faith, to the culture in which we live?

During my studies, Southern Baptist Theological Seminary was in turmoil. When I graduated in 1995, the fundamentalists, under the leadership of incoming president Al Mohler, literally took over the power structures of the seminary. Ironically, as the seminary moved to the conservative far right, I started tilting toward the far left, becoming at the end, a self-identifying liberation theologian. My conversion occurred in the school library, long after all my class assignments were completed, reading the works of South American liberation theologians that were never assigned in class. The takeover of the seminary (which I first supported, only to deeply regret said support as my consciousness was raised by the time I graduated) became a hostile environment for professors who made students think beyond simplistic answers and supposed doctrinal truths. They were either purged or they "voluntarily" left before the inevitable. Not surprisingly, Stassen was among the first to leave Southern. As for myself, unable to find a pastoral assignment within a rightward moving denominational milieu, I did what any unemployed college student does: I pursued my PhD.

Years passed, I obtain my doctoral at Temple University under the tutelage of ethicists Katie Cannon and John Raines and started teaching social ethics at Hope College in Holland, Michigan, thanks mainly to ethicist Allen Verhey. It wasn't long before Stassen and I reconnected at the Society of Christian Ethics. He honored me by offering an invitation to teach a summer course in 2003 at Fuller Theological Seminary. During this time, I had the opportunity to get to know him better. One sunny California day, while walking through Fuller's campus, Stassen rode up on his bike. He stopped and we began an impromptu conversation on the concept of needing a "thicker Jesus," a theme that he was at the time developing. He was concerned that the discourse of ethics used a Jesus that was way too thin and anemic for his liking. He argued that Jesus is thickened when the faithful move beyond compartmentalizing Jesus, relegating him to religious rituals and events and, instead, make him Lord over every aspect of their life. Only then can one participate in what he called "incarnated discipleship" as modeled by individuals like Dietrich Bonhoeffer and Martin Luther King Jr.

That Sunday I visited Stassen's Sunday school class where his lecture paid close attention to the Sermon on the Mount. Obviously, Stassen grounds his ethical thinking on the biblical text, believing that the Bible can provide realistic guidance in dealing with a broad set of ethical dilemmas faced by humanity. Since that summer, Stassen has consistently challenged me to thicken my own Jesus. Others, more disturbingly, have argued that the liberation theological project does not seriously consider Jesus; rather, the social justice it seeks is more a faithful response to the Enlightenment Project than it is to the Gospel. For Christians to participate in such justice-based praxis is to become complicit with the hegemonic liberalism of the world (Hauerwas 1997:190–91, 195).

Not surprisingly, it has become popular among comfortable Euroamerican churches (and churches of marginalized communities seeking assimilation) to preach a Gospel that requires no quest for justice. Such churches follow the ancient practice of voiding the teachings concerning God for the sake of some orthodox tradition. We can witness this practice during the time of Jesus when religious leaders circumvented the commandment of honoring one's mother and father by declaring that the money that was to be used to help their parents was instead *Corban*, "devoted to God," thus forbidding them to use it for their parents' care. "You hypocrites!" Jesus thundered as he quoted the prophet Isaiah, "You honor me with your lips, but your hearts are far away. You worship me in vain, but your teachings are merely human rules" (Mk. 7:8–13).[1] Likewise, today's religious leaders nullify the call of the good news of Jesus by circumventing his teaching concerning justice with a sectarian call to simply be the church, to simply be religious, or simply make a public acceptance of Jesus as one's savior, or simply follow some personal piety code.

In a perverted twist of Scripture, the argument is made that emphasizing justice, as a primary norm that guides the Christian witness, is a mistake (Hauerwas 1991:45). To ask why the least among us are hungry, thirsty, naked, undocumented, lacking health care, or caught up in the prison-industrial complex is somehow not the task of the church. Instead, the church is supposed to remain aloof to "political change and justice," as well as "progressive forces" (Hauerwas 1985:185), because justice-based praxis, in the final analysis, is but a gesture (Ibid.:186).

When we consider, as sociologist Robert Bellah did, that "individualism lies at the very core of American culture . . . deeply rooted in America's social history" (1985:142, 147); we should not be surprised when this hyper-individualistic culture focuses on a self-centered Christianity. Individual faith to a personal Savior based on correct doctrine trumps communal responsibilities to the God of humanity that is based on correct actions. Being a Christian has less to do with what one says or thinks and more to do with what one does in relation to the least among us. But while the church slumbers in the light, Jesus gazes with compassion upon the needy multitudes that are harassed and helpless before oppressive structures, for they are like sheep without a shepherd. His words to his disciples are as true today as when he first uttered them, "The harvest is plentiful but there are few laborers. Ask then the Lord of the harvest to send more laborers to the fields" (Mt. 9:36–38).

This book is an evangelical call for laborers to harvest among the harassed and helpless, serving with Jesus as shepherds in solidarity with lost sheep seeking a more just social order. What I hope to do in this book is demonstrate to the critics of liberative ethical approaches, who claim we Christian liberationists ignore Jesus and his narrative by exchanging the good news for some enlightenment quest for human rights and justice, that our work is instead deeply rooted in the Jesus story. The problem is that these critics don't recognize the Jesus that Hispanic Christians follow. My Jesus is already thick, thank you very much, demonstrated by an employed praxis for social justice that signals the outward expression of an inward conversion to this Jesus. This book will argue that the sure sign of a Christian apostate is someone who verbally claims Jesus but fails to produce just fruits by rejecting to follow his radical call to praxis.

The goal of this book is to delineate a biography of Jesus as understood by marginalized Hispanics; recognizing the reality that all biographies of Jesus reflect more the life of the author and her or his social location than most authors are usually willing to admit. As I embark on this venture, I am reminded of the words of Brazilian liberation theologian Leonardo Boff: "No matter how much [authors] attempt to abstract from themselves as subjects, they can never escape the self and arrive at the object. For this reason, every life of Jesus will necessarily partly reflect the life of the author. . . . [I]n defining Christ we are defining ourselves. The more we know ourselves, the more we can know Jesus. . . . [W]e ought to speak of Jesus Christ, not with a view to defining him but rather ourselves, not the mystery but our position when confronted with the mystery" (1978:5, 32, 47). And here is the starting assumption of this book that differs from other books written by so many Euroamericans. While they present a so-called objective biography of Jesus, I unapologetically and with willful intent present a subjective biography. I simply claim what they deny they also do.[2]

INTRODUCTION
Jesus or Jesús?

In his 1972 groundbreaking book, *The Politics of Jesus*, Howard Yoder, a pacifist Mennonite, attempts to fill the gap between biblical exegesis and contemporary social ethics by providing us with what he deemed to be a nonconformist messianic ethics based on a Christology where Jesus serves as a model for radical political action. Employing biblical realism, Yoder presents us with a Jesus that resonates with many Euroamericans. While I appreciate Yoder's methodology, I remain troubled by the conclusions of his Christology, specifically the construction of the politics of a (pacifist Mennonite) Jesus. In all honesty, we should not be surprised, for we all create Jesus in our own image. Christology at times tells us more about the culture from which the Jesus narrative is interpreted than anything specific about who historically or theologically was Jesus. If this is true, then all the Jesuses constructed serve the important function of uniting people into communities that share a similar Christian-based worldview. Christian groups spanning different eras, occupying different geographical locations, and comprised of different ethnic and/or racial groups all created a Jesus that gave meaning to their particularity while justifying their political actions, especially if those political actions ended up being oppressive.

The Jesus creators, in their cosmic fight against whomever they designated to be the enemies of Jesus, all too often have implemented oppressive structures that politically protect privileges amassed. One simply needs to think of the witch burnings, the Inquisition, the crusades, the conquistadores, or the militarism of *pax americana* for examples of a Jesus created by political leaders to justify repression and subjugation. In an earlier work co-authored with historian Albert Hernández, we claimed that "No evil ever dreamed-up by Satan can outdo the atrocities committed by good, decent people attempting to purge such evil forces from this world. . . . Some of the most diabolical actions, enough to make the very demons of Hell cringe in shame, are committed by those who consider themselves to be righteous chosen ones in the spiritual battle against the forces of evil" (2011:8).

How Jesus has been constructed throughout history by those wielding political power is probably responsible for most of the misery and bloodletting experienced by humanity. Native American religion scholar George "Tink" Tinker, wrestling with the role Jesus played in the lives of his people, concludes that liberation for indigenous folk begins with a clear understanding that Jesus, in whose name well-intending missionaries justified cultural and physical genocide, is not the answer. Salvation for those crushed under Christendom begins by saying no to Jesus (2004:243). How can the symbolic justifier of so much global oppression ever be redemptive? Can Jesus be saved from Jesus? The insightful popular social commentator, Woody Allen, probably said it best in the movie which he wrote and directed, *Hannah and Her Sisters* (1986): "If Jesus Christ came back today and saw what was being done in his name, he'd never stop throwing up."

I hold no desire to become an apologist for all the horror done in Jesus' name. Only the ignoramus ignores the chasm that separates the history of humanity from how Christians remember their place in that history, full of the bodies of those labeled enemies of the true faith. It is tempting for me to wash my hands of Jesus and seek some other foundation upon which to build ethical liberative thought, a path several of my colleagues have taken, and in all honesty, who can blame them. As I peruse the historical record or simply read today's daily newspaper, I am struck with how hopeless is the situation for today's marginalized, not only for those claiming faith in Jesus, but pretty much everybody else. Neoliberalism,[1] and the oppressive political structures designed to economically privilege the few, seems to have won. So why, then, insist on holding on to a Jesus that seems so complicit with, or mute concerning, the neoliberal economic consequences under which the vast masses of humanity are forced to endure?

We live in a nation where the rich are getting richer, and the poor are slipping into greater stomach wrenching poverty. By 1999, at the close of the century, the top 1 percent of U.S. taxpayers each had on average $862,700 after taxes, more than triple what they had in 1979. Meanwhile, the bottom 40 percent had $21,118 each, up by 13 percent from their average $18,695 in 1979 (all numbers adjusted for inflation). And while median household incomes reached their peak that year at $53,252, nevertheless, the year 2000 proved to have the greatest economic disparity since 1979, when the U.S. Budget Office began collecting such data. The National Bureau of Economic Research, a nonpartisan, nonprofit research group, claimed that the top 1 percent enjoyed by the close of the millennium the largest share of before-tax income for any year since 1929. For the next decade, all incomes, except for the ultra-rich steadily dropped. By 2010, real median household income dropped by 7.1 percent to $49,445, literally wiping out almost two decades of accumulated prosperity, according to the Federal Reserve.[2]

The U.S. poverty rate in 2012 was 15 percent, with 46.5 million people (the largest number in 54 years) living in scarcity.[3] Meanwhile, the richest 10 percent share of market income captured surged from 30 percent in 1980 to 48 percent by 2012, while the share of the richest 1 percent increased from 8 percent to 19 percent. More disturbing is the fourfold increase in the income share of the richest 0.1 percent, from 2.6 percent to 10.4 percent.[4] The share of income that goes to the top 1 percent within the United States is higher than in any other developed country (a rise of 135 percent from 1980 to 2007).[5] Because the 1 percent controls the vast majority of the wealth, by extension, they also control the political systems that protect their riches.

The consequences of a growing income gap are not limited to the United States. The neoliberal economic policies that undergird the wealth accumulation of the top 1 percent within the United States make an economically disproportionate world possible, responsible for much of the planet's poverty, hunger, destitution, and death. We live in a world where during the 2010–2012 period, 850 million people (or 12.5 percent of the global population) were malnourished (FAO, 2012:8). In 2010, of the seven billion inhabiting the earth, about 1.75 billion people in 104 countries (about a third of their population) lived in multidimensional poverty, reflecting acute deprivation in health, education, and standard of living. This block of the population exceeds the 1.44 billion people in those countries who live on $1.25 a day or less, but not the 2.6 billion living on $2 a day or less. The 2008 Great Recession only exacerbated the situation, pushing 64 million more people under the $1.25-a-day poverty threshold. In Africa alone, it is estimated that an additional 30,000 to 50,000 children died as a direct result of the 2008 financial crises (UNDP, 2010:78, 80, 96).

Global inequality is at its highest levels in twenty years. While it is true that in recent decades the world has made dramatic progress in cutting global deaths of children and improving their opportunities, nonetheless, in 32 developed countries, the rich increased their share of national income since the 1990s while in a fifth of the countries, the incomes of the poorest fell over the same period (Espey et al. 2012:vi–x). This has led Save the Children's chief executive, Justin Forsyth, to conclude: "Unless inequality is addressed . . . any future development framework will simply not succeed in maintaining or accelerating progress. What's more, it will hold individual countries—and the world—back from experiencing real growth and prosperity."[6] In spite of these immoral and unethical global and national economic conditions, the Jesus of Empire that undergirds this economic structure lacks the credibility to challenge the status quo. For those who attend Eurocentric Christian churches, think of the last time the sermon message dealt with income inequality or the growing wage gap. More than likely these sermons never touched on economic justice; rather, emphasis was placed on learning how to live a more joyous life in Christ or walk closer with Jesus or even how to faithfully tithe. When we think that the main message of the biblical prophets usually revolved around the theme of economic justice, or that Jesus spoke more about money than any other topic, we are left dumbfounded as to why churches within prosperous nations like the United States, who claim to be Bible-believing disciples of Jesus, seldom broach one of the main themes (if not the main theme) of the biblical text.

And even if the church does discuss economic justice, the Jesus they present usually calls for reform without questioning the very economical foundation of neoliberalism or if the prevailing global economic model is beyond reform. If one of the foundational messages of capitalism, as expressed by Adam Smith, is that by placing one's self-interest first, the general welfare is promoted,[7] then how do we reconcile this with the foundational message of the New Testament of placing the interest of others before oneself?[8] We are left asking if capitalism and Christianity are compatible or irreconcilable. Could it be that the Jesus who supports "the American way" is in reality an anti-Christ? I am left wondering where the pathos of indignation is over the acceptance of the Jesus of Empire by Latina/os (and other marginalized communities). Hispanics seeking to be subjects instead become self-subjugated when they uncritically bow and kneel before the Lord Jesus whose silence makes him complicit with Empire.

And yet, Jesus' purpose is to serve, not be served (Mt. 20:28); even to the point of washing the feet, as if a slave, of his disciples (Jn. 13:5). I argue that the purpose of religious and theological critical thought concerning the personhood of Jesus is neither to perceive the mysteries of the metaphysical nor to deductively ascertain a list of dogmatic truths and ethical acts to unquestionably follow. After washing his disciples' feet, Jesus states that they are right to call him teacher and Lord. Now, if a servant is not greater than the master, then they, the disciples should do likewise and serve (Jn. 13:13–17). Hence, the purpose of religious and theological critical thought concerning the personhood of Jesus is to serve humanity by transforming the normative oppressive social structures to a more justice-based reality preached by Jesus. Why is this important? Because the purpose of humanity is unconditional liberation, freedom from all oppressive structures so that humans can live to their full potential. In fact, one cannot be ethically responsible unless one is radically liberated, for the guilt of participation in the unethical in order to physically survive blotches the souls of those whom oppressive structures benefit, not those whom they victimize. If the hungry, who are refused a living wage, steal from the employer to feed themselves and their children, they have not sinned; rather, the sinner is the employer who robs the worker of their humanity by refusing to pay a living wage, thus providing the laborer no alternative but to take their rightful share from the employer, even if the employer calls it theft and even if the employer employs the power of the state to legitimize their interpretation of the term "theft." The struggle for unconditional liberation is the process that transforms human-as-object to human-as-subject. To be denied liberation, in the final analysis, is to be denied one's humanity.

If this is true, then what the wretched of the world need is a Jesus that serves not paternalistically, but in solidarity, as one who also comes from the underside of global power and thus understands the plight of those negatively impacted by oppressive social and cultural structures. The modest project in which we'll engage in this book will be a quest for a Jesus not captured by the dominant culture, for such a Jesus cannot serve Hispanics well; rather, we search for a Jesus that resonates specifically with the U.S. Latina/o community (with the hope that this Jesus will also resonate with other marginalized groups). In short, this book unapologetically rejects the Eurocentric Jesus for the Hispanic Jesús.[9] Because all Christologies are contextual, not all contexts can be conceived as liberating for Hispanics. In fact, many contexts (specifically the context of the U.S. dominant culture) have historically proven to be quite oppressive. Jesus may be desirable, but not all Jesuses are beneficial.

Hispanics (as well as Euroamericans) must avoid the Jesus of history that launched crusades to exterminate so-called Muslim infidels; the sexist Jesus that burned women seeking self-autonomy as witches; the genocidal Jesus who decimated indigenous people who refused to bow and kneel to the European White God; the capitalist Jesus who justified kidnapping, raping, and enslaving Africans; and today's neoliberal Jesus that is ignorant to the pauperization of two-thirds of the world's population so that a small minority of the planet can consider themselves blessed. It is these Jesuses, as James Cone would remind us, that are satanic (2010:10). To say no to oppression and its symbol (even when that symbol is Jesus) is the first step toward saying yes to the self, yes to liberation, and yes to the Hispanic symbols of that liberation (of which, this book argues, Jesús is one such symbol). Because liberation is never a given (oppressors never willingly give up their power and privilege), it is a goal toward which humanity struggles, where Jesús, at least for Hispanics, as a symbol of liberation, can inform the strategic political praxis that require implementation. For Jesús to be congruent with the Hispanic quest for liberation from oppressive structures, Jesús must unashamedly be Hispanic.[10]

There is no one true Jesus that can be objectively known; there only exists subjective interpretations of Jesus. The social, cultural, political, and global economic power of Euroamericans allows them to impose their subjective interpretation of Jesus as the objective Truth (with a capital T) for everyone else, including Latino/as. What would happen if, rather than denying that we do indeed create Jesus in our own image, we embrace this methodology? What if we recognize that there is no such thing as some universal Jesus upon which every Christian can agree? What if we radically employ a hermeneutical suspicion to Christology—not simply to debunk the normative Eurocentric understanding of Jesus but to construct a new Jesus? If Yoder could give us a pacifist Mennonite Jesus created in his own image, why then can I not provide us with a liberative Hispanic Jesús created in my and my community's image? The difference is that while Yoder made his subjective Jesus objective for all people, I recognize that my Jesus, or better yet, my Jesús, is definitively subjective. While I may hope that some of the traits of my Jesús might resonate with other disenfranchised communities, I lack the hubris to claim that my constructed Jesús is universal for all.

I propose that we engage in creating a Jesus that resonates with our particular marginalized community (for me, it would obviously be a Latina/o community). But rather than focusing on some essentialized characteristics of what it means to be Hispanic, I will argue for a preferential option in the creation of Jesús. Whoever this Jesús ends up being, it is a Jesús whose mission is to give life and give life abundantly (Jn. 10:10). Jesús, as the symbolic representation of Emmanuel (God with us), resonates with the Latino/a existential experience of disenfranchisement and commits, in solidarity, to walk toward a more just social order. And yes, while I recognize that not all Hispanics are monolithically dispossessed, the Jesús being constructed here focuses only on those relegated to the underside of history and those who stand in solidarity with them (including Euroamericans seeking their own liberation and salvation). The Jesús of privileged Hispanics is no different from the Jesus of the dominant culture that justifies a status quo detrimental to the disenfranchised and, thus, for the sake of our own salvation, must be rejected.

No doubt a danger exists in our quest for a Jesús created in the image of Latino/as, where twenty-first century ideas of the Hispanic community are projected upon a two thousand-year-old historical figure in order to justify the praxis our community advocates. While every interpretation of Jesus or Jesús reflects the life of the author, our task is to remain as faithful as possible to the biblical narrative while exploring aspects of the text that might indicate how Jesús would understand and sympathize with the plight of today's Latino/as. In defiance of Rudolf Bultmann, we must not hesitate to reconstruct the story of Jesús because of the shortcomings of historical exegesis, thus solely concentrating on the Christ of faith. Reading the text with our own Hispanic eyes has the potential of freeing the text from the institutionalized Eurocentric church by reinterpreting the text through a more liberative lens.

This approach moves beyond historical criticism so that the text can address issues of power relations and the doctrines created to mask those relations.

The purpose of this book is to develop an understanding about the character of a Jesús rooted within the U.S. Hispanic disenfranchised milieu that can lead toward liberative praxis. But not abstract liberative praxis: rather, praxis with a political vision (something liberation theologians have not done very well) that can serve as a roadmap toward justice. The Christology this book embraces and, in fact, the liberative theological and ethical discourses in which we engage, is not the sole perview of the intellectuals. Liberation-type theological and ethical works cannot allow themselves to be captured by seminaries and universities, a perspective to solely comprehend. The liberative work proposed here is rooted in actual acts and requires a doing that takes these perspectives out of the classroom and into the streets. This is a methodology that relies more on dirtying one's hands in the struggle for justice than on the presentation of scholarly papers in the safety of five-star hotel conference rooms where academic symposiums are usually held, or the security of sectarian churches where preaching is only heard by the choir.

Before we totally reject the Jesus of the dominant culture, allow me to begin by clearly stating why I find the questions raised by Yoder important. Christian thinkers all too often ignore the Good News of Jesus (in my case, the Good News of the liberation proclaimed by Jesús). Since the beginning of the twentieth century, Christian thinkers from the dominant Eurocentric culture have moved away from considering the actions (the praxis) that should be employed whenever an ethical dilemma is faced. Instead, Christians devote too much of their energies to issues that deal with the ethereal, specifically abstract questions concerning what is virtue and what is the good. Pursuing such philosophical truths, I believe, makes Jesus the first casualty of Eurocentric Christian thought. Jesus is not a thought—Jesús is a praxis. The question Christian thinkers encounter is not to determine some abstract understanding of what should be done, but rather, in the face of dehumanizing oppressive structures and hopeless no-win situations, how do people of faith adapt their actions to serve the least among us. Rather than reducing the Christian ethical discourse to explaining what is or is not ethical, Christian ethics becomes the process by which the marginalized enter a more human condition, overcoming the societal mechanisms that relegate them to history's underside.

The second concept articulated by Yoder with which I resonate is that the biblical text has something important to say about ethical dilemmas faced by those who claim to be followers of Jesus. While I recognize that the biblical text is not for everyone, and that at times is highly problematic—advocating sexism, classism, ethnic cleansing, and heterosexism—still, within its pages I believe are liberative gems that can propel humanity toward justice. The quest then is to avoid the dominant culture's biblical read that might be complicit with the uncritical hermeneutics held by those with power and privilege. The audience of this book is therefore those who believe Jesus the Christ can make a moral contribution to the establishment of justice. And even if the reader rejects Jesus as Lord, participates in a different religious tradition, or claims to be a humanist, agnostic, or atheist, the fact remains that how Jesus has been constructed for the past two millenniums undergirds a global worldview that impacts everybody, especially as the religious justifier of conquerors and colonizers. More importantly, to ignore Jesus-speak is to ignore signified words and terms by which a majority of those with power and privilege constructed a worldview that they claim to be moral and just. How Jesus is imagined provides language and symbols for the disenfranchised, which the dominant U.S. culture understands, which could foster a comprehensible conversation concerning justice. Regardless of any faith or lack of faith in Jesus, it behooves all of us to imagine and construct a Jesús that stands in solidarity with the wretched of the earth for liberation over and against neoliberal oppression. The focus of the book challenges all, believer and nonbeliever, to read the biblical text through Hispanic eyes that belong to the dispossessed, the disinherited, the disenfranchised, the disempowered for the sake of actively moving toward a more just and humane society.

So, while I totally agree with the exercise of paying closer attention to Jesus to inform how we deal morally and ethically within a world stifled with oppression and repression, my only question is whose Jesus are we to pay closer attention, whose Jesus are we to remember? A danger exists in constructing a Eurocentric Jesus when Jesus is uncritically remembered through a romanticized understanding of what was the early church. Scholars like Allen Verhey call us to remember Jesus by remembering the early church's remembering Jesus so that today's congregations "can discern the shape and style of lives 'worthy of the gospel' (Ph. 1:27) and 'in memory of Jesus' (cf. 1 Co. 11:24–25)" (2002:13). But how much of what we say was the early church's remembering of Jesus but an imposition of some unified pristine consensus of what is accepted as remembered? Can we, today, with any certainty know what they remembered? And whose memory do we consider: the memory that won the internal Christian power struggles of that time? What about the different memories of Jesus that were labeled unorthodox and silenced? If indeed knowledge is a product of power, then how much of the knowledge we claim to possess about how the early church remembered Jesus tells us more about those who won the early church power struggles than anything about who Jesus actually was?

For the dominant Eurocentric culture today to maintain the position of Subject whose remembrance of Jesus is superior and truer than any interpretation arising from their margins, they must operate within, what postcolonialist Homi Bhabha terms, the "syntax of forgetting" (1994:160–61). Dominance that appears normal and legitimate requires epic tales of triumph, heroic figures, and awe-inspiring achievements. Remembering a false construct of the early church elevates the dominant culture's production of Christian knowledge while dismissing and/ or silencing the remembering done by their Other. How Euroamericans remember Jesus, or their interpretation of the early church's remembrance of Jesus, creates a dominant narrative that not only disguises the complex political forces responsible for bringing forth Christianity and its understanding of Jesus; but more important, it suppresses differences based on racial, ethnic, and class divisions or conflicts.

All too often, remembering Jesus as articulated within traditional Eurocentric Christian institutions tends to justify, legitimize, and normalize oppression. Jesus and the Eurocentric construction of Jesus that is mute to dysfunctional complicity with structures of oppression is too often fused and confused during the remembering process. Hispanics (and other disenfranchised communities) need to be careful about uncritically adopting a Eurocentric Jesus that might be detrimental to their marginalized social location. For those in power to remain in power, a constructed Jesus is needed that either explicitly or implicitly maintains the status quo. Even when such a Jesus is critical of political power or privilege, little if any praxis is put forward to dismantle the mechanism responsible for maintaining oppressive societal structures. Usually, cosmetic reforms are offered, indicative of not seriously considering structural forms of injustices or social sin. As long as oppressive social structures persist, actions by individuals, no matter how well intended, are incapable of liberating those existing on the margins of society. Worse, some Eurocentric Christian thinkers denounce and discard the implementation of any praxis that could lead to a more just social order as an error, as in the case of ethicist Stanley Hauerwas who proclaims, "The current emphasis on justice and rights as the primary norms guiding the social witness of Christians is in fact a mistake" (1991:45).

The failure of many well-meaning Euroamerican religious scholars is their lack of hermeneutical suspicion, how their interpretation might reflect more their societal complicity with oppression than they are willing to admit. While they accuse scholars of color in general, Latina/os in particular, for not paying much attention to the Jesus narrative, or for advocating a very thin Jesus, they ignore how their own Jesus, more often than not, advocates an individualistic, subjective, liberal bourgeois spirituality that justifies their power and privilege within society as God's will for the good of all. Reading Scripture from a position of "objectivity" becomes a myth constructed to protect the privileged space of those with power to claim their subjective interpretations as objective. So for example, when Eurocentric scholars read in their biblical texts of Jesus' condemnation of the rich over and against the poor, the text must be reinterpreted so as not to challenge the privileged space many of these same scholars hold within society. Hence, the text is spiritualized to insist that Jesus really was talking about the spiritual poor, and thus even the rich are spiritually poor and hence among the chosen.

To suggest such Eurocentric interpretations concerning Jesus are at the very least problematic is to be written off as being too subjective (or too angry) and refusing to employ interpretational methodologies accepted by an academy deeply rooted in Eurocentric thought, regardless of the ethnicity or skin pigmentation of the one participating in the discourse. Eurocentric subjectivity is usually masked as academically or spiritually superior, purer than any reading that comes from their periphery. A Eurocentric Jesus, no matter how appealing or seductive he may seem to be, cannot save Latino/a Christians who come from a very different social context. Only a Hispanic Jesús can save them; hence the title of this book: *The Politics of Jesús*, with the accent mark placed over the letter *u*.

An attempt is made here to literally do Christology with an accent— and not just over the *u*, but also the linguistic accent of Hispanics attempting to speak the language of the Empire. The gospel recounts the story of Pedro, who, incognito, sneaks into the courtyard of the high priest after the arrest of Jesús to see what will become of him. While there, he is recognized as one of Jesús' disciples, not by appearance, but by his Galilean accent. "Surely you are one of the followers of Jesús, *your accent gives you away*" (Mt. 26:73). We Hispanics who speak with a "funny" accent know all too well how we are "given away" whenever we open our mouth. To speak with an accent, unable to speak a pure English (whatever that is) has been internalized as a mark of shame. And yet, in this book, not only will we embrace our accent, we will proudly ensure that Jesús is also heavily accented.

Why is Jesús, over and against Jesus important? Because the Euroamerican Jesus has historically been used (or muted) to divinely justify societal actions that have silently contributed to or loudly maintained the marginalization of U.S. Hispanics. The Euroamerican Jesus is the Jesus of President James Polk, who following the quasi-religious ideology of Manifest Destiny, led the United States in the military conquest of northern Mexico, preventing the future ability of that nation to build wealth, and disenfranchised those for whom the border "crossed over." The Euroamerican Jesus is the Jesus of Theodore Roosevelt who instigated a "gunboat" diplomacy that denied Latin American nations their sovereignty and provided U.S. corporations the freedom of and protection for extracting the cheap labor and natural resources of a people. These first imperialist steps resulted in the pauperization and migration to the United States of Spanish-speaking peoples from Central America and the Caribbean northward. The Euroamerican Jesus is the Jesus of present day presidents and politicians (conservative and liberal) whose main purpose is the maintenance of U.S. global hegemony. This Jesus is silent as tens of thousands of Brown bodies die along our southern border, attempting to follow the resources and cheap labor stolen from their home nations. Or the millions of undocumented Latina/os who live in the shadows of Empire because their labor is wanted but not their physical presence.

Latina/os are not saved by the Bible but by the justice-based praxis that can be rooted in the reading of the Bible, a reading done through Hispanic eyes. Such readings require a turn away from Eurocentric theological triumphalism. For the salvation of Hispanics to occur, they might need to say no to the Euroamerican Jesus. The Jesus presented to Hispanics by well-meaning Euroamerican scholars and clergy is incongruent with the Hispanic culture, and as such, detrimental and destructive. To accomplish the task of becoming a Christian disciple, I must first reject Jesus and make a preferential option for a Jesús who provides my particular Latino/a community (as well as other marginalized communities) with realistic spiritually based political praxis that could lead us toward a more just social order.

As long as Latino/as bow and kneel to a White, blond, blue-eyed Jesus who is silent about what it means to live at the margins of Euroamerican power and privilege and as long as this Jesus refuses to motivate action among Euroamerican churches to speak out about what the marginalized face throughout the *barrios* of this nation and as long as this Jesus does not elicit Euroamericans to stand in solidarity with the thousands who die in the Sonora desert of Arizona because of unjust immigration laws that target Brown bodies, those Hispanics insisting on worshipping the Jesus that looks and acts like the dominant culture would in fact be worshipping the symbolic cause of their oppression. Our goal is more than simply creating a Jesús that looks Hispanic (whatever looking Latina/o means) for the sake of political correctness. The thick Jesús called for understands what it means to be Hispanic and thus has something important to say to the marginalized, a message that is usually indecipherable to those accustomed to their power and privilege.

In attempting to sever the link between the colonizer and the colonized, between power and disenfranchisement, between privilege and marginality, Jesús, and the politics derived from his being, must be recognized as ontologically Hispanic. Just as Euroamericans have for centuries worshipped a Jesus created in their own image, it becomes significant for Latina/os to also see and understand the Divine through ethnic Hispanic signs and symbols. In the name of this White Jesus, White Christian civilization is protected from so-called Hispanic inferiority, thus normalizing and legitimatizing in the eyes of White America the marginalization of Hispanics. The extent of the pervasiveness of this White Euroamerican Jesus can best be demonstrated through a colonialization of Hispanics' minds taught to not only worship the image of this Euroamerican Christ but also the social order it signifies.

Jesús' Latinoness is not due to some psychological need existing among Latina/os to see a Divine through their own cultural signs. Jesús is Hispanic because the biblical witness of God is of one who takes sides with the least among us against those who oppress them. The biblical Jesús, upon which Latino/as construct a messianic ethics is, like them,

Hispanic, informed by the historical identification of Jesus with those who suffer under oppression. But if we all create Jesus in our own image, are all manifestations of Jesus therefore relative? Are some Jesuses closer to the biblical witness? And if so, how do we decide which ones? The oppressed and marginalized have an epistemological privilege concerning reality unavailable to those who have no need to know what is occurring among those relegated to their underside. Not only must the marginalized learn how to function in a world where they lack the power and privilege unquestionably assumed by most from the dominant culture, they must also know how to survive within the confines of their own world. This double consciousness, à la W. E. B. Du Bois, and at times triple or quadruple consciousness, provides an insight to which an understanding of Jesus is closer to the intent of the biblical text. The Jesus interpreted by the dominant culture usually misses the mark when done from the center that is customarily privileged by society. We should never forget that all biblical hermeneutics are a constructed discourse, legitimized and normalized by those who have the ways and means of making their subjectivity objective. Those who have been born within and/or assimilated to a Euroamerican culture are products of a society where White supremacy and class privilege have historically been interwoven with how Americans have been conditioned to see and organize the religious world around them. Whether consciously or unconsciously, the racist and classist underpinning of the dominant culture influences how they develop and participate in their understanding of who Jesus was. Meanwhile, those who are oppressed understand, for the sake of their own survival, what it means to live in the world of the dominant culture as well as within their own culture; thus, they have a better grasp of reality than those of the dominant culture who have no need, incentive, or motivation to learn what it means to be Hispanic within the United States.

Religion scholars of color are required to master the theological and ethical analysis of Euroamericans in order to be awarded a coveted PhD, while no one from the dominant culture needs to learn anything about the Hispanic margins to earn that same degree. One can argue therefore that Latino/as (along with all who are marginalized) hold an epistemological privilege over and against Euroamericans. This does not mean they are smarter or holier, just that they master the world of the dominant culture and their own marginalized spaces. Hence, their understanding of Jesus is much broader, richer, thicker, and more complex than those who only master the official Eurocentric canon. The multiple consciousness possessed by the disenfranchised generally makes their perspectives closer to any type of "truth" than the opinions and views of those who benefit from how society is structured.

While this epistemological privilege makes it clear for Hispanics that the Eurocentric Jesus is problematic to their very being, they also realize and propose that the White Jesus is also impotent in bringing salvation for Euroamericans. In the famous biblical parable of the sheep and the goats (Mt. 25:31–46), Jesús divides those destined for glory (the sheep) from those destined for damnation (the goats). The salvation of those with power and privilege is contingent upon how they treated those who were starving, thirsty, aliens, unclothed, ill, and imprisoned—a space often occupied by Latina/os. The dominant culture finds its life (salvation) when it struggles along with those who are oppressed by attempting to alleviate, if not dismantle, the structures that, while benefitting from them, cause death among the disenfranchised. Crucial to the understanding of this passage is the radical revelation made by Jesús. At the end of the parable, he states: "Then [the Lord] will answer [the condemned], saying, 'Truly I say to you, inasmuch as you did not do for one of these, the least, neither did you do it to me'" (v. 45).

The question Latino/as must ask themselves is: Does the Euroamerican Jesus provide life and provide it abundantly for Hispanics (Jn. 10:10)? If history is any guide, the Euroamerican Jesus has mostly provided disenfranchisement, despair, and death. Again, salvation for Hispanics will never be found in the divine symbols of the Euroamerican culture. Consequently, only a Latina/o Jesús can liberate Hispanics. Why? Because Eurocentric Jesuses, no matter how benignly they are presented, will always be incongruent with the marginalized reality Latino/as are forced to occupy. To commune with a Hispanic Jesús is to incarnate the gospel message within the marginalized spaces of the *barrios* so that the actions and words of Jesús can infuse *la comunidad* (the community) with the hopeless hope of survival and liberation. For this reason, the Euroamerican Jesus that has served as the Hispanic anti-Christ, needs to be rejected for a Jesús constructed from within the Latino/a ethos.

Not only is the Latina/o Jesús salvific for Hispanics, it is also salvific for Euroamericans. If the Eurocentric Jesus of the dominant culture is responsible for spiritually justifying much of the oppressive structures faced by Hispanics and other non-White groups, then Euroamericans are at risk of worshipping a false messiah with no ability to save or redeem them, or anyone else for that matter. For the sake of their own salvation, Euroamericans must put away their Jesus idols and learn to walk in solidarity with the Jesús of the oppressed and the people with whom Jesús identified in the parable of the sheep and the goats. It is not enough to insist that a Euroamerican Jesus needs to be rejected. We must also envision how Jesús is incarnated in the historical social location of Latina/os. We begin by realizing that whatever Jesús means for Hispanics, he must be understood within the sociohistorical and the eco-political contexts of the Latina/o community of faith that is responding to the biblical message of liberation. From the underside of U.S. culture, where Hispanics (along with other communities of color) are forced to suffer under the yoke of domination, a quest for a Hispanic Jesús from the margins becomes a quest for liberation, liberation from racism and ethnic discrimination.

Why is it important to understand who Jesús is through the lens of Hispanics? By making those humbled by the dominant culture of Jesús' time the recipients of the Good News, Jesús emphasized the political edge of his message. Any quest for understanding Jesús within the U.S. political sphere requires making marginalized communities of color the starting point of all inquiries. This is not an attempt to romanticize Hispanic marginalization (for there is nothing romantic about disenfranchisement); rather, it is an attempt to understand Jesús as a unifying symbol for Latina/o Christians.[11] Whoever this Jesús is, Hispanics see him through their own eyes as being quite different from the Eurocentric Jesus. Following Yoder's lead, this book turns to the Gospels in order to discover who this Hispanic Jesús is and what, if anything, he has to say to Latino/as today. But before we explore the biblical text, it should be noted that when recalling the narratives of Jesús, I am not interested is searching for the historical Jesus. Attempting to prove the reliability of the Gospels as true is an intellectual luxury that provides fascinating speculations with no concrete conclusions. For Latina/os who are Christians, caught in oppressive relationships, the Jesús narrative is not read to determine if he really turned water into wine but rather to seek Jesús' face and discern a divine word that can sustain the spirit in the midst of hopeless disenfranchisement. We search for the politics of Jesús to find guidance as to what praxis can be implemented to realistically bring about a more just society, not solely for Hispanics, but for all. Hence, the narratives of Jesús are real. Not necessarily because they may have literally occurred as recorded by the early church, but because they reveal ethical precepts concerning God and God's call for love, mercy, and justice as understood by those who claimed to be disciples of Jesús. Remembering Jesús from the Hispanic margins is to read the narratives as *prima facie*, at face value that, nonetheless, require a certain (dis)membering in the remembering process. The goal is not to prove or disprove the narrative's validity; the goal is to learn what those who claim to be disciples of a Jesús constructed within our disenfranchised Latino/a context are to do politically. In a very real sense, this book attempts to answer Jesús' question to his disciples, "Who do you [Hispanics] say I am?" (Mt. 16:15).

I

FOR UNTO YOU IS BORN THIS DAY A LIBERATOR

During the early 1980s, as a young Latino in college, I decided one spring break to take a road trip to the Big Apple. I left Miami, Florida, and headed north toward New York City in my prized possession, a fiery red sports car. Somewhere on the New Jersey Turnpike, I was pulled over. I was politely informed that I was traveling five miles above the speed limit. The officer then proceeded to acquire my permission to search my vehicle. When I inquired as to the probable cause for this search, he responded that sports cars driven by Hispanic males with Dade County license plates were suspected of transporting cocaine to the northeast. Finding no narcotics, he simply gave me a speeding ticket. Before racial and ethnic profiling ever made the headlines, I learned what it meant to be a suspect simply for driving while "under the influence" of being Hispanic.[1] This was not the first time I was stopped and frisked by law enforcement. My very first encounter occurred when I was a fourteen-year-old-lad walking home after my night shift at Burger King, where I worked part-time. A police cruiser pulled up in front of me and, without asking permission, proceeded to search me. Finding nothing, he let me go, advising that I shouldn't be walking the streets so late at night. Today, most might find these two encounters and subsequent other stops by law enforcement troublesome, an abuse of power toward a young Hispanic. But if I am honest, "problematic" was more my reaction.

As a teenager continuing my walk home, and as a young adult driving to New York City, the same thought crossed my mind: "Thank God the police are being vigilant in protecting society from potential criminals." It wasn't anger that I felt for being ethnically profiled; rather, I was thankful the police were keeping the community safe. My mind was so colonized that I did not, I could not, see how my identity was being constructed through the gaze of those in authority (De La Torre 2013b:3–4). To accept the myth of my own inferiority as defined by those whom society empowers is madness. The insanity of accepting the criminality of Latino/a bodies leads to gratitude for the punishment doled out as I learned to domesticate my body to conform to a normalized and legitimized social order that accepted Hispanics as thuggish. In *Madness and Civilization*, the twentieth-century philosopher Michel Foucault looked to Philippe Pinel (liberator of the insane who were confined during the French Revolution), who established a moral system linked to the dominant middle-class understanding of the world. Those from lower classes who refused to conform to the way the middle class understood reality were seen as a threat. To reject what society accepts as true is insane. The danger of madness, nonconforming, had to be cured through "professionals" who constantly observed and judged, quick to mete out punishment for minor transgressions from the norm. Repetition of judgment and punishment continued until the one defined as "mad" internalized the proper behavior required to avoid further discipline. But it is not enough to simply internalize one's own discipline; the one being punished for failing to conform "must feel morally responsible for everything within him [or her] that may disturb morality and society, and must hold no one but [her- or] himself responsible for the punishment received" (1965:246).

Foucault provides us with the example of a "maniac" who had a habit of tearing off her clothes. The asylum keepers responded by giving her cold showers and placing her into straitjackets until she appeared "humiliated and dismayed." Fearing that the shame she felt might be transitory and her remorse superficial, the asylum director impressed a feeling of terror upon her, threatening her with harsher punishments. Foucault continues: "'Her repentance was announced by a torrent of tears which she shed for almost two hours.' The cycle is complete twice over: the transgression is punished and its author recognizes her guilt" (Ibid.:267–68). Like this woman, many Hispanics (myself included), through years of constant terror and punishment geared to make us conform to structures wherein we do not belong, have learned to be grateful for being relegated to the underside of those who are considered sane by society.

To a certain extent, physical punishment is really no longer needed. A simple gaze from those in authority should be enough. The police officer who gazed upon a young Latino male body is able, through the power of that gaze, to define it by aligning said body with how it is normatively constructed by society. This gaze can lead to a physical imprisonment of the Latino body[2] or to its psychological domestication as Foucault illustrated in *Discipline and Punish*, reintroducing us to the perfect prison paragon known as "panopticon." Foucault analyzes panopticon, as originated by eighteenth-century philosopher Jeremy Bentham, as a model prison designed to keep inmates under constant surveillance and scrutiny without their being aware of their observers. Theoretically, constant surveillance coupled with an inability of knowing when they are being watched reduces the inmates' bad behaviors, since they are always fearful of being caught. The gaze of the guard confers power to the observer while serving as a trap to those being observed, even when the surveillance is not constant. The mere possibility of being watched forces the object of the gaze to internalize the power relationship. The prisoners who are being subjected to a field of visibility assume responsibility for policing themselves (think of how you no longer speed up when the traffic light turns yellow, due to surveillance cameras at most city intersections). The prisoner assumes the power relationship in which he or she plays the roles of both disciplinarian and disciplined, becoming the principal enforcer of his or her own subjugation. Basically, prisoners learn to see themselves through the eyes of their guards (Foucault 1995:202–3). To have a domesticated mind, an imprisoned mind, a colonized mind is to see and define the Hispanic body attached to said mind through the eyes of the colonizer. To see oneself through the eyes of the society that benefits from one's repression and subjugation is to self-police.

Since childhood, those of us who resided on the underside of U.S. history have been taught to see and interpret reality through the eyes of the dominant culture, specifically White, heterosexual, middle-upper-class, patriarchal eyes. Seeing myself through the eyes of the colonizer was so normalized within my worldview that I accepted, without question, my so-called suspicious nature. The triumph of the colonizing process is best demonstrated when scholars of color define themselves and their disenfranchised communities through academic paradigms that consciously or unconsciously continue to contribute to their marginalization. Even today, if I am honest with myself, regardless of all the work that I do in liberative ethics, I would have to admit that my mind continues to be colonized— and I would suspect, I would propose, that the minds of many who are children of the colonization process might still contain its corroding residues. This is best illustrated by the uncritical acceptance by Latina/os of a Jesus who is silent and complicit with the oppression of Jesús— and José, and María.

Whenever someone from the dominant culture is pulled over by the police, the individual usually analyzes the situation in one of three ways: 1) I was speeding and got caught, 2) the police officer must be having a bad day, or 3) the police officer must not have made his or her ticket quota for the month. But when a Latino/a is pulled over, there is a fourth consideration that those from the dominant culture need never consider. Was I pulled over because I'm a Hispanic? Maybe I was speeding, maybe the officer is having a bad day, maybe the officer has not yet made his or her quota. It matters not if any of these reasons are true. I am left with the nagging suspicious feeling that maybe, just maybe, the real reason was because I'm Hispanic (De La Torre 2013b:4).

The power to domesticate is most effective when coercion appears neutral and natural. For those whose minds are colonized, submitting to societal norms and adopting the dominant culture's worldview are rewarded with inclusion in the privileges the culture has to offer. But for those who challenge the prevailing mores, punishment occurs in the form of marginalization and exclusion from power and privilege (Foucault 1984:60–61; 1978:93–101). The dilemmas caused by a colonized mind are not limited to driving. Everything Hispanics (and other people of color) do, every interaction in which they engage— even when good things happen (tokenism? paternalism?)— result in their inability to fully shake off this fourth consideration. Is what's occurring because I am Hispanic? Of course, those whose identities have been constructed to be the norm can never fully understand what they dismiss as being overly sensitive. But for those who continue to struggle against such false consciousness—how can they ignore a lifetime of conditioning? This false consciousness, as myth, keeps the oppressed silent because they accept, through religious and educational socialization, a false reality that benefits the privileged space of the one with the vantage point to gaze.

Before anyone can speak about the liberation of the marginalized from societal, political, and economical structures of oppression, we must begin by liberating ourselves from our own colonized minds, from equating the apex of rigorous thought with Eurocentric subjectivity. The real issue is not that police traversing this nation's highways and byways disproportionately stop Hispanics or that Latino/as are disproportionately incarcerated. The real issue is that as a Latino, I saw myself through the eyes of the police officer searching my vehicle or my person. The real tragedy is that my mind, and I will argue the minds of many of my fellow Hispanics, were and remain colonized. But how do we Latina/os decolonize our minds? We begin the decolonization process by not perpetuating the Eurocentric Jesus that contributes to our own oppression. We begin by recognizing that in Jesús we can find a kindred spirit, for Jesús too was a colonized man. If this is true, then maybe we can find in the life, teachings, and actions of Jesús strategies that can be employed to raise consciousness in the Latina/o community as it struggles for a more just social order.

JESÚS: A COLONIZED MAN

In the colonized land of Judea, poor marginalized shepherds abided in the field, watching over flocks belonging to others, when suddenly a messenger of the Lord came upon them, and the glory of God shone forth. They were filled with great fear. But the messenger said unto them, "Do not be afraid, for behold, I bring you, and all peoples of the world, good tidings of great joy. For onto you is born this day, in the city of David, a Liberator, who is Christ the Lord! And this will be a sign to you, you will find an infant wrapped in swaddling-clothes lying in a trough located in a filthy, manure-filled barn." Suddenly there appeared with the messenger a multitude of the heavenly host praising God, and singing, "Glory to God in the highest, and on earth peace, good will towards humanity" (Lk. 2:8–14).

The Christmas story has been retold so often, through sermons, church plays, popular literature, and movies that a false memory, detached from all reality, has been constructed. This memory romanticizes the birth of Jesus, thus masking the radical political implications of the event. Today, under our Christmas trees, we usually place a nativity scene among the multitude of conspicuous gifts, which we cannot afford to give to recipients who seldom need what we bought on credit. The baby Jesus, usually White with blue eyes and blond hair, rests comfortably in a wood-frame crib as angelic cows and donkeys gaze upon the miracle. The proud parents survey the sanitary scene as regal kings and peasant shepherds come to worship. Winged white angels surround the scene as if singing the glories of this event. And yet, stripping through the mythology, we are left with a tale of the liberator of people being born in a dirty, grimy barn. Barns are smelly soiled spaces where animals and the malodorous manure they produce, and the flies attracted to the manure create unsanitary conditions. In addition, a young maiden, either a teenager or someone who is not much older, goes through the bloody and messy process of childbirth. María was forced, like any other barn animal, to give birth amid the unhygienic surroundings of an outbuilding (De La Torre 2002:109).

We do not know if a midwife was present for the actual birthing event. The text is silent on that matter. But if there wasn't one, the birthing process could only be considered to have been scarier and more traumatic. Upon the birth of Jesús, a place was needed for him to rest. Proper furniture did not exist. The text tells us that he was placed in a manger (Lk. 2:7), which our Christmas nativity scene interprets to be some type of crude crib. In reality, a manger was either a wooden box or a hole on a cave wall. The manger was the place where the cattle ate. If the barn itself was not antiseptic enough, the newborn was placed in an animal trough. In a very real sense, Jesús physically entered this world homeless.

The radicalness of the Gospels, usually missed by those who are privileged by houses within the empire, is that the Jesús narratives are anticolonial literature about a native resident displaced by the invading colonial power. The opening words of the Gospel of Luke set the stage. Luke begins by stating that, in those days, an imperial decree was ordered from the colonial center of Rome by Caesar Augustus. To increase the revenues flowing toward the colonizer, all within the empire would be taxed. This revenue theft occurred when the Roman aristocrat Publius Sulpicius Quirinius served as governor of Syria. To facilitate the taxing, with no regard to what hardship it might cause to the colonized, everyone had to return to their city of origin. So José left the city of Nazareth located in Galilee, traveled toward Judea to the city of David, which is called Bethlehem, for he was of the house and lineage of a once heroic and mighty king. This descendant of royalty now made his living as a laborer, a carpenter. To Bethlehem he traveled with his espoused wife María who was great with child, in order to be taxed (Lk. 2:1–5). Remembering Jesus all too often ignores the destitution of Jesús caused by the colonization process, missed when the Scriptures are read from the center of empire.

The Gospel narratives depict a careful dance, which takes place between Rome the colonizer and Jesús the colonized. Not far from the storytelling surface is the real-world dynamics and consequences of colonization. We see it throughout Jesús' everyday experience and how he responded to the circumstances brought about by the economic and political occupation of Judea, as made evident by questions posed concerning paying tribute to Caesar (Mt. 22:20), constantly facing danger for preaching of another reign or kingdom more powerful than the one to which Jews were subjugated (Mk. 1:15), or given a death sentence under the charge of being "king of the Jews," hence a rival sovereign (Mk. 15:2). Even the very audience that first heard the words of Jesús were fellow colonized compatriots, many of whom held an abiding hatred toward the Roman oppressors. From this colonized space, the Gospel message is shaped and formed, and ignoring this historical reality leads to false remembrance, if not pure illusions.

We are told that among Jesús' entourage was Mateo the tax collector (Mt. 10:3), and Simón who was called the Zealot (Lk. 6:15). Tax collectors and zealots were deadly enemies. Given an opportunity, zealots or revolutionaries were known for ramming their blades into the backs of any tax-collecting collaborator upon whom they could lay their hands. And yet, these politically sworn enemies, the one colluding with the colonizer and the one violently rebelling, were counted among Jesús' disciples. What held them in fellowship? Could it be that Jesús modeled a new strategy between the two extremes represented by Mateo and Simón? If so, what is this reconciling praxis?

Jesús tells us to render to Caesar what is Caesar's and to God what is God's (Mt. 22:21). Although Jesús is specifically referring to the colonizer's tax when he states what to render to Caesar, it seems that this imperial tax as sign signifies some deeper meaning. The tax to the empire underwrites the very structures that make the colonization of Judea possible. Without the tax, colonialism would be useless. Such taxes, as illustrated by Caesar Augustus' need for a census, create devastation for the colonized, that is, having to return to one's city of origin and having a greater financial tax burden leading to greater poverty.

Yes, we are to give Caesar his tax, not because it is a civic duty, as many modern Euroamerican Christians would argue in regard to filing their own IRS tax returns, but because failure to do so only provided the colonizer with the excuse to send the full force of the empire's military to domesticate the people with the threat of obviation for the sake of compliance. This is not some hypothetical possibility; it actually occurred in 70 CE, which concluded with the destruction of the Temple.

To render unto Caesar what is Caesar's may mean to pay the imperial tax as an act of survival (not civic duty), but also it could encompass returning all of the misery, pain, and despair that colonial rule engenders. The issue raised by Jesús' call is how to render unto Caesar what Caesar deserves without bringing about the iron fist of Caesar, while still planting liberative subversive seeds that may, in some distant future, blossom into salvation from evil powers, including colonial powers. The question raised for us by Jesús, the colonized man, is how to display compliance for survival's sake while disrupting the very social structures that create, force, and demand compliance.

JESÚS: PEDIGREE

For many Latino/as, families are a crucial unit that influences and shapes who we are and what we can become. To know whence we came shapes our understanding of where we are going. Our very identity is based on the *familia*, the family, a concept usually dismissed by more hyper-individualist societies. Reverence for our ancestors helps strengthen our current families and communities, providing meaning to our identity. Unfortunately, individualist-based cultures seem to disregard, if not outright ignore, the stories of those who came before. Many traditions, specifically in the southern regions of the globe, have recognized the importance of, and provided respect for, the ancestors. And while we can look to the long lists of biblical genealogies as a positive attempt to record and provide reverence to ancestors, it still remains deeply disturbing that within the biblical text, the natural order of women bearing children is reversed for the sake of patriarchy. In the biblical record, men beget men. Women are seldom mentioned, unless in the rare instances that their inclusion has historical significance, for example, Ruth as King David's great-grandmother (Rt. 4:17), or whose inclusion serves as a counter-narrative, that is, an alternative to ethnic cleansing of "putting away your foreign wives!" that became a cry during the restoration of Jerusalem after the Babylonian captivity (Ezr. 2:59–63; 10:9–44; Ne. 13:23–28).

To read the story of Jesús reveals that the writers of the gospels recognized the importance of detailing Jesús' pedigree. Unfortunately, we are presented with two conflicting linear genealogies for Jesús. These two lists found in Matthew (1:1–17) and Luke (3:23–38) are mainly designed to prove his King David lineage, which for Christians signals the fulfillment of the messianic hope. A quick comparison of these two genealogies reveals that after King David, the names listed are totally different. Even though the ancestors listed from Abraham to David are nearly identical, the accounts differ from David to Jesús, with only two names, Shealtiel and Zerubbabel, appearing on both lists.[3]

Although both genealogies lack harmonization, the Matthew passage does include four women: Tamar (who played the prostitute), Rahab (an actual prostitute), Ruth (a foreigner), and the wife of Uriah (Beersheba who either participated or—more likely—was forced into adultery). It is troublesome that when women are mentioned in these genealogies, the male biblical reader views them in a negative light based on their gender or what they supposedly did sexually. Nonetheless, it presents us with a Jesús that has a "checkered" pass. Ignoring for the moment the larger question that the active sexuality of women somehow taints their moral character, for the male misogynist reader, these women have historically been perceived to be less than holy or pure, thus problematizing Jesús' ancestral list with the inclusion of prostitutes, adulterers, and migrants—women of so-called questionable morals. What does it mean to have a God whose ancestors included such "indecent" characters? Can a God in-flesh, who supposedly is pure and holy, have prostitutes in God's lineage? It forces us to reexamine more carefully the stories of these women to seriously consider a politics of survival that the pious in positions of power and privilege may deem too indecent, yet are necessary so that these women, along with others, may experience life. Jesús' genealogy forces our pietistic gaze to be taken off these women and instead focus on historical cultures' misogynist structures that forced these women, and many like them, to participate in what we have defined to be "indecent" behavior.

JESÚS: A MIGRANT

Las Posadas, literally "the inns," is a reference to a Hispanic community celebratory tradition based on the biblical story of when María and José found "no room in the inn" (Lk. 2:1–7). This four-hundred-year-old yuletide ritual physically reenacts the search for shelter prior to the birth of Jesús.[4] Usually occurring nine days before Christmas, this marks the start of the season. For nine days, *los peregrines* (the pilgrims) accompany the Holy Family, walking through darkened streets carrying candles. Men, women, and children travel from house to house requesting lodging and singing Christmas carols. They are turned away by *los mesoneros* (the innkeepers), but before the procession leaves, it is invited inside to enjoy food and drink. Today many Latina/o churches orchestrate *posadas*, as do some business communities for tourist and commercial purposes.

Rooted in the people's existential lives and spirituality, the community at large is invited to participate in the pilgrimage and also await the birth of Jesús. But this is more than simply a reenactment of a familiar biblical story. At a time of increasing homelessness and immigration restrictions, reenacting the story reminds participants of the challenge of providing a home for all (Fernández 2009:687). A God who calls us to hospitality, lest we too leave Jesús out in the cold, is remembered. But remembering is not just a thought process. Remembering is an act. Reenacting *Las Posadas* signifies the risk-taking and life-seeking migrations that Hispanic families are often called to undertake due to neoliberalism and the consequences of colonialism. Participating in *Las Posadas* reveals the most basic understanding of who God is and what political act we are called to enact. Former U.S. ambassador to the Vatican Miguel Díaz reminds us that "the God of [Jesucristo] is the God of life-giving migrations whose offer of life crosses over into human reality and stands in solidarity with life-deprived persons" (2009:644).

The exchange that takes place between José and the innkeeper during *Las Posadas* celebration is worth noting in some detail, for this reflects a political dialogue that seems to be repeated daily between today's undocumented migrants and the U.S. innkeeper:

> *José*: Who will give lodging to these pilgrims, who are tired out from traveling the highways?
>
> *Innkeeper*: However much you may say you are worn out, we do not give lodging to strangers.
>
> *José*: In the name of Heaven I beg you lodging, since my beloved wife can travel no longer.
>
> *Innkeeper*: There is no lodging here, keep on moving. I cannot open to you, don't be stupid.
>
> *José*: Don't be inhuman and have pity, for the God of the Heavens will reward you for it.
>
> *Innkeeper*: Now you may go away and not bother me, because if I get mad I'm going to beat you.
>
> *José*: We come worn out from Nazareth, I am a carpenter by the name of José.
>
> *Innkeeper*: Your name does not concern me; let me sleep, since I already told you that we are not to open to you. (Hughes 1996:13)

The script continues until the innkeeper, upon discovering José's true identity, relents and welcomes him and his family. But what about all the other Josés who are left out, who are no one of note, beyond the borders of marginality and disenfranchisement?

Dr. Ana María Pineda, of the Sisters of Mercy, reminds us that when Hispanics partake in the annual Advent practice, they "ritually participate in being rejected and being welcomed, in slamming the door on the needy and opening it wide. They are in this way renewed in the Christian practice of hospitality, the practice of providing a space where the stranger is taken in and known as one who bears gifts" (1997:31).

Among the crowd that accompanies the Holy Family are actual descendants of migrants and strangers. Some in the throng may themselves presently be unwelcomed migrants who are undocumented, criminally labeled as "illegals." Standing in solidarity with the Holy Family who themselves are unwelcomed migrants reveals a Jesús, who, himself a migrant, understands the pain and humiliation of having to go door-to-door begging to be let in.

Jesús, according to biblical scholar Leticia Guardiola-Sáenz,

> live[s] between borders, in a hybrid space which is an experience similar to that of Hispanics/Latin Americans in the postcolonial and neocolonial era. [Jesús], *the border-crosser*, the traveler between cities and villages, between heaven and earth, between suffering and bliss, comes to redeem the border-crosser who refuses to conform to the limits and borders of a society that has ignored her voice, her body and the borders of her identity as Other. (2002a:151)

And while most border crossers today do so as an act of desperation, Jesús, theologically speaking, chose to be a border crosser as an act of solidarity with the least of these. The biblical text reminds us that, although divine, Jesús became human, assuming the condition of the alienated. Accordingly: "[Jesús], who subsisting in the form of God thought it not robbery to be equal with God, but emptied himself, taking the form of a slave, in the likeness of humans, and being found in the fashion of a human, he humbled himself, becoming obedient until death, even the death of the cross" (Ph. 2:6–8). The radicalness of the incarnation is not so much that the Creator of the universe became human but rather that God chose to become poor, specifically a wandering migrant. This reveals a God willing, through Jesús, to assume the role of the ultra-disenfranchised. Because God incarnated Godself into marginalization, being born a migrant who lived and died in poverty, Jesús signifies a political ethics lost on those accustomed to the privilege of citizenship within the empire who miss the significance of a Jesús who is an "illegal."

Not only is Jesús born a migrant, he quickly becomes a refugee. The biblical text remembers José as a simple man who worked with his hands. He built things. He tried to make a living as a carpenter, but times were hard and taxes were high. Regardless of the foreign military occupation of his homeland, there simply was no time for him to become involved with any of those revolutionary groups doing maneuvers and hiding in the wilderness. He just worked hard, barely keeping food on the table for his rapidly growing family. Although wed for fewer than nine months, his wife, María, had already given birth to his first child, a healthy boy.

On this particular night, José was scared. He ran through the sleeping town, silently making his way toward his makeshift home, praying and hoping that he wasn't too late. He had to save his family from certain death. He burst into his shack and went straight to the sleeping mats on the dirt floor. "*Despierta mi amor*. Wake up, my love," José told his wife as he gently shook her. "A messenger just warned me that *la guardia nacional* will be coming for us. I fear we will disappear! *Apúrate*. Hurry up. We must leave this moment for a safer land, far from the reaches of this brutal dictatorship backed by the hegemonic military empire." There was no time to pack any belongings or personal mementos, nor was there time to say goodbye to friends and family. In the middle of the night, literally a few steps before the national guard, José took his small family into *el exilio*, the exile. That night they traveled south toward the border (Mt 2:14).

They would go to a foreign country, wearing only the clothes on their backs. Even though they could not speak the language, nor understand the strange customs and idiosyncrasies of the dominant culture, at least they were physically safe. Over two thousand years ago this family arrived in Egypt as political refugees, fleeing the tyrannical regime of Herod, who served as Rome's vassal. Rather than fleeing to *el norte* as so many Latin Americans do today, this family crossed borders and headed south. Although I recognized that "papers" were not required during this time to cross borders, nevertheless, Jesús still had to deal with the stigma of being a foreigner, a sojourner, an "undocumented alien" (De La Torre 2002:112–13).

That Jesús experienced alienation should not be surprising. The story of God's people is the story of aliens. The first refugees recorded in the Scriptures are Adam and Eve, forced— against their will—to leave the land from which they emerged for another land that they considered inferior. All the patriarchs of Genesis were also aliens. The stories of Abraham, Isaac, Jacob, and Joseph are narratives of aliens trying to survive among a people who are not theirs in a land that they cannot claim. If they were living today, we would probably call them "undocumented immigrants," if not the more pejorative term "illegal aliens." The people who would come to be called "Jews," were formed in the foreign land of Egypt. They became a nation while traversing the desert, having no land to claim as their own. Eventually, they would experience exile in a far-off place called Babylon and disenfranchisement on their own terrain due to military occupation by competing colonial powers.

Is it any wonder that the second most common phrase used throughout the Hebrew Bible exhorts the reader to take care of the alien among you, along with the widows and orphans? For those who claim to be Christians, responsibility toward aliens is paramount; after all God incarnated Godself as an alien—today's ultra-disenfranchised. Jesús understands what it means to be seen as inferior because he was from a culture different from the dominant one. I imagine he was mocked as a child for speaking with a "funny" accent or looked down upon for dressing differently from all the other Egyptian boys. Did Jesús cry himself to sleep, like so many children of immigrants today, feeling the same shame of inferiority imposed by the dominant culture? Did he have to become the family translator, as I did, between a dominant culture who looked down with disdain at the parents who cannot speak the language and the parents needing to endure the role reversal of having to learn from their children about the wider world? And of course, the shame felt by the child translator toward those parents for appearing "less-than" the dominant culture that masters the language, and yet simultaneously, having the tremendous fear and burden of knowing that a mistranslation can lead to precarious situations as some within the dominant culture seek an opportunity to defraud the migrants. Those of us who have been the intermediates between the dominant culture and our families discover in Jesús a savior, a liberator who knows our fears and frustrations.

And yet, for those of us with proper documentation who wish to mitigate the plight of the aliens in our midst, we find ourselves within a United States that prohibits us from being faithful in following Jesús' admonishment of imitating the example of the Good Samaritan (Lk. 10:29–37). Those today who go to the desert, walking the migrant trails with food and water strapped to their back, looking for those crossing the border to provide physical, spiritual, and medical assistance, come across Jesús often. On these trails of terror, thousands of brown bodies die torturous deaths in fulfillment of a U.S. policy, called Operation Gatekeeper, designed to deter future immigration through the death of those who, out of desperation, attempt the crossing. But among these migrants, like lambs sent to their slaughter, is Jesús. Jesús was once an immigrant escaping Herod's reach, and Jesús today is an undocumented immigrant escaping the poverty caused by our economic policies in neighboring countries.

We are told that Saint Martin of Tours (316–397 CE) once came upon a nearly naked beggar at Amiens. Cutting his cloak in half, he clothed the wretched figure. That night, in a dream, Jesús appeared to him wearing the cloak Saint Martin gave the beggar. When we feed the hungry, give water to the thirsty, clothe the naked, and welcome the stranger, we are doing these things to Jesús. Not figuratively, but literally. The honor and privilege of ministering to Jesús is available, for Jesús comes disguised as an immigrant, walking on secluded migrant trails. And yet, laws have been enacted that make us accomplices if we give food to the hungry or water to the thirsty or provide care for the alien in our midst. Those who come across an undocumented immigrant in the wilderness, beaten and dying, are prohibited due to present legislation from doing as the Good Samaritan did—take the stranger to a facility to have her or his wounds bound up. When attempts are made to follow the example of the Good Samaritan, harassment at the hands of border agents can be expected.[5] Today a "Good Samaritan" can receive up to twenty years in prison for providing transportation to the closest hospital for a dying immigrant. Could it be that the United States is the only country in the world in which providing humanitarian aid is a crime? We can muster our resources to save the whales but certainly not Hispanics.

Jesús' parable of the Good Samaritan teaches that we must care for all humans regardless of their documentation. It was the religious folk, in Jesús' parable, who found justification as to why it was God's will not to minister to the dying stranger by the side of the road. To deny preventive health-care services to any person based on that individual's documentation status is inhuman[6] and directly repudiates the teachings of Jesús. The story of the Good Samaritan lies not only in some distant past. Christians today are called to heal the wounds of the strangers in their midst. It's interesting to note that because Samaritans were viewed as the dirty foreigners of Jesús' time, this particular one was singled out as good. If this parable were to be updated for today's audience, it might be titled the "Parable of the Good Illegal Alien"— maybe even the Good Spic—a story of someone who doesn't fit the predominant negative stereotypes of society. This updated parable might sound something like this true story that recently happened to us.

As we walk through the desert, we yell in Spanish: "We have food and water. We have medicine. We are with the church. Do not be afraid." Migrants, hearing us coming usually hide, afraid we are the border patrol, or worse, one of the numerous vigilante groups patrolling and terrorizing the border. Our words are meant to encourage migrants to reveal themselves and receive the lifesaving supplies we carry. One of our groups, while on patrol, saw several migrants running away, so they quickly cried out the familiar phrase. Their Spanish was not fluent, so their words were misunderstood. The migrants stopped in their tracks and returned to our group. They said, "We don't have much food or water, but what we do have, we'll share with you." These refugees misheard the cry to offer assistance as a cry for help. They who had so little were willing to share their meager resources with those of us who have so much. We went into the desert to be like the Good Samaritan only to be humbled when we actually came across Jesús (De La Torre 2009a: 98–101).

While Jesús' solidarity with today's aliens should emphasize the eternal worth of temporary and disposable immigrants, his social location also stands as a warning to a dominant culture responsible for much of the present immigration debacle. Today's U.S. immigration dilemma is a direct result of over a century of colonialism. Conservative U.S. politicians portray Latin Americans, specifically Mexicans, as an invading army that crosses the border in order to take advantage of American generosity and social services. Terms like "anchor babies"[7] are used to illustrate the depths of Hispanic immorality and cunningness. In response to this supposedly Brown invasion, necessary draconian legislation is enacted that causes hardship, oppression, and at times death to those whom the United States insists on calling "illegal aliens."

Jesús' physical presence in Egypt forces us to ask why he was there. Jesús being in Egypt is due to the colonial consequences of living under Roman rule. Over two thousand years ago, the Holy family arrived in Egypt as political refugees, migrants fleeing the tyrannical regime of Herod that was imposed upon the local population by distant colonial powers in Rome. Herod's ultimate job was to ensure that profits flowed to the Roman center with as little resistance as possible. Of course, he financially benefited from this relation, as do many elites within Latin American countries today who sign trade agreements that are disadvantageous to their countries. Jesús was an undocumented alien, a victim of political circumstances beyond his comprehension or control. Not only do we need to ask why Jesús was in Egypt, but also why Latino/as are in the United States. The reasons are similar.

As the Romans benefited from *pax romana*[8] brought about by territorial expansion, Americans benefited from the nineteenth-century jingoist religious ideology of Manifest Destiny,[9] which justified Anglo territorial expansion in North America. The massive land acquisitions from northern Mexico were based on a theology that conceived the dominant Euroamerican culture as chosen by God who destined Euroamericans to acquire the entire continent. The expansionist war against Mexico was minimized by the false creation of the U.S. historical mega-narrative that masked the fact that it was the borders that crossed over Mexicans—not the other way around. Absent from the rhetoric is the true motive for the invasion of Mexico, acquisition of land and its resources, specifically the gold of California, the silver of Nevada, the oil of Texas, the copper of Arizona, and all the natural harbors needed for commerce along the western coast.

Besides territorial expansion, an attempt was made to control the economies of other nations. While empires of old, like Rome, relied on brute force, the U.S. Empire relies mainly on economic force (not to disregard the fact that it also has the largest military apparatus ever known to humanity). Through its economic might, the United States dictates terms of trade with other nations, guaranteeing that benefits flow to the U.S. center and the elites from the countries that agreed to the trade agreements. This strategy became a neoliberal-based foreign policy during the twentieth century, which moved the focus from acquiring the lands of others toward a hegemonic control of the economies of others. Nevertheless, the military might of the United States remained at the disposal of multinational corporations like the United Fruit Company so as to protect their business interests. During the twentieth century, the United States invaded at least twenty-one countries and participated in at least twenty-six CIA-led covert operations throughout the Caribbean basin to institute regime change, even when some of those countries, like Guatemala, had democratically elected governments.[10]

The political situation brought about by colonization during the time of Jesús pushed his family, out of fear for their lives, toward Egypt. This push factor remains operative in the lives of so many Latin Americans. The economic, political, and foreign policies of the United States cause this push factor in Latin America, specifically Central America, as people either lose their farms and livelihoods or flee in fear of the governments established in their countries through the might of Washington. Simultaneously, in the quest for cheap labor within the United States, a pull factor is also created. Crossing the border, described as a festering scar caused by the First World rubbing against the Third World, becomes a life-threatening venture. Whenever one nation builds roads into another nation for the purpose of extracting their cheap labor and/ or natural resources, why should we be surprised when those same people take those same roads and follow all that has been stolen from them? The United States has a Latin American immigration problem because, for the past two hundred years, its wealth was based on stealing the cheap labor and natural resources of it neighboring countries through the foreign policy known as "gunboat diplomacy."[11]

Euroamericans, reading the Jesus narrative through White eyes have attempted to respond to the immigration moral crises by advocating the virtue of hospitality. It is our Christian duty to be hospitable to the stranger among us. But hospitality assumes ownership of the house where Christian charity compels sharing one's possession. But to read the biblical narrative of Jesús from the perspective of the undocumented alien is to argue that it was Latin American cheap labor and natural resources that built the house; hence, advocating hospitality is the wrong approach. Instead, the moral initiative should be restitution. The Jesús biblical narrative forces us to ask: What does the colonial U.S. Empire owe Latin America for all it has stolen (De La Torre, 2009a:16)?

JESÚS: ONE OF THE POOR

The Law of Moses dictated that any woman who became pregnant and gave birth to a son would be ceremonially unclean for seven days, similarly unclean as during her monthly menstrual cycle. On the eighth day the boy was to be circumcised. Afterward, the woman had to wait thirty-three days to be "purified" from her bleeding. During that time, she was prohibited from touching anything sacred or visiting the sanctuary until the days of her purification were over. It should be noted that if she instead gave birth to a daughter, then for two weeks the woman would be considered unclean. Afterward she must wait sixty-six days to be purified from her bleeding. Giving birth to girls made women unclean for twice as long as giving birth to boys.[12]

When the days of her purification for a son or daughter were over, she was to bring to the priest a year-old lamb for a burnt offering and a young pigeon or a dove as a sin offering. The priest would then offer them before the Lord to make atonement for her. Only then would she be ceremonially clean from her flow of blood. But what if she is so poor that she was unable to afford a lamb? Then she must bring two doves or two young pigeons, one for a burnt offering and the other for a sin offering (Lv. 12:2–8). When the days of María's purification ended, she and José traveled to Jerusalem and brought Jesús so as to present him unto the Lord and offer the necessary sacrifice. Because José and María were poor, they fulfilled their obligation by bringing a pair of turtledoves (Lk. 2:24). Jesús was born into poverty, attested by the sacrifice offered by his parents that made use of the offering of the poor.

Without any hesitation, Jesús, throughout his life, claimed to be among the marginalized poor, incarnated among those who are most disenfranchised. He gives us a vision of a day when the heavens will roll away and the son of humanity returns in all his glory, accompanied by the host of Heaven. He will gather all the people before him, separating them as a shepherd divides the sheep from the goat. He would invite the sheep to enter the reign that has been prepared for them since the foundation of the earth. "I was hungry and you gave me some food to eat. I was thirsty and you gave me a glass of water to drink. I was naked, and rather than debate the morality of my appearance, you clothed me. I was an alien, without proper documentation, and you welcomed me. I was infirm, wasting away, and you visited me. I was incarcerated, and you took the time to come and encourage me, regardless if I was or was not guilty" (Mt. 25:31–36).

When the virtuous, as well as the condemned, ask how their salvation, or lack thereof, was determined, Jesús responds by indicating that it was he who was the person most normatively avoided, ignored, or shunned. Jesús does more than simply show empathy for the poor and oppressed, more than simply express some paternalistic concern. Jesús *is* the poor and oppressed. "Inasmuch as you did it to one of these, the least of my people, you did it to me" (Mt. 25:40). If you want to gaze into the eyes of Jesús, look into the eyes of the undocumented immigrant caught and abused while crossing artificial borders. If you want to place your hand in the hand of the one who calmed the waters, then shake the hand of the homeless. The sheep are not separated from the goat due to the denomination to which they proclaim membership, nor by what church they attend, nor by the doctrines that they profess to believe, not even by their confession of faith. Walking down an aisle and giving your heart to Jesus guarantees neither liberation nor salvation. Sheep and goats are separated by what they did or did not do to the least of these, personified in the materiality of Jesús' body. Jesús clearly states that when the Son of Humanity comes in all of God's glory, "each person will be rewarded according to what they have done" (Mt. 16:27), not rewarded according to what they said they believed. In dividing the sheep from the goats, Jesús asks if the grace of God, freely given, manifested itself in acts leading toward liberation or condemnation of others. Specifically, did we feed the hungry, give water to the thirsty, welcome the alien, clothe the naked, visit the sick and prisoner? The radicalness of salvation is that Jesús ties those destined for paradise with how they interacted with those dispossessed by society. Why? Because Jesús is an old, indigenous, poor, dark-skinned ex-convict, undocumented, Latina lesbian with AIDS who has no place to lay her head. Those who are most disdained and despised by society are the material forms our Savior, our Liberator takes.

We have a God who intimately understands marginalization and rejection because Jesús experienced disenfranchisement. Even though Jesús was born into poverty, within the normative imagination, the poor are usually seen as simply lazy or backward, whose hope solely rests on the generosity of the wealthy who can provide them food, education, or loans. The artificial link created between the poor and rich is one based on the liberality of those who have toward those who have not. Charity eases the conscience of the wealthy and obscures the need to consider why the poor are poor in the first place. The true link between the wealthy and the poor is based on the reality that many of the poor today are made poor by economic forces that cause the prosperity of the few to be rooted in the poverty of the many. Treating workers as objects means they are defined only by what they contribute to the profitability of others. Seldom are they defined by their humanity. Human rights are defined, first and foremost, around removing obstacles so as to engage in trade and commerce rather than achieving human flourishing or self-fulfillment. For reasons like this, neoliberalism is incapable of incorporating the basics of the politics of Jesús. How does one reconcile the biblical mandate to forgive debts with the insistence that foreign debts be paid off at the expense of people obtaining basic human needs? Ironically, toward the end of the 1970s in Latin America, as growing foreign debt was negatively impacting the lives of most people, some Catholic and Protestant clergy changed the words of the Lord's Prayer from "Forgive us our debts" to "Forgive us our offenses" (Mt. 6:12). Fears existed that Christians, pauperized by the policies of the World Bank and IMF that benefited the Empire, might take the Lord Prayer's literally and actually demand that debts be forgiven so that they could have their daily bread. Churches succumbed to economic pressures by neutering the potency of the biblical message (Hinkelammert 1995:333–34).

And yet, the stone rejected by the builders has become the corner-stone of God's designs, which "is God's doing, and a marvelous thing to see" (Mt. 21:42). For Jesús to occupy the space of the rejected is pregnant with political possibilities. The politics of Jesús forces us to contemplate how to achieve salvation and liberation from the oppressive paradigms that permeate our culture and churches. If Jesús is the least of these, then the quest for justice occurs through the perspectives of those whom the culture and church oppresses and then blames for their own disenfranchisement. For this reason, the Christian church, for the sake of its own salvation, needs those whom it marginalizes. For only by how we interact with the least of these are we able to discover our own liberation. No one gets to reside in Heaven without a letter of recommendation from the homeless. The voices of the outcasts, the ones who are marginalized because of their gender, their class, their race, their ethnicity, or their orientation are needed by all believers so that God's holy word does not become imprisoned by the social location of the dominant culture. Those residing on the periphery of power and privilege are being called by God to be the cornerstone that brings a message of redemption and salvation to a church that at best ignores them, at worst contributes to their dispossession. Patriarchal churches need women if they hope to hear the Word of God. Homophobic churches need lesbian, gay, bisexual, and transgendered folk if they ever hope to see the glories of God. And Euroamerican churches that demonize the undocumented, that pauperize Hispanics, that discriminate against Latina/os, need Jesús much more than they need Jesus if they ever hope to be saved.

This may sound totally unfair for the disenfranchised, but this has always been the way God operates. Those who for generations suffered under Eurocentrism may find more affinity with Jonah, who simply wanted to sit under the shade of a gourd and watch the wrath of God pour out upon his people's oppressors. Many desire fire and brimstone to consume the tormentors of Latino/as. But Jesús' solidarity with the rejected becomes the political path by which the marginalized become cornerstones. This strategy is nothing new to God. God has historically chosen those from the margins of society to be agents of God's new creation. Pharaoh's court was not blessed with God's revelation; rather, it was his slaves who were chosen to witness the manifestation of the Divine. The house of Caesar was not the recipient of the incarnation, nor was the House of Caiaphas[13] the means by which the Good News was proclaimed; rather, it was impoverished Galilee. This theme of solidarity between Jesús and the victims of oppression makes the people on the margins salvific agents for the recipients of society's power and privilege.

JESÚS: OUR UNCLE

Putting on flesh means Jesús is one of us, living with us in *lo cotidiano* (in the everyday). In fact, for many of us, Jesús is our uncle, an argument made by theologian Luis Pedraja, who recalls next-door neighbors, church deacons, and of cause, his uncle—all named Jesús. Yet an English-speaking Euroamerican culture finds it sacrilegious to name anyone after the name of God's only begotten son. Thus, an attempt is made to correct the Hispanic irreligious act of naming their children Jesús. Hispanics who are named Jesús find their name, the signifier of their identity, changed (usually without their permission) to Jesse. To name another is to exert power over what is being named. Parents name children and humans name pets; likewise, the powerful name the powerless. The unwelcomed name change becomes an imposition by those with the power to determine what is normative through the erasure of the Hispanic cultural, religious, and family values. As ethicist Hugo Magallanes reminds us, "When 'Jesús' becomes 'Jesse,' it is not simply a matter of pronunciation, but is a sign of theological domination" (2009:112).

The Latino/a worldview is also erased through the comical way of trying to say Jesus in Spanish. In an attempt not to offend the sensitivity of ears that privilege English as normative, Jesús is exaggeratedly rendered "Haysue." Regardless of this linguistic violence, Pedraja notes that, growing up in a Latino/a community, he came to understand God's child as "someone who lived near me and who had a human face like those who bore his name. He was close to me and concretely present in my life. Just like my neighbor, relatives, and friends, [Jesús] also lived in our community. He was someone we could call upon to understand our plight and to give us hope" (1999:15). Naming our children Jesús reflects our familiarity with divinity.

Refusal by Euroamericans to call Latino men by their given name, Jesus, becomes a theological statement that reinforces the belief that there exists only one way of understanding Christology. The existence of some stereotypical gardener named Jesus is a deviant understanding of the one true faith, in effect, an act of blasphemy by giving some

Hispanic "nobody" an exulted name that is above all names. All too often, Jesus, for Euroamericans, is a name reserved for a faraway kingly deity sitting on some heavenly golden throne detached from the experiences faced by common folk. And yet the gospel narrative is clear that this Jesús is one of us. When the crowds wondered where Jesús obtained wisdom and power to perform miracles, they asked themselves, "Isn't he the carpenter; the son of María and the brother of Santiago, José, Judas, and Simón? Aren't his sisters also here with us?" (Mk. 6:3).

Intimacy with Jesús is evident in diminutive terms of endearment employed by Latina/os, which find no direct correlation in English, terms like "Jesusito" (little Jesús) or even nicknames like "Chuy," "Chucho," or "Chus." Ethicist Ada María Isasi-Díaz reminds us of the Spanish linguistic norm of combining the word "Jesus" and "Christ" into one word: *Jesucristo*. While learned Eurocentric theologians write theses about the differences between the historical Jesus and the Christ of faith, Latino/as collapse these distinctions in the personhood of Jesucristo (2009:40). One is hard pressed to find among Hispanic scholars the rigid dichotomy found in the Jesus versus Christ discourse normative among Eurocentric scholars. In fact, theologian Roberto Goizueta clearly states that in popular Hispanic religiosity, there exists "no separation between the concrete, particular 'Jesus of history' and the spiritual, universal 'Christ of faith'" (1995:67).

JESÚS: *ACOMPAÑAMIENTO*

Jesús does not walk to Golgotha alone. As the soldiers led him away through the narrow byways of Jerusalem, they found and seized a man named Simón de Cirene, who had recently arrived from the countryside. They placed the cross on his back and made him carry it behind Jesús. Many people followed, among them women who were beating their breasts and wailing (Lk. 23:26–27). The crowd that walked with Jesús invites us to do likewise. During Jesús' darkest hour, as he headed toward a humiliating death due to his political and religious views, ordinary people, the nobodies of history, demonstrated for his disciples how to accompany the least among us, a model to be emulated as Hispanics implement a communal political methodology that emphasizes that no one should stand alone to face the overwhelming oppressive structures designed to rob their humanity, their personhood, and their dignity. *Acompañamiento*, accompanying, is how a preferential option for the politically, economically, and culturally oppressed is made. This option becomes an act emphasizing the term "we," an ethics *de acompañamiento* in the struggle for survival based on the concept of a God who accompanies God's people in their struggle. Being befriended by God restores to the so-called nonpersons of history their humanity, worth, and dignity. According to Goizueta, the preferential option for the poor implies a preferential option for the home, the city, and the crossroads where home and city meet. The option for flesh-and-blood persons is an option for particular places, the places where the poor live, die, and struggle for survival. Opting for the least among us is to place ourselves with them, accompanying the marginalized. To walk with Jesús, who walks with the poor, is to walk where Jesús walked and where the poor walk (Ibid.:191–92).

Jesucristo is not alone, for he is accompanied on his way to the cross during his struggle. The historical act is repeated each year throughout many *barrios* on Good Friday. Known as *Via Crucis*, the Latina/o community gathers during the reenactment of the Passion narrative to walk with Jesús on his way to the cross. During the procession, a litany is sung where the people respond *"Caminermos con Jesús"*—"Let us walk with Jesus" (Ibid.:33). Participating in the *Via Crucis* changes the Eurocentric theological discourse from "Jesus suffered for" to the Hispanic witnessing that "Jesús is suffering with." As historian Justo González observed, "The suffering Christ is important to Hispanics because he is the sign that God suffers with us. An emaciated Christ is the sign that God is with those who hunger. A flagellated Christ is the sign that God is with those who must bear the stripes of an unjust society" (1990:148–49). This act of solidarity reaffirms the community's bond to a God who suffers and struggles alongside them. In spite of the hopelessness of Good Friday, the act of *acompañado* Jesús, teaches us to also accompany our disenfranchised neighbors. Any politics that derives from the life of Jesús must contain a component that emphasizes *acompañamiento*, learning to not only walk with Jesús but with all who are being led to the slaughter, the marginalized today who are being crucified on crosses designed to maintain and sustain oppressive structures.

This radical *acompañamiento* as modeled by Jesús is noticeable in his self-reference as the good shepherd. Even today, popular art either depicts Jesús with a shepherd's staff guiding the flock or carrying the lost sheep on his shoulders, bringing it back into the fold. "I am the good shepherd," he says, "it is the good shepherd who lays down his or her life for the sheep" (Jn. 10:11). Because Jesús referred to himself as the good shepherd, we tend to romanticize the occupation of herding sheep. Many of us have come to envision shepherds as brave, wise, humble pastors who lovingly care for the flock. After all, does not the psalmist sing "the Lord is my Shepherd" (Ps. 23:1). In reality, there was nothing romantic about being a shepherd, neither during Jesús' time nor our own. No occupational social status was so limited and tenuous, so close to no status at all, so marginalized from the rest of society than that of the shepherd. The shepherd lived apart from what was considered civilization, among the company of the most miserable outcasts of society. From the margins, the shepherd occupied a slave-like space, usually guarding someone else's flock. The sheep of another was more valuable than the shepherd's own life, who, if need be, would be required to lay down their life for the sheep (MacMullen 1974:1–3). Hence, when Jesús referred to himself as the good shepherd, he was doing more than simply using a clever metaphor; he was stressing his solidarity with the ultra-disenfranchised.

JESÚS: A HEALER

Jesús heals. The Gospel narratives are pregnant with stories of Jesucristo healing the infirm. He heals the blind (Jn. 9:1–12), the deaf (Mk. 7:31–37), lepers (Lk. 17:11–19), paralytics (Jn. 5:1–18), a bleeding woman (Mt. 9:18–26), Pedro's mother-in-law (Mt. 8:1–15), a man with dropsy (Lk. 14:1–6), and a man with a withered hand (Lk. 14:1–6). Jesús was all about providing healthcare to the poorest of the poor, who were unable to pay so as to remain healthy. He also exorcises demons (Lk. 9:37–49) and even raises the dead, bringing them back to life (Mk. 5:21–43). To read the Gospels is to encounter a narrative of the supernatural. Liberals are quick to dismiss these miracles as myths. Embarrassed that they appear prominently in the tradition, these frequent occurrences are usually downplayed. Conservatives, meanwhile, take these stories literally, debating among themselves if the ages of miracles ended with the first Christian church or if they continue to occur to this day. Many Pentecostal churches hold healing services where parishioners come to expect miracles (usually the healing of a backache or headache). What liberationists bring to the discussion is the reason why these healings appear in the biblical text. Their appearance is not to make Jesús into some sort of magician who stands at our beck and call, but rather to emphasize the importance of Jesús' ministry to bringing peace (*shalom*) and completeness (*shlemut*) to lives lacking healthy physical and/or spiritual harmony.

Jesús' acts of healing demonstrate one of the goals of faith, holistic well-being for those heavily burdened by the everyday. Jesús' healing grace moves beyond curing physical illness to encompass all that prevents humans from fulfilling Jesús' mission as found in John 10:10, to give life and give life abundantly through *shalom* with *shlemut*. The Hebrew concept of *shalom* is complex, denoting peace, solidarity, and wholeness. When *shalom* is connected to the Hebrew word *shlemut* (which connotes a concept of completeness), the highest level of peace is attainable. *Shalom* without *shlemut* can simply imply the absence of hostilities, but *shalom* with *shlemut* moves further, toward harmonious completeness, what today we can call liberation. To be healed is to be saved, liberated from all that limits humans from achieving fullness. This *shalom* with *shlemut* can be achieved through spiritual union with one's God and physical commitment to one's neighbor. Achieving *sha-*

lom with *shlemut* moves beyond just being a private matter, as it becomes an achievable communal reality.

JESÚS: A LIBERATOR

Salvation is liberation. Jesús is first and foremost a Savior, that is, a Liberator. For onto us is born this day a Savior/Liberator. The Hebrew word translated in the Scriptures for "save" (*yāša'*), along with the Greek term (*sōzō*) are also used to connote "liberate." Etymologically, to be saved is to be liberated. Hence the question: salvation/liberation from what? From what (or from whom) are the wretched of the earth rescued and delivered? Salvation is neither an abstract concept nor a personal warm, fuzzy feeling; rather, it is a state of being that encompasses rescue and deliverance. Justice occurs when we are saved/liberated from sin, when sin is understood as the forces (individual or corporate) that bring oppression, enslavement, and death. To be liberated from this type of sin is to be saved. Salvation, thus, means more than simply acknowledging that Jesús died for our sins, where salvation is obtained through right beliefs. Santiago, the brother of Jesucristo, reminds us that salvation is more than orthodoxy, right belief. "So," he writes, "you believe that there is only one God, fine. But the demons also believe, and tremble. You fool; don't you know that faith without works is dead?" (Jm. 2:19–20). But it's not just the demons who believe in God and tremble at God's name; "good" Christian folk prospering from power and privilege obtained at the expense of the disenfranchised also believe. The emphasis then is not on which doctrines are believed to obtain salvation but, rather, on which actions are committed that lead to liberation.

The gospel message of liberation that is found in Jesús becomes a message of liberation from all forms of human oppression, such as social, economic, political, racial, sexual, environmental, and religious ones. Believing becomes the process of integrating faith with the sociopolitical everyday in which the oppressed find themselves. The goal of salvation, of liberation, is to break with sin through a new life in Christ, achieved through the process of consciousness raising, learning how structures of oppression prevent believers from experiencing the abundant life promised by Christ (Jn. 10:10). Thus, the evangelical goal is not to convince nonbelievers to believe doctrinal tenets but to convince nonpersons of their personhood, their infinite worth because they, regardless of what the world tells them, are created in the very image of God (*imago Dei*).

All humans, regardless of their faith or lack thereof, regardless of their race, ethnicity, gender, or sexual orientation, and regardless of their immigration status, are created in the very image of God. All are created in God's image, meaning all have dignity and intrinsic worth. Because every life contains the sacred, every life is sacred. To ignore this *imago Dei* violates the inherited rights of all humans. Because the spark of the Absolute exists within every person, all possess dignity. Even so, social structures are constructed to deny the worth of those who are relegated to the margins or, worse, cause the oppressed to question even whether they possess the *imago Dei*. What does it mean to possess the *imago Dei*? It means that basic human rights should be safeguarded. All who are human have the right to be safe from physical harm and receive basic healthcare. All who are human have a right to work and receive in return a wage sufficient to sustain life. All who are human have a right to be united with their families. These are the minimum rights humans can expect and that Christians are called to ensure.

Liberation does not come about by having the right beliefs, doctrines, or ideologies. The very essence of Jesús is action, praxis. The Gospel of John starts with the proclamation that "in the beginning was the Word [*logos* in Greek], and the Word was with God, and the Word was God" (Jn. 1:1). To read the Bible in English is to be introduced to a Jesus who is equated with the Word, word being a noun. But to read this text in Spanish is to discover that "*en el principio era el Verbo*," which when translated into English is rendered: "in the beginning was the Verb." The Greek word *logos* is usually translated as *Verbo* when it refers to Jesús, as opposed to the more common translation *palabra* as in *la palabra de Díos* (the word of God). In English, Jesus is a static noun; in Spanish, he is an action word. Jesús, according to theologian Luis Pedraja, can lead us to think of him not as "passive observers" of world events but as caring "agents of history" (1999:95). When Jesús sees hungry multitudes, he feeds them; when he sees the infirm, he heals them; when he sees injustice, he whips the bankers out of the Temple. Could language explain why one culture is more focused on correct doctrine (orthodoxy) while the other emphasizes correct action (orthopraxis)? Just as Jesús, the incarnated verb, participated in the everyday of his time, so too are we called to engage in politics of our present moment by feeding the hungry, providing healthcare to the uninsured, engaging in bringing about justice. To read Jesús as a verb is not an exercise of creating a new abstract theological understanding; rather, it is to discover new revolutionary ways of doing our Christology. As theologian Benjamín Valentín concludes: "if we truly want to know who [Jesús] was and is, and if we truly want to understand why people came to believe that [Jesús] reveals the nature and will of God, we need to take into consideration his public activity" (2010:104).

Latino/a-based Christology is less concerned with metaphysical or ontological conjectures concerning the nature of Jesús and more concerned with his politics, what he actually did. As Pedraja asserts, Christological concerns need to shift "from ontology (the structure of being) to ontopraxis (the act of being)" (1999:106). Praxis becomes the cornerstone of Latina/o-based faith, a responsibility of followers of Jesús to engage in transformative acts that lead society toward a more liberative and just future. And while, for many Eurocentric theologians, theology is abstract concepts created from the comfort of armchairs in prestigious ivy towers, Hispanics insist that Jesús as *verbo* moves theology toward a critical reflection of the praxis employed in light of the narrative of Jesús. Any Christological purpose propels the believer toward raising the consciousness of people to imitate the justice-seeking actions of Jesús and then to reflect on said action that becomes the bases of constructing a theology for this moment in time, a fluid theology destined to change as the political structures of oppression shift. Through the engaged praxis of faith communities, Jesús becomes present in the here and now, and, in fact, a lack of praxis signals a lack of faith because Jesús linked praxis to salvation.

To follow Jesús the Liberator becomes an existential response in the here and now to the inhuman conditions to which the vast majority of the world's population, containing the *imago Dei*, is relegated. One of the phrases often repeated by Jesús is that the reign of God is at hand. For Jesús, God's reign was not some future event. Historically, the reward of some hereafter has been used to encourage submission to oppression as an earthly trial in preparation for heavenly riches. But the proclamation that God's reign is at hand signaled that liberation/salvation is for the here and now, not some by-and-by. The birth of Jesús ceases to be the grounds for the creation, expansion, or sustention of traditional doctrinal beliefs, but, rather, Jesús' birth becomes a divine response to the inhuman conditions that the vast majority of humanity, created in God's image, are forced to endure. Hence, the good news is that onto us is born this day—and every day—a Liberator!

2

CAN ANYTHING GOOD COME FROM NAZARETH

Normally I'd say "Hello America," but here's the one thing: This can't be the same country I grew up in, because in the America I grew up in the headlines would be a whole lot different today. — Glenn Beck[1]

We believe that the best of America is in these small towns that we get to visit, and in these wonderful little pockets of what I call the real America, being here with all of you hard working very patriotic, um, very, um, pro-America areas of this great nation. —Sarah Palin (Praising North Carolina's small towns)[2]

If you are thirty-five or older, chances are good that your childhood in America was pretty much like mine, no matter where you grew up. . . . How times have changed. — Bill O'Reilly[3]

Several themes run throughout most ultra-conservative political rhetoric. Among the prominent themes voiced by many senior Euroamericans belonging to Tea Party–type organizations, is the demand to return to the America of yesteryear—the America in which they and I grew up—the America of the 1950s and 1960s. They voice frustration that the type of neighborhood in which they were raised was somehow "taken away" due to liberal social engineering. If only we can return to a simpler time, before political correctness and affirmative action, where everyone respected their place, their station within society. They demand that this America be returned to them. They express real fear about today's America, concerned that it has moved away from the family values supposedly prominent within their childhood neighborhoods. And yet, whenever I hear such nostalgia for the good old days voiced, cold chills run up my Hispanic spine, mainly because I am old enough to remember, all too well, the America to which they want to return.

Regardless of O'Reilly's tendency of reducing all Americans to some mythical White experience similar to a 1950s sitcom, this particular Hispanic lived in a very different America from his, even though our homes were just a few miles apart. I, unlike Mr. O'Reilly, emanated from Nazareth, where nothing good ever comes. His Long Island experience could not be enjoyed by my family, relegated to the New York slum of Hell's Kitchen, thanks to the prevalent segregation of the America for which he pines. This was an America where Brown bodies throughout the Southwest, like Black bodies throughout the South, were often the strange fruit hanging from trees. This was an America where the killing or the disappearance of non-White bodies was a common occurrence. Laws, customs, and traditions made sure that the neighborhood deprivation of my Hispanic childhood was segregated from the good old days of O'Reilly's childhood.

The headlines Beck longs for are found in an America where I would have remained trapped in my first job—a job I took when I was nine years old as an assistant janitor for $5 a week (child labor laws didn't apply to Hispanic kids), where I pushed a mop that was taller than me, and where my only aspiration was to succeed my father as the tenement building's superintendent. It was an America where most Hispanic kids lacked opportunities to advance. If the America for which Beck hopes was still with us, I would more than likely be mopping the floors at my seminary rather than teaching in its classrooms.

Palin believes that real America is comprised of small North Carolina towns—towns reminiscent of the mystical North Carolina community of Mayberry, from the sitcom *The Andy Griffith Show*, popular during our childhood. This is an America where lovable characters like Aunt Bee, deputy sheriff Fife, and little Opie lived in an uncomplicated, simple, and rustic America. More importantly, this is an America that, in spite of the fact Mayberry is located in the heart of the South, there are no Black people, and even fewer Hispanics, an America where a correlation of greater invisibility interconnects with darker skin pigmentation.

The nostalgia for their lily-white neighborhoods devoid of people of color only occurred thanks to segregation. But as bad as segregation was growing up, living in Nazareth has only gotten worse half a century later. As disenfranchised as our Latino/a barrios were, today they experience greater deterioration due to persistent unofficial segregation that exists, separating White from Brown, privilege from privation. To come from Nazareth today means Hispanics find themselves living in disempowered neighborhoods with dilapidated houses. In 2003, almost 10 percent of all Hispanic homes (compared to 4 percent of non-Hispanic White houses) lacked a complete kitchen, plumbing, or electricity. What they did have plenty of was rodent activity. And yet, Latina/os, according to the Bureau of Labor Statistics, pay more for shelter (about 33 percent of their pretax income in 2003), compared to 26 percent by non-Hispanics. These practices lead to Whites being more likely to own their homes, occupy better quality homes, and live in safer, more opportunity-rich neighborhoods (Turner et al. 2013:1–2).

Poor segregated neighborhoods translate to inadequate educational opportunities. According to the U.S. Department of Education, schools where more than half of the student body belongs to a racial/ethnic minority group, or schools where 70 percent or more of the students are poor, major repairs to an estimated tune of about $223 billion are needed (Chaney and Lewis 2007:1). Exacerbating the conditions is overcrowding, where minority populations of over 50 percent experience 25 percent or more congestion in classrooms, requiring the usage of multiple portable buildings (Ibid.:7, 9, 14–16). Nothing good comes from Nazareth because as a society we refuse to invest equally in neigh-

borhoods dominated by Latina/os. School districts that are predominately Hispanic (and Black) spent on average $908 less per student than
mostly White school districts (Wiener and Pristoop 2006:6).

We should therefore not be surprised, nor feign shock, when 27
percent of Hispanics aged 25-plus years failed to complete ninth grade,
compared to 4 percent of non-Hispanic Whites (Acevedo-Garcia and
Bates 2008:102). Or that our schools are as segregated today as during
the days longed for by O'Reilly, Beck, or Palin. Euroamericans, who
represent the majority of the population, attend schools where 76.6
percent of their classmates are White. By contrast, Hispanics (and
African Americans) are in schools with almost three-fourths minority
students, while about 40 percent find themselves in intensely segregated schools. In our schools, ethnic discrimination is linked to poverty,
when we consider that Latino/as attend schools where 57.4 percent of
the students (58.8 for Blacks) are poor, compared with the majority of
White students who attend schools where the percentage of poverty
ranges from 0 to 30 percent (Orfield 2009:13).

Yes, I do remember the America to which conservative pundits wish
to return. This is an America where neither I nor my Jesús are welcomed. Those of us who hail from Nazareth are a threat to those who
see as their birthright an America that protects their power and privilege. Many of those who wish to return to that America, no doubt, love
Jesus. They are just not too comfortable with Jesús moving in next door
or attending their schools. For those of us who come from Nazareth,
the Jesus of the America these pundits pine for is irreconcilable with
the Jesucristo to which Hispanics turn. Because such a Jesus was silent
back then in the good old days about the plight of Latino/as (and continues to be muted today), such a Jesus, as James Cone reminds us, is
Satanic not just for the Black community, but also for Hispanics
(2010:10). Jesús, like Latina/os, is from Nazareth, and it is to Nazareth
we must turn if Hispanic Christians hope to understand the politics of
Jesús.

JESÚS: FROM THE BARRIO

Jesús makes a preferential option for the marginalized, for the outcast, for the dispossessed, not because they are smarter, holier, or better, but simply because they are the disenfranchised. When commenting about Juan *el baptista* (the baptizer), Jesús notes that among those born of women, no one has risen who is greater than Juan; and yet, the one who is least, who is discounted now will, in the reign of God, be greater than Juan (Mt. 11:11). The greatest in the reign of God is the one who takes the lowly position of a child, and whoever welcomes the child welcomes Jesús, but woe to whoever causes the least among us to stumble. Better for them if they would have a millstone hung around their neck and be drowned in the depths of the sea. God is simply unwilling that any of these who are lowly perish (Mt. 18:4–7, 14). Not only does Jesús make a preferential option for the least, the lowly, the powerless, Jesucristo becomes the disinherited and dispossessed. Those from the barrios are the least among us, the dispensable, the rejected. As theologian Father Virgilio Elizondo reminds us, "What human beings reject, God chooses as his [*sic*] very own. . . . It was said that nothing good could come out of Galilee. God ignored them and chose it as his starting point" (1983:91–92). Those who are among the least become the cornerstone of any Christology. Why? Because the Divine, as we saw in the last chapter, was incarnated as one of the least.

Hence, Jesucristo is a street rat, a barrio kid, a spic from the "wrong side of the tracks." Those who came from Nazareth, like Jesús, were looked down upon, mainly because large portions of the Jews living in the area were Hellenized. Being Hellenized meant being of mixed races. The region's inhabitants were too multiethnic in the eyes of the more pureblooded Jews living in Jerusalem. Jesús also experienced the disdainful dismissal experienced by those today that come from impure and mixed neighborhoods, from today's barrios. No respectable member of society hails from *those* types of neighborhoods.

The barrios of today are irrelevant locations where nothing important occurs and ignorant lowlifes are believed to live. Similarly, Nazareth was insignificant to the religious life of Judaism. Nowhere in the

Hebrew Bible is it mentioned, not even as a trading route or major highway. This was a secluded village in the middle of nowhere. To come from Nazareth was considered by the privileged urbanites of Jerusalem to be uncouth, primitive, and backward. If it were not for Jesús being a Nazarene, Nazareth would have been destined to become some un-known and unimportant spot of the world, lost to human history. Jeru-salem dwellers considered Nazarenes to be on their periphery, econom-ically surviving through sordid labor. These so-called ignorant peasants were believed to be so uncivilized that they could not even be trusted to fulfill the basic duties of citizenship (MacMullen 1974:34).

Galileans were part of the economical margin whose purpose was to serve the Jerusalem center, similar to the ways today's barrio spaces serve the city's centers of power. Jerusalem's wealth was derived from being the religious and political capital of the region, with most of the property in the countryside being owned by the wealthy of Jerusalem. The bulk of the land didn't belong to Galilean peasants; they just la-bored upon the fields for an urban elite who neither worked the land nor lived in the vicinity. For example, Ptolemy, Herod's chancellor, owned the whole city of Arus, while the priest Eleazar ben Harsum inherited from his father over one thousand villages with so many slaves that few knew who their master was (Jeremias 1969:92–100). Jerusalem was a city with no single trade whose product made it famous. All raw materials were imported from her neighbors, specifically Galilee. The center attempted to extract economically all that could be taxed from the provincial peasant, as absentee landlords from the city sent their agents for a share of the crop during the harvest (MacMullen 1974:36–37). Today's Hispanics, crowding our urban barrios, can relate to this, with similar feelings of anger and frustration derived from ex-ploitation at the hands of distant slumlords, as did Jesús' neighbors.[4]

Peripheries like Nazareth back then and barrios today are needed if centers are to thrive. Those today who are most removed from the "White ideal" disproportionately occupy the most menial jobs and live in the most economically deprived neighborhoods. This economic real-ity faced by Hispanics must continue because New York's Park Avenue profits by the surplus cheap labor extracted from Spanish Harlem, while the households and businesses of California's Los Angeles thrive by utilizing "illegal immigrants." The luxury houses of the exclusive gated "vanilla" neighborhoods are established at considerable cost. Their privileged space protects them from the menace of the "chocolate" barrios, while drawing upon this marginalized space for cheap labor and economic exploitation. In addition to this economic dependency, the reserve army of the underclass is systematically barred from economic opportunities that would significantly raise its status. Both exclusion and exploitation contribute to the conditions prevalent in this nation's barrios.

These economic social structures provide new eyes from which to read the Scriptures. Consider the third commandment: "Remember to keep the Sabbath day holy. Six days you shall labor and do all your work. The seventh day is a Sabbath to Yahweh your God, you shall do no work that day" (Ex. 20:8–10). Euroamericans usually interpret this commandment by focusing on taking a break during a demanding work week, to carve out of their busy lives one day in seven to study God's word and worship God's holy name, where fellowship with family and other believers can also take place. Such interpretations betray the reality that the vast majority of Christians have been taught to read the biblical text through the eyes of those who do not hail from the barrio. Historian Justo González provides us with an alternative interpretation to the commandment, an interpretation rooted in the Hispanic barrio experience. He recounts a sermon heard at a church composed mainly of poor Latina/o parishioners. The minister began by asking how many within the congregation worked four days last week. Five days? Six days? Few in the congregation were able to raise their hands to any of these questions. Then the minister asked how many would have wanted to work six days last week but were unable to find employment. Almost every hand went up. To this response, the minister asked, "How, then, are we to obey the law of God that commands that we shall work six days, when we cannot even find work for a single day?" (1996:59–60).

The privilege of employment influences how the commandments (or the rest of the biblical text for that matter) are read: consequently the dominant culture's emphasis on taking a day off. To read the Bible from the barrio reveals to those with economic privilege that God's commandment is more than the capricious imposition of a deity to choose one day in seven to do nothing. Rather, God establishes symmetry and balance in the created order. Working six days is counterbalanced with resting one. When we read this text from the position of economic privilege, we assume employment. We are unaware of the reality that segments of our society lack opportunities for gainful employment due to their race and ethnicity. By imposing upon the text our assumptions of class privilege, we are oblivious to the first part of the commandment, "six days you shall labor."

Consider the unemployment figures for any given year. Regardless of whatever the rate happens to be—a conservative number nonetheless when we don't include those who have given up looking for jobs or are working at part-time positions—we ignore who is disproportionately unemployed. For example, in November 2010, the unemployment rate was at 6.2 percent. Among Euroamericans, the unemployment rate was 5.3 percent, below the national average. But for Hispanics, the rate stood at 7.8 percent (11.4 percent for African Americans).[5] These figures remind us of the failure of our society in disallowing non-Whites to keep God's commandment, "six days you shall labor." Our entire economic system comes into question. For our economy to work at top efficiency, an "acceptable" unemployment rate is required, usually at about 5 percent. In fact, when the unemployment rate drops too low, the stock market gets jittery and begins a downward turn. Why? Because more money must be spent on wages to compete for, attract, and retain workers. Full national employment means companies are paying too much to retain employees, which negatively affects their profits. When we consider that those who are unemployed are disproportionately people of color, we realize that our economic system is geared to prevent certain segments of our population from keeping God's commandment, "six days you shall labor." Corporate America needs a reserve army of underskilled and undereducated laborers to keep overall wages depressed, ergo high dividends for stock portfolios and retirement plans of those who can afford such financial planning. Why then are we surprised with Hispanics' high school dropout rates? According to the Center for Labor Studies, our nation had a 16 percent dropout rate in 2007. The Latino/as dropout rate was 30.1, while the African American rate stood at 18.8 percent. Nearly three out of every ten Latina/os drop out of school (2009:3). One can only wonder what would happen if the White community suffered a 30.1 percent dropout rate. All of the nation's resources would be made available to reverse this national tragedy. Failing our White children is simply unacceptable! Fortunately, these are not White students but barrio kids whose employability benefits corporate earnings as long as they remain undereducated and underskilled.

Coming from Galilee (or the barrio) signified marginality, nothing to brag about. When the people debated if Jesús was the Messiah, some retorted, "How can the Messiah come from Galilee? Search the Scriptures and see that no prophet out of Galilee has ever been raised" (Jn. 7:41, 52–53). Natanael, a future disciple, when realizing where Jesucristo comes from asked if "any good thing can come out of Nazareth" (Jn. 1:46). You can hear the biting ethnic bias in Natanael's question. Can anything good come from Spanish Harlem? Can anything good come from East L.A.? Because Jesús experienced cultural prejudices for being from the margins of society, today's inhabitants of barrios have a God who is also from the 'hood and thus understands their social location. All too often, we read the Gospels with middle-class privileged eyes, thus transforming Jesus into some middle-class carpenter. Unable to read from the social location of the marginalized, we often miss the radicalness of the disenfranchised body that Jesús occupied and how that body has come to be signified.

JESÚS: AMONG THE ALIENATED

Barrios are mixed spaces where different groups are forced to live together. The borderlands of Galilee have always been a place best known for foreigners and outsiders, a region that the author of Isaiah (9:1) and the author of the Gospel of Matthew (4:15) refer to as "Galilee of the Gentiles." The term "Galilee of the Gentiles" can also be found in several rabbinical writings, such as the Babylonian Talmud where its appearance seems to reflect a derogatory connotation.[6] As theologian Orlando Costas reminds us,

> Galilee was a cultural crossroads. It was a commercially oriented region that had long been inhabited by Gentiles as well as Jews. During the time of [Jesús], Jews lived side by side with Phoenicians, Syrians, Arabs, Greeks, and Orientals. This racial mixture had given it the name Galilee (literally "the circle"), which came to mean "circle of heathens." (1989:51)

For Jesús to come from the barrio, the disenfranchised social location of his time, means that Jesús was alienated. The vast majority of Hispanics knows what it means to not belong, to be alienated from the dominant culture. Latina/os need not live nor grow up in the barrio to experience this alienation. Regardless of where Latino/as live or how they or their ancestors ended up within the boundaries of the United States, Hispanics live with the alienation caused by borders. *Border* can no doubt refer to the militarized international line separating the United States from Latin America. Cultural theorist Gloria Anzaldúa refers to this "U.S.-Mexican border [as] *una herida abierta* [an open wound] where the Third World grates against the first and bleeds. And before a scab forms it hemorrhages again, the lifeblood of two words merging to form a third country—a border culture. Borders are set up to define the places that are safe and unsafe, to distinguish *us* from *them*" (1987:3). But borders also exist in every state, county, city, town, and village throughout the United States. These borders are invisible walls that are just as real in New York City, Washington, D.C., Omaha, Nebraska, and

Chapel Hill, North Carolina as the visible walls of Chula Vista, California, Douglas, Arizona, or El Paso, Texas. To be a Latina/o living anywhere in the United States is to exist in a state of alienation, constantly separated from privilege, power, and whiteness, that is, from the benefits and fruits that society has to offer its inhabitants. Through the extraction of cheap labor from the barrio periphery, Hispanics have contributed for centuries to the wealth building of this nation. Yet alienation from the product of their labor occurs mainly because Latino/as are perceived by the dominant Euroamerican culture as not belonging, as unwelcome aliens. They are, as were the Nazarenes of Jesucristo's time, seen as inferior as they cluster at the lower stratum of the economy, receiving the lowest weekly wages of any major group in the labor market. Alienation from the wealth they produce is due in part to how many Latina/os are seen specifically as inferior due to their mixture (specifically racial mixture).

Marginalized spaces like Jesús' Nazareth or today's barrios are usually occupied by racially or ethnically impure people, with "impure" understood as not being from or belonging to the race or ethnicity of the dominant culture for which society is geared. Even though we recognize that Jesús was Jewish, his compatriots perceived him to be of mixed races, what today Latino/as call *mestizo*. Elizondo captures the similarities between today's mestizos and the Nazarenes of Jesús' time. He writes, "The image of the Galileans to Jerusalem Jews is comparable to the image of the Mexican-American to the Mexicans of Mexico. On the other hand, the image of the Galileans to the Greco-Romans is comparable to the image of the Mexican-American to the Anglo population of the United States. They were part of and despised by both" (1983:52). I would add that this phenomenon is not exclusive to Mexican Americans but exists among most (if not all) U.S. Hispanic groups regardless of nation of origin. It should be noted that some Latina/o scholars, based on a lack of sufficient archeological and literary evidence to indubitably conclude the *mestizaje* of Galilee, reject the area's *mestizaje* concept (Valentín 2010:94–97). Nevertheless, the economic periphery Galilee occupied, and questions concerning Jesús' parentage that lead his contemporaries to wonder about his mixed race status, makes him *mestizo* in the minds of his contemporaries, regardless of the actual demographics of Galilee.

Most of today's Christians unquestionably accept the doctrine of the Immaculate Conception, that Jesús was conceived by the Holy Spirit who came upon María. For those today who reject the virgin birth, they at least assume that Jesús was the product of a premarital relationship between María and José. Still, during Jesús' lifetime, it appears that there was some question of whether he was a bastard child of a mixed sexual relationship. Even José suspected that María was unfaithful and planned to quietly break off the betrothal (Mt. 1:18–19). At best, Jesús' contemporaries assumed José was the father, even though José knew that he wasn't. No one accepted the claim of María's being pregnant while still being a virgin, assuming such a claim was even made and circulated during Jesús' lifetime. After all, the earliest New Testament writings, the Gospels of Mark and John and the Pauline epistles, fail to mention the virgin birth of Jesús. It wasn't until the second century that the virgin birth was considered true, and the need to include it in the Apostle's Creed (which of course was not written by the apostles) hints that the miracle was not universally accepted.[7]

At worst, rumors and innuendos concerning who impregnated María existed, rumors that could have dogged Jesús throughout his life. A hint of such gossip might be found in an exchange that took place between the Pharisees and Jesús. The story begins with sexual impropriety when a woman is brought to Jesús caught in the very act of adultery (Jn. 8:1–11), leaving us to wonder, if she was caught in the very act, why the man was not also brought to Jesús. After forgiving the woman, an argument erupts over his authority to do so. At one point the Pharisees ask, "Where is your father?" To which Jesús responds, "You do not know me or my Father. For if you knew me, then you would have also known my Father." Let's not forget, this conversation is a response to adultery. Jesús might have been speaking about God the Father, but the Pharisee missed the point. They claimed that they knew their father, Abraham (Jn. 8:33), a possible dig that they, unlike Jesús, are true descendants of the patriarch. Then they make an interested comment, "We are not illegitimate children. The only Father we have is God" (Jn. 8:41). Their innuendos that Jesús was a half-mixed bastard is more clearly evident when charged thus: "Are we not correct in saying you are a Samaritan?" (Jn. 8:48). Samaritans were considered to be half-breeds, *mestizos*, by the pure Jews of Jerusalem.

If indeed the Pharisees were stating that unlike Jesús they at least knew who their father was, then who did they suspect was Jesús' father? According to the writings of Origen of Alexandria, the Christian apologist, it was believed by the deniers of Jesús that he was the bastard child of María the Jew and Panthera, a Gentile Roman soldier, even though no historical evidence exists. In Origin's *Contra Celsum*, written in the middle of the third century, way after Jesús' encounter with the adulterous woman caught in the act and her accusers was recorded, Origin writes, "Let us return, however, to the words put into the mouths of the Jew, where the mother of Jesus is described as having been turned out by the carpenter who was betrothed to her, as she has been convicted of adultery and had a child by a certain soldier named Panthera" (I:32). The term *Jesus ben Panthera* (Jesus son of Panthera) also appears in several places throughout the Talmud.[8] While we do not know if such rumors existed when Jesús encountered the Pharisees concerning the issue of adultery, it still might explain the verbal jab: "We are not illegitimate children. The only Father we have is God" (Jn. 8:41).

The question is not whether Jesús is a product of a mixed marriage, son of an unwed mother. What is important is that Jesucristo might very well have been perceived by those around him as being a product of a mixed marriage, son of an unwed mother. And if perceived in said fashion, he was more than likely treated as such. Jesús then knows the feeling of being treated as a *mestizo* as well as being familiar with the difficulties of being raised by a single mother. Remember, José drops out of the narrative shortly after Jesús' childhood, last seen when he finds Jesús teaching the elders at the Temple (Lk. 2:46–47), leaving us to wonder if he died young or if he abandoned the family due to the rumors of being cuckolded. Certainly by the time of Origin, María's unfaithfulness was the common belief held by those who were not Christians, hence the importance of the virgin birth becoming doctrinal truth.

To be a "half-breed," in Spanish, is to be a *sato/a*. *Sata/o* is a Spanish idiom that refers to a mongrel dog, a mutt. Jesús was a *sato/a*. The term, when applied to humans as in *qué sato* denotes a person of dubious moral character. According to theologian Loida Martell-Otero, "*Satos/as* are mixed breeds who are not perceived to be beautiful or of pleasing aspect. They are unwanted. They seem to lurk from the peripheral edges of polite society. People shoo them away. Stones are thrown at them. Shelters teem with them. *Satos/as* are the rejected ones. . . . To use *sato/a* as a Christological term is to raise the specter of the theological scandal of the incarnation" (2009:77). To be a *sata/o*, to be part of a *mestizaje* or *mulatez*, is to occupy the radical periphery. We do not know what Jesús looked like, and the Bible seems silent about this except for one possible exception in the Book of Revelation where the resurrected Christ is physically described. The apostle Juan, exiled on the island of Patmos, sees the Alpha and Omega, whom he describes as having "wooly white hair" and feet whose skin is like "burnished bronze" (Rv. 1:14–15). Bronze skin and wooly hair are not terms usually used to physically describe Euroamericans. In fact, if Jesús did have European physical characteristics, then it would give credence to the rumors concerning his father really being the Roman soldier named Panthera. Although it may be satisfying to imagine Jesús as a Brown person, for our purposes, what is important is not Jesús' skin pigmentation, but rather that his compatriots saw Jesús, like so many others from blended families, as a *mestizo* or as a *mulatto*.

Jesús experienced the discrimination of occupying a hybrid body, falling short of ethnic purity. To be a "half-breed," a *sato*, as are so many Latina/os who are the result of clashing cultures and the children of colonialism, means never being pure White (regardless of how light the Hispanic's skin might actually be). Being neither a pure Jew during Jesús' time nor a pure White today is to be relegated to the margins of power and privilege, along with the societal institutional violence that has historically accompanied *mestizo/as* and *mulatto/as*. To exist in the hybridity of an "in-between" space, is to exist in a *nepantla* location. The term *nepantla* originates among the indigenous contributions made to the overall Hispanic identity. Coined by one of the indigenous roots of Latina/os, specifically the Aztecs, the word connotes being in the middle or in "that situation," as anthropologist Jorge Klor de Alva reminds us, "in which a person remains suspended in the middle between a lost or disfigured past and a present that has not been assimilated or understood" (1982:353). To be in the middle means neither denying the indigenous customs and traditions of Hispanics nor the new religions and concepts brought about by the vicissitudes of conflicting cultures.

The Latina/o *mestizaje* and/or *mulatez*, that is, the cultural, political, religious, social, and physical "mixing" born from the pain and anguish of continuous conquest, contributes to a notion of *nepantla* that describes the recognition that within most Latino/a's veins flows the blood of both the conquerors and the conquered. From the *nepantla* social location of being in the middle, or on the border, any analysis that is to be called "Hispanic" originates with the goal of finding justice-based alternatives to the everyday struggles of the Latina/o hybrid community. Jesús understood these struggles, knowing what it means to be discriminated against because those of the dominant culture consider the hybrid mixture of races and/or ethnicity an abomination whose consequence is inferiority and marginalization.

JESÚS: *UN AJIACO*

For Hispanics, Jesús is not only rooted within our community, *nuestra comunidad* but also represents the multiple roots that comprise our community. This rootedness of Jesucristo can be captured in what I have previously referred to as an *ajiaco* Christ, an understanding of Jesús that attempts to consolidate the vastly different backgrounds of the Latina/o experience. Ethnographer Fernando Ortiz was the first to use *ajiaco* to describe the Cuban diverse experience. *Ajiaco* is a consommé made from a variety of roots. As such, *ajiaco* becomes the collection of our indigenous roots—roots that symbolize the diverse ethnic backgrounds of Cubans and how they came together to form a *cubanidad*, a Cuban community. The term *ajiaco* refers to a native Cuban dish, a renewable stew consisting of different indigenous roots that symbolize a particular people. Ortiz used this term within the context of a Cuba composed of immigrants who, unlike those who came to the United States, reached the island on the way to someplace else. For him, *ajiaco* was a stew where the original Native nation contributed the *maíz, papa, malanga, boniato, yuca*, and *ají*. The Spaniards added *calabaza* and *nabo*, while the Chinese added Oriental spices. Africans contributed *ñame* and, with their culinary foretaste, urged a meaning from this froth beyond mere creative cooking. Ortiz did not use *ajiaco* to mean that Cuban culture has achieved complete integration; rather, Cuba remains "a *mestizaje* [mixture] of kitchens, a *mestizaje* of races, a *mestizaje* of cultures, a dense broth of civilization that bubbles on the stove of the Caribbean" (1940:165–69). In effect, Cubans eat and are nourished by the combination of all of their diverse roots.

Ortiz recognizes that the Cuban culture (and I would expand this concept to the overall Hispanic U.S. culture) is not a finished product. Like the *ajiaco*, the culture is a "vital concept of constant fluidity" (1939:3–15). For Ortiz, the culture becomes a "condition of the soul, a complexity of sentiments, ideas and attitudes . . . a heterogeneous conglomerate of diverse races and cultures, which agitate, tremble, and disintegrate in the same social effervescence" (Ibid.). While the inhabitants (with the exception of the indigenous people) representing the "ingredients" of this *ajiaco* originated elsewhere, they nevertheless repopulated this new space called the "United States" as displaced people (even though some of our ancestors occupied these lands before the founding of the United States or the arrival of the northern European colonizers). While not belonging, they made a conscious decision to be rooted in this particular land. For this reason, *ajiaco* is and should be an unapologetically authentic space from which to approach and understand Jesús as well as the wider world. This space collapses the dichotomy existing between those who have historically been called the "oppressors" and those whom they have oppressed. We construct an *ajiaco* Jesús that honors and celebrates the diverse and contradictory roots of the stew that come together somewhat harmoniously to establish a new Latino/a creation (De La Torre 2009b:69).

Usage of *ajiaco* to better understand Jesús becomes a radical employment of the liberation theological concept known as the *preferential option for the oppressed*. Rooting Jesús takes seriously the diverse Latina/o roots that are located among the very least. Additionally, the *ajiaco* paradigm becomes a clear rejection of the melting pot concept historically popular within the dominant culture. Unlike the North American melting pot paradigm maintaining that all immigrants who arrived to these shores are somehow placed into a pot where they "melt down" into a new culture that nevertheless remains Eurocentric in nature, an *ajiaco* retains the unique flavors of its diverse roots while enriching the other elements. Some "ingredients" may dissolve completely while other "ingredients" remain more distinct, yet all provide flavor to the simmering stew, a stew that by its very nature, is always in a state of flux. Employing the term *ajiaco* surpasses the melting pot metaphor. As many people of color have said concerning melting pots: the scum usually rises to the top while those on the bottom usually get burned.

JESÚS: ANDROGYNOUS?

Part of the Latino/a *ajiaco* identity, which is all too often masked, is our gender diversity. We know Jesús was born as a male. There is no question that he was physically male, a fact proven when we consider that the Roman custom was to strip the condemned and crucify them naked to increase their humiliation, shame, and vulnerability (Burge et al. 2009:143–44). But if Jesús is the ultimate reflection of the Divine, does this imply that God is also male? Such an assumption has led to centuries of patriarchy. And yet, if Jesús is a liberator, then how does the materiality of his body engender liberation for nonmales?

We are told that God dispatched a messenger named Gabriel, whose name means, "God is my strength," to the town of Nazareth, an insignificant barrio located in Galilee. There he approached a young teenaged virgin, a nobody, a "lowly servant girl" who was betrothed to a man named José, a distant descendant of Israel's famed King David. The messenger went to her and said, "Rejoice, O blessed one, for the Lord is with you. Blessed are you among women." His words greatly troubled María, and she wondered what this messenger's words might mean. "Do not be afraid María," Gabriel continued, "for you have found favor in the eyes of God. You will conceive and give birth to a child, and you will call him Jesús. He will be great and will be called the son of the Most High. The Lord your God will give him the throne of his father David, and he will forever rule over Jacob's descendants, his reign will know no end." "But how could this be," María asked the messenger, "since I am still a virgin, unknown and untouched by man?" The messenger responded, "The Spirit of God will come on top of you, and the potency of the Most High will overshadow you. Thus, the holy one who is begotten will be called the Son of God" (Lk. 1:26–35, 48).

Central to Christian thought is the immaculate conception of Jesús who was born of a virgin. This assertion has led biologist Edward Kessel to draw very interesting conclusions concerning Christ's androgynous identity due to his parthenogenetic birth. We are taught by biology that males have XY chromosomes. Women, on the other hand have XX chromosomes. Upon conception, each parent contributes one of their chromosomes to the fetus. Women only have an X chromosome to contribute, while the male can contribute either an X or a Y chromosome. If the man contributes his X chromosome, then the fetus will develop into a girl because it has the combined XX chromosomes. If, however, the man contributes his Y chromosome, then the fetus will develop into a boy because it has the XY chromosomes.

Further complicating Jesucristo's conception is the understanding that the Spirit who came on top of María has consistently been viewed throughout the biblical text as feminine. Both the Hebrew word (*ruah*) and the Greek word (*pneuma*) for Spirit are female gendered. So, if there is no human male figure with an XY chromosome involved in María's pregnancy (remembering she is unknown and untouched by man), then Jesús cannot contain a Y chromosome required to deter-mine male physical identity. The literal acceptance of Jesús' virgin birth would conclude that he cannot be biologically a male, although he obvi-ously was physically a male as attested to by his crucifixion, and much earlier, his circumcision (Kessel, 1983:129–36). When we consider that Scripture and centuries of Christian theology have taught us that Jesús is the exact imprint of God's very being (He. 1:3), we can begin to better appreciate the inclusiveness of Genesis 1:27, where: "God creat-ed humanity in God's image, in God's image God created them, male and female God created them." Both male and female and everything in between and beyond find their worth and dignity in the image of God fully revealed in the intersexuality of Jesús. To say that Jesucristo exists in the in-between spaces of male/female, human/divine, Jew/Gentile is to say that Jesús is a *bilingüe*, a bilingual.

JESÚS: *UN BILINGÜE*

The ultimate signifier of the Hispanic *mestizaje* existence, rooted in living in the space of *nepantla*, celebrating the *ajiaco* of the Latino/a identity, is being *bilingüe*. Desi Arnaz, best known for playing the role of Ricky Ricardo in the 1950s hit sitcom *I Love Lucy*, had a sign hang-ing on his dressing room door that stated, "English is broken here" (Pérez Firmat 1995:200). "Spanglish" is that broken English of Latino/as that serves as the verbal expression of a new space that expresses the *mestizaje* where Hispanic bodies reside and the disenfranchised reality where their souls are imprisoned. For Latina/os whose identity is rooted in the nations of origin from which they hail, Spanglish becomes a corrupt vernacular of the mother tongue signifying neglectfulness at best, or at worst, a rejection of Hispanics' original indigenous cultures through the Americanizing of the language. And yet, to speak Spanglish allows the converser to convey nuances in meaning that are better ex-pressed through a particular word existing in one language where a direct translation does not exist in the other. To the dominant Eurocen-tric culture, Spanglish is heard as linguistically deficient, a humorous

attempt to imitate the legitimate English language. In a real sense, to be
bilingüe is to belong to two cultures that equally rebuff Latino/as. To be
bilingüe or to speak Spanglish moves beyond simply being able to con-
verse in two languages (after all, many Hispanics are monolingual);
bilingüe and Spanglish signifies "two-ness." The construction of Spanglish does not imply fluency in Spanish or English; rather, Spanglish,
more than a language, becomes a space where the concepts, ideas,
dreams, and visions represented by linguistic signs create a Latinoness
that superficially unites diversity.

When a people are denied economic and cultural capital, a new way
of expression is usually devised in the diverse setting of everyday life.
Spanglish reflects the reality that forces Hispanics to live with one foot
in the Latina/o world whence they come and the other foot in the
present physical country where they reside, switching between two different sets of symbols depending on which signs (i.e., words or phrases)
best provide nuances of the intended meaning. Rather than a rejection
of heritages or cultures, an attempt is instead made to carve out a
distinctive, separate, social space. The construction of Spanglish becomes a Hispanic sociopolitical project toward the unification of "who
they are" and "where they live." Spanglish represents the irremediable
"two-ness" of cultures that dwells within the materiality of Latina/o
bodies.

Jesucristo also found within his flesh the "two-ness" of being, being
one with God yet dwelling among humans. When the Word took on
flesh, uniting divinity and humanity, Jesús became a *bilingüe*. His nei-
ther/nor, and/also resonates with the social location of many Latina/os
who discover they are too Hispanic to be accepted within Eurocentric
culture and too Americanized to be accepted in their countries of ori-
gins. Hispanic identity is not derived from any given race (for Latino/as
represent the rainbow of races and ethnicities), but from language,
regardless of whether the Latina/o can or cannot speak Spanish. Holding ethnically and racially diverse Hispanics together is this two-ness.
According to ethicist Ada María Isasi-Díaz, "The Spanish language
functions for Latinas[/os] not only as a means of communication but as

a means of identification [becoming] 'the incarnation and symbol' of our whole culture, . . . 'the bearer of identity and values.'. . . [T]he importance of Spanish for Latinas[/os] is . . . to be able to identify each other, grammatical and pronunciation correctness is totally secondary" (1993:52–53).

Language then, is more than simply a collection of words; it constructs an identity by becoming a conveyer of thought that forms, creates, and impacts theological and theoretical concepts. Usage of English, Spanish, or Spanglish to ponder Jesús' politics does more than simply name a praxis; it creates action which becomes linked to either Jesus (if English becomes the lens through which we gaze) or Jesús (if Spanish or Spanglish becomes the lens). For Ferdinand de Saussure, the linguist and semiotician, words as "linguistic signs unites, not a thing and a name, but a concept and a sound-image." This sound-image is a mental notion created by the name that is uttered. Thus sound-image is complex, with the power to connote or mask relationships that the concept has with other sound-images. The mental entity of the concept is what is signified while the signifier is the mental entity of the sound-image to which the concept is linked through the linguistic sign. Although linguistic signs are arbitrarily chosen to engender what is being signified, still, a power relationship is created between those who name the object and those who accept the naming (1959:66–67).

If words (as a collection of sounds) signify constructed concepts, what is important, then, is not the sounds arbitrarily chosen to point toward a particular concept but the signified concept itself. This means that being *bilingüe* has less to do with reading or speaking English and Spanish and more to do with possessing a dexterity of thinking within the fluidity where the Hispanic and Euroamerican culture meet and overlap. And while possessing the ability to speak in the language of the angels is always preferable, for our purposes, to read and speak Spanish moves beyond any ability to master the language in favor of the ability to conceptualize worldviews born within the disenfranchisement and struggles of the Hispanic community. Not surprisingly, there exist Latina/os fluent in both languages who, due to their lack of solidarity with

the Hispanic marginalized, are culturally monolinguist and Euroamericans (as well as Hispanics speaking only English) who, due to their
solidarity with *la comunidad*, are *bilingües*.

The linguistic sign *Jesus* provides coded access to the object it signifies, which masks a relationship of power. *Jesús* provides a very different coded access that masks a different relationship of power. Jesus is
not Jesús, for Jesus means something different that masks certain power
structures that justify the power and privilege of the dominant culture,
while Jesús signifies liberation and resistance. Of course, all languages
fall short of fully describing the reality of deity. Finite words as signs fail
to fully signify the infinite concept of God, hence the importance of
metaphors, imagery, and aesthetic expressions. Yet regardless of the
limitations of language, to the dominant culture, Jesús represents the
ethnic stubbornness (or stupidity) that resists assimilation to what is
perceived as an intellectually superior culture possessing a correct theological interpretation of divinity.

Hispanics by choice continue to preserve what their language signifies by passing it onto the next generation. With the act of being
Spanglish speaking and holding onto Jesús, Latina/os place themselves
in direct conflict with the sociopolitical structures that would have all
Hispanics articulate self-oppressive expression with each linguistic ut-
terance of Jesus' name. The insistence on speaking and dreaming in the
dominant language, according to sociologist Pierre Bourdieu, has been
constructed to endow the status of sole legitimacy upon the official
language and way of being of the dominant group. Language, in the
hands of this group, becomes an instrument of action and power that
creates knowledge and truth. The purification of thought through the
purification of language legitimates the dominant group's monopoly of
political power (1991:1–37, 46–49). Latina/os desiring to produce successful discourse as a means of fully participating within the structures
of society must observe the "cultural capital" of that society, which is to
speak a fluent English without a Hispanic linguistic or cultural accent.
Not only must they speak, think, and dream in English, they must adopt
a Jesus whose name and being is also absent of an accent. Regardless of

the effort exhausted, the attempt to sound Eurocentric is viewed as a parody. This inability to master the dominant language signifies that Hispanics are in a symbolic system that they will never command, rather, a system that commands.

Defenders of linguistic assimilation often insist on its predominance because of some alleged intrinsic virtue. In reality, they are defending their position of power. Power need not be overtly exercised. Rather, power can be transmuted into a symbolic form through the routine flow of day-to-day life that is conducted in the linguistic symbols of the dominant group. This process empowers the dominant group by bestowing a kind of legitimacy. Language, as a symbolic power, presupposes the values of the dominant culture in such a way that Hispanics assimilating to Eurocentric linguistic patterns participate in their own subjection. The tacit acknowledgment of the dominant culture's legitimacy, and the power relation in which Hispanics are embedded, prevents them from recognizing that the present system is but an arbitrary social construction designed to serve the interest of the dominant group (Ibid.:1–31, 45, 57).

Still, to insist upon the validity of Spanglish dooms Hispanics to being oppressed because English (manifested in language and culture) is a precondition for both economic and political success in the United States, and, because English is *la lingua franca*, it also becomes a precursor for global success. If knowledge and power work through language, then which language used to recount the Jesús narrative imposes power of "correct interpretation," making the arbitrary use of any particular language universal and normative for all? And yet, the miracle of Pentecost is specifically that Divinity communicated with humanity in each of their tongues (Acts 2:4–6). To read about Jesús in Spanglish provides the reader with different significations to the words serving as signs from those reading about Jesus in English. To insist on reading about Jesús rooted within Hispanic concepts raises different significations alien to Euroamericans. A few examples can illustrate this point.

The English word *love* usually characterizes how we feel toward diverse objects, persons, and experiences. "I love my spouse," "I love chocolate," "I love my children," and "I love soccer." In all of these phrases, *love* is a sign that signifies feelings and sensations for something or someone that provides us with great joy, happiness, and fulfillment. And yet, if pressed, I honestly do not have the same emotional attachment to soccer that I have toward my wife. Forced to make a choice, I would willingly live a life without chocolate rather than a life without my children. Obviously, different degrees and intensities exist for feelings toward diverse objects of my affection. Regrettably, when the same word, *love*, is used to describe different levels of affections, the word loses its intimacy and significance. The Greek language understood this, therefore providing us with four words to describe the nuances of love. *Philia* describes the friendship and affection shared by equals, as illustrated in the name Philadelphia, the City of Brotherly Love. *Storge* is used to depict the "natural" affection that exists within familial relationship, as in the case of parents toward children. *Eros* portrays the sexual attraction and passion. And *agape* connotes an unconditional love best illustrated in the love God has for humans, and best described in the biblical passage of 1 Corinthians 13, which has come to be known as the "love chapter."

Reading Jesús in Spanglish and through Hispanic symbols provides the reader with radically different interpretations of the biblical text. *Te amo* (I love you) is only reserved for spouses or lovers. *Te quiero* (literally—I want you) is used to connote love toward family and friends. *Me gusta* (I like it) usually refers to soccer, chocolate, and other things or experiences we enjoy. These different Spanish connotations for the English word *love* create an understanding of God when read through Jesús. When the biblical text refers to the affection of the Spanish reader to God, the more intimate term, *te amo*, is used. To read of the love we are to have for God is to read about the intimate relationship between lovers, a relationship to which we are called. This is a love that moves beyond some fuzzy feelings toward a lover's desire demonstrated through one's actions, specifically faithfulness to God and God's ways. The mutual trust and vulnerability that are supposed to serve as the foundation for intimacy between lovers is the same love and affection Jesucristo calls us to have for God.

Another example concerning language can show the richness of a *bilingüe* Jesús. The English word *you*, can be translated into Spanish as either *tú* or *usted*. When addressing those who occupy a higher station in life, one's elder, patron, employer, mentor/teacher, or political/community leader, the formal pronoun *usted* is used as a sign of respect. However, when addressing equals or those who occupy lower social standing, friends, coworkers, children, or employees, the informal pronoun *tú* is used. Most with a Eurocentric worldview might assume that when referring to God, *usted*, the term reserved for royalty is used. Nonetheless, God is addressed as *tú* when read in Spanglish. Calling God *tú*, recognizes God's solidarity with the station of life of the disenfranchised.[9] God is not far away sitting on some throne in the heavens; rather, God is here among God's suffering people. God is not some unapproachable ruler, we can approach God in the same way we approach someone with whom we are intimately familiar. God is one of us, from the margins of society.

Reading the Bible in Spanglish even provides a different understanding of what justice is, as both English and Spanish create different significations for these linguistic signs. When a biblical text is read in English, the word "righteous" is mostly used, but when the same text is read in Spanish the word *justicia*, which is translated into English as "justice," is used. While those reading the Bible in English read about righteousness, those reading the Bible in Spanish read about justice, creating a clear Jesus/Jesús dichotomy. The dictionary defines "righteous" as "morally right or justifiable, acting in an upright, moral way." The definition implies an action that can be performed privately. Stuck on a deserted island, one can be righteous by maintaining a prayer life that honors God, by maintaining self-control, and by praying without ceasing. To read the Bible through Jesus is to discover a very individualistic faith. However, to read "justice" in Spanish is to assume a communal faith for justice can only be exercised in community, requiring others to whom justice can be administered.

James tells us that "the effectual fervent prayers of a righteous person avail much" (5:16); that is, one who is pious, whose relationship with God is based on an individual conversion, has his prayers answered. When we read the same verse in Spanish, *"La oración del justo es poderosa y eficaz"* (NIV), it tells us that the prayer of the *just one* (the one doing justice within the community in obedience to God) has much power. In English, Matthew quotes Jesus as saying, "Blessed are those who hunger and thirst for righteousness, for they will be filled" (5:6); in other words, those who hunger for moral purity and thirst for chastity will be rewarded. In Spanish, *"Dichosos los que tienen hambre y sed de justicia, porque serán saciados"* (NIV), those who hunger for justice to be done to all members of the community, especially to the disenfranchised, and who thirst for justice against all oppressors, these are the ones whom God will fully satisfy. Scripture admonishes us to be righteous if we hope to enter God's reign, "Truly I say to you, unless your righteousness surpasses that of the Pharisees and the teachers of the law, you will definitely not enter the reign of heaven" (Mt. 5:20). But in Spanish, Jesucristo claims, *"Porque les digo a ustedes, que no van a entrar en el reino de los cielos a menos que su justicia supere a la de los fariseos y de los maestros de la ley"* (NIV); that is, one's work in justice must surpass the Pharisees and the teachers of the law to enter God's reign. Based on these translations, the politics of Jesus becomes alien to those who read about Jesús through their Spanglish cultural eyes detecting the clear call throughout the pages of the Bible to participate in a politics that seeks justice.

JESÚS: THE INCARNATION

God is not over and against the joys and sufferings of human experiences; instead God enfleshes Godself in the concrete events of human history. The Gospel proclaims that, "the Word became flesh and dwelt among us. We beheld God's glory, the glory of the only begotten who came from God, full of grace and truth" (Jn. 1:14). The Word dwelling among humans means we have a God who understands our delights and pleasures as well as our trials and tribulations because God in the flesh experienced the highs and lows of human existence. But the incarnation of God is not a onetime event, for this God who became human continues to enflesh Godself in the everyday lives of those who consistently are today crucified on the crosses of oppression—the crosses of Latino/a ethnic discrimination. By saying that God took on flesh, we signal the importance of contextualizing one's social location as fundamental to the construction of knowledge. For Christians, what we perceive to be ethical is based on the experiences of flesh, what we humans experience in our own flesh informed by what Jesús also experienced in his flesh. Crucial to our understanding of the politics of Jesús is which flesh was chosen for the incarnation. It was not Rome, the most powerful city of the known world, where God chose to perform the miracle of the incarnation, nor was it Jerusalem, the center of Yahweh worship; rather, it was impoverished Galilee where God chose to first proclaim the message of liberation. The starting point of liberating news is the margins of power, the periphery to which the disenfranchised are relegated. This is the same pattern adopted by Moses centuries earlier, who while in Pharaoh's court cast his lot with the Hebrew slaves. "God made flesh," assuming the materiality of Jesús' body, means that God chose to become marginalized. Jesús denied some heavenly abode to dwell among the least of these. God stands in solidarity with all who suffer under unjust religious and political structures because through Jesús God experienced this oppression in the flesh.

Because Jesús experienced humanity in the flesh of the poor, the ethical is perceived not by ethereal philosophizing but by determined experiences. All too often, ethical structures are based on the experience of those who write books, preach at influential churches, or teach at prestigious academic centers whose social location differs from the poor of the earth. The experience of religion professors, professional ethicists, and clergy ministering in economically privileged congregations or seminaries usually becomes the norm for the construction of what is moral. By contrast, because Jesús put on the flesh of the marginalized, I argue for an ethics rooted in the experiences of the marginalized, an experience that was, and continues to be, shared by God. Those marginalized in Jesús' time occupied the privileged position of being the first to hear the Good News. Not because they were holier, nor better Christians, but because God chooses sides. God makes a preferential option for those who exist under the weight of oppression, demonstrated by God's physical solidarity with the disenfranchised through the incarnation. Jesús willingly assumed the role of the ultra-disenfranchised, becoming the paragon for disciples to emulate. Followers of Jesús are called to imitate God, an imitation that excludes those who hold onto power and privilege, those who lord over humans. The difficulty for the privileged in finding salvation is usually their refusal to imitate Moses and Jesús in accompanying the disenfranchised in their daily struggle. Salvation for today's powerful and privileged, those who made for themselves heavenly abodes on earth, is to also incarnate themselves among the marginalized.

Incarnation is clearly understood as an abstract theological Eurocentric term. Yet among Latina/os reading their Bibles in Spanglish, the translated term, *encarnación* connotes a more meaty meaning. Sociologist Caleb Rosado argues that Jesús is our *hermano*, our brother, who by putting on flesh (*carne*) becomes our *carnal* (slang: buddy, pal, which connotes the sharing of the same flesh), thus suggesting that Jesús becoming one *carne*, one meat, with humanity (1992:76). To be of the same flesh, the same meat makes Jesús family, or as the apostle Pablo puts it, firstborn among many brothers and sisters (Ro. 8:29). Theologian Luis Pedraja illustrates how Hispanics perceive the usage of the word *carne* when he points out that the common Latina/o walking through his or her *barrio* might notice a common sign found over most butcher shops (*carnicería*) advertising sales on meat (*carne*) as the butcher (*carnicero*), wearing a blood splattered apron, stands next to the slabs of meat (*carne*). The in*carna*tion, Jesús in-meatedness, becomes a concept that is hard to ignore among Latino/as (1999:76).

The individual, to whom divinity was incarnated, as subject and supreme object of all philosophical, theological, and theoretical thought is a tangible creature who is born, suffers, and dies. Philosopher Miguel de Unamuno provided an anthropocentric view of the universe where humans are understood as persons consisting of *carne y hueso* (flesh and bone),[10] struggling to answer the unanswerable human question. An intensity for life is called for due to the realization of death's ultimate victory, forcing one to override logic lest it obstruct passion; thus, a passionate response to the everyday of life becomes as valid as Eurocentric systematic reasoning (1968b:925–38). For Unamuno, the existential self becomes an expressive constituent element of physical reality viewed as an independent, indivisible, and impenetrable unit of substance, à la Leibnitz. This self, while attaining personal awareness, becomes conscious of its own internal contradiction: a contradiction that realizes the self as a unique living being whose *raison d'être*, while being eternal life, must die. The sorrow, or tragedy of human life, which takes its being from the world that moves from created to creating, from formed to forming, as a self-formation of the historical world, lies in this paradox. Becoming conscious of this existential contradiction, the self develops awareness of the religiously problematic dilemma wherein the self is located. Recognizing one's eternal death confirms one's individuality.

For Unamuno, and the rest of us, the agony of Christianity refers to the tension between his feelings for a God who is incommunicable knowledge and the truth that is social and collective, a position that Hegel labels the "Unhappy Consciousness." Unamuno was the unbeliever who believed. The kernel of his philosophy is his mystic hunger for personal immortality through an ambivalent hope for the existence of God. God's existence is not a "rational necessity but vital anguish that leads us to believe in God . . . (that is) to hunger for divinity, to feel the lack and absence of God, to wish that God may exist" (1967:305–65). Such tension must exist, for agony means struggle, and as long as there are struggles there is life, thus averting death.

Faith can be defined as pure faith in God, apart from any special doctrine (orthodoxy) that represents God. This faith is not a rational concept but an imperative of the heart where Jesús, as a clearly defined figure, counters historical criticism. A religious awareness of faith supersedes any attempt to confine it within a paradigm of reason. This does not mean that the lack of reason leads to the illogical. Rather, the paradoxes and mysteries of the everyday of life that are beyond the comprehension of the rational can be known through experience. Faith in God can only be believed and confessed; it can never be achieved rationally. Because there exists little in religion that is capable of rational resolution apart from "subjective logic," Unamuno looks to the mystics for valid expressions of faith. In a letter to fellow philosopher José Ortega y Gasset, Unamuno writes: "They say we do not have a scientific spirit. But ours is of a different sort. . . . If it were impossible for one nation to produce both a Descartes and a Juan de la Cruz, I would choose the latter" (1956:104). The core of faith becomes the *dolor sabroso* (the delicious or exquisite pain) of Santa Teresa that monopolizes God and stresses God's nexus to each separate individual. Eurocentric rationalism, unlike mysticism, fails us because the world of abstract concepts can never transcend this existential historical world. Ironically, Ortega y Gasset (who began his career as a neo-Kantian) agrees. To him, rational reflection became utopian and unhistorical. He maintained that reasoning is but the combination of unreasonable views.

Forsaking rationalism, Ortega y Gasset turns to the philosopher Martin Heidegger to construct a world where the pragmatic individual encounters an environment that is nothing more than a mere combination of advantages and obstacles (1939:93). Reality becomes subordinated to subjective exigencies. Life's problems and struggles cease primarily being of an intellectual or scientific nature, requiring solutions that do not call for the discovery of a new scientific law. Ortega y Gasset's exhortation to doubt science because of its inability to satisfy the volition needs of humans (their mortality) is echoed by Unamuno, who concurs that scientific proof leaves life's essential and final questions unanswered (1942:67–72). Ortega y Gasset argued against a philosophical thought elevated to divine status, calling instead for its dethroning and subjugation to serve humanity. He came to view all lofty Eurocentric thought (specifically German) from Immanuel Kant until the 1900s, as the bigotry of culture that simply transferred values, which previous Christian philosophers called "God," to what contemporary Germans dubbed "idea" (Hegel), "primacy of the practical reason" (Kant), or "culture" (Cohen) (Gray 1989:129). Likewise, Unamuno's work vindicates human existence by demythologizing philosophical abstractions, forcing us to deal with the passionate anxiety generated by their emphasis on life's mortality.

No longer can philosophies attempt to crystallize thoughts into an absolute pristine system based on objective principles. Philosophy must strain beyond its systematic thought toward its purpose and reason for existence: humans—complex humans made of *carne y hueso*. Philosophies and/or theologies that fail to channel knowledge for the benefit of humanity become, as per Unamuno, "a cemetery of dead ideas" threatening the tyrannization of humanity. For Unamuno, "science robs [women and] men of wisdom usually converting them into phantom beings loaded with facts" (1925:55).

This human dilemma that Unamuno wrestles with is one that the divine inhabited. Because the Word took on *carne*, God does not stand aloof from human experiences, but rather enfleshes Godself in the chaos of human history, not to direct it, but to suffer in solidarity with those ruined by the human conflicts that create history. Probably the most powerful verse of the entire Bible also happens to be the shortest verse. "Jesús lloró" (Jn. 11:35). God in-flesh weeps over the everyday sufferings of humanity. Not only do we learn from the Gospel how to be more like Jesucristo, but also God, through Jesús, "learns" how to be human-like. The crucifixion of Jesús signals God's solidarity with the countless multitudes that continue to be crucified today. The civil and religious leaders who saw him as a threat to their power put Jesús, as fully human, to death, like so many today. The importance of the cross for the marginalized is having a God who understands their trials and tribulations because God in the flesh also suffered trials and tribulations. This God who became human continues to enflesh Godself in the everyday lives and experiences of today's crucified people. An important element in ethical reflection is what Hispanic theologians have

called *lo cotidiano*, the Spanish word for "the everyday." Ethics from
the margins is contextual, where the everyday experience of the disenfranchised, in our case Latina/os, becomes the subject and source of
ethical reflection. To do ethics from the margins is to reflect on auto-
biographical elements to avoid creating a lifeless ethical understanding.

Church historian Zaida Maldonado Pérez reminds us that among
Latina/os "Jesús [is] preached as Emanuel, God with us in the barrio, in
the factory, in the welfare office, in the dark when the electricity got
shut off because of an unpaid bill" (2009:122). The methodological
inclusion of the everyday of one's story into an ethical dilemma powerfully connects reality with theory. Such an inclusion challenges the predominant assumption that all ethical deliberations must occur apart
from and independent of the interpreter's social location or identity.
Rather than verifying what is truth as explicated by those who are tradi-
tionally viewed as authorities (such as clergy or ethicists) or through
sacred texts as historically interpreted by experts, the source of ethical
deliberation begins with *lo cotidiano*, as experienced and understood by
those existing on the margins. The perspective of those who are considered nonpersons because of their ethnicity, race, class, orientation, or
gender becomes the starting point for any Christian ethical action. And
this shatters the grip of those at the top of theological hierarchies on
being the sole legitimate interpreters or arbiters of what is ethical.

Jesucristo lived in *lo cotidiano*. All too often, Eurocentric theological
thought is constructed in the prestigious ivy towers of academia. Jesús,
on the other hand, constructed his theology out of the everyday experiences of the people, recounting parables of a woman who lost her coin,
a shepherd searching for a lost lamb, or the planting of a mustard seed.
Jesús is rooted in the materiality of Latina/o life, and thus can only be
understood by focusing on the everyday trials and tribulations of the
marginalized. For Jesús, the mysteries of God found expression on the
daily existence and struggles of common folk, critically analyzing the
good and bad that shapes and forms daily life. Theologian María Pilar
Aquino reminds us that our daily relationships become the basis for all
social relations. "This is why analysis stress that daily life permeates the

public as well as the private spheres, because the activities carried out in both spheres 'imply a level of dailyness, daily actions that confer upon this oppression, day after day, an air of naturalness'" (1993:40). This was a theological perspective comprised from the *carne y hueso*, the flesh and bone contextual reality of the marginalized, not the ethereal contemplation of intellectuals who claim neutrality or objectivity. To engage in the politics of Jesús is to recognize and understand the everyday experience of Hispanics, to do theology from the space of living on the borders between belonging and perpetual alien.

Latino/as understand a God who took on flesh in the form of Jesús, enfleshing Godself, then and now, in the everyday lives and experiences of the dispossessed. Because Jesús had flesh, humanity can encounter the divine in the midst of the everyday. An "epistemological privilege" exists for Hispanics who know how to live and survive in both the center and periphery of society, unlike the dominant cultures, which generally fail to understand the everyday experience of their periphery. This is why Hispanics must remain suspicious of Euroamerican theological thought that teaches to distinguish between the "sacred" and the "profane" history. Such a dichotomy is a false construction. Jesús transcends these categories by fulfilling his mission, standing over and against all repressive structures, be they religious or secular. By living in *lo cotidiano*, Jesús provides a spiritual response to the everyday sociopolitical realities of oppressed Hispanics.

Theological reflections are understood as being more than simply creating, expanding, or sustaining doctrinal beliefs. As important as salvation from sin may be, personal or corporate salvation, understood as liberation, is achieved through the consciousness-raising process of learning how current oppressive structures prevent Latina/os from living the abundant life promised by Jesús (Jn. 10:10). Theology is understood as a reflection of praxis by Jesús, responding to inhuman conditions experienced by the majority of humanity. A salient characteristic of Jesús' use of parables rooted in the everyday was the ability of such short stories to reconcile the theoretical and theological with pastoral

concerns, rooted with the people's daily experience of disenfranchisement.

From the underside of power and privilege, a religious view is developed from which to address structural injustices. The methodology employed in reading the Bible from the margins fuses the biblical narrative
with the everyday experiences of Hispanics, producing a biblical witness
capable of addressing oppression. The everyday trials and tribulations
of Hispanics, as our theological starting point, become the bases by
which Jesús' actions and message is understood. The politics of Jesús is
manifested where the everyday brings the margins to the center and
when the process challenges those accustomed to setting the parame-
ters of theological discourse. Moving beyond simply the analytical, *lo
cotidiano* has the potential to become the catalyst for structural political
changes.

JESÚS: EVIL AS TRICKSTER

To claim that God was incarnated within the everyday flesh, the everyday meat of humanity is to recognize an immanent God who stands in
solidarity with those who suffer. All who are in the flesh have faced, or
will face, tragedy, misery, illness, and death. Events will occur that
appear unfair, leading most of us to question if any sense of cosmic
justice and mercy truly exists. The real question is not if the moral
universe bends toward justice, but if there is anything moral in the
universe. Natural disasters will claim thousands of lives, and the victims
will include the innocent. Many have referred to this dilemma as the
"theodicy question." How can an all-loving, all-powerful God allow evil
to occur? Jesús asks, "What person among you, if asked by their child
for a loaf would give a stone? Of if asked for a fish will give a snake? If,
then, you, who are evil, know to give good gifts to your children, how
much more will your Father in Heaven give good things to those that
ask?" (Mt. 7:9–11).

Yet, reading the morning paper, one finds stories where many suffer
under moral evils (those actions caused by humans) and natural evils

(those actions caused by nature). Tornadoes have wiped out good Christian families, innocent children have perished at the hands of murderers with semiautomatic weapons that society condones, and good, decent individuals have died in freak accidents. When we consider the billions of senseless deaths, tragedies, and atrocities that define human history, it would seem that history denies, more than it confirms, the paternal love of a caring and merciful father God. And if we were to solely focus on the atrocities committed by the hands of Jesus-loving Christians, which include, but are not limited to, genocide of indigenous people, burning as witches of independent-thinking women, enslavement of Africans, colonization of the vast majority of the world's people, and countless wars over doctrines, we are forced to ask: Where is God?

Comparing Jesús' words with the reality of evil in our global economy seems to indicate that earthly parents, rather than God, know better about how to care for their children. It is God who appears to be giving the tens of thousands who die each day of hunger and preventable diseases a stone when they are begging for bread, or hands them a snake when they are praying for fish. In a very real way, we need a Satan to justify God's grace while legitimizing the reality and presence of evil in human history. It appears that the development of a Satan was, to a certain extent, trying to save God from appearing as the source of evil that is so much a part of the reality of human suffering and death. The Scriptures attempt to convince us that God is still worthy of our worship despite the presence of evil, even though the most troubling conclusion derived from the Judeo-Christian biblical text is the discovery of a God who is the cause and author of all that is good—and all that is evil. "If there is evil in a city, has Yahweh not done it?" (Am. 3:6), "I form light and create darkness, make peace and create evil, I Yahweh do all these things" (Is. 45:7). This is a God who sends evil spirits to torment, as in the case of Saul (1 Sa. 18:10) or Jeroboam (1 Kg. 14:10).

Evil befalls a person like Job because God directs it to be so. We are left with the troubling answer from God as to why evil befell such a faithful person: Over scores of chapters we finally hear the heavenly response: "Because I wanted it to." The early shapers of sacred texts and religious traditions found themselves in the position of having to protect God from accusations of being the source of evil. As it became less acceptable to have aspects of God represented in evil elements or events, independent evil figures had to be brought forth. If Satan did not exist, then perhaps he would have had to be invented to serve as an adversary so as to vindicate God. As troublesome as it may be to conceive of God as being the author of malevolent acts, more bothersome yet is the creation of another supernatural being in competition with God within a strictly monotheistic religion. A simple good-versus-evil binary understanding of reality leads to ethical perspectives that might cause more evil than good. A world where everyone and everything is either with or against God leads to great atrocities by those "with God" in their defense against the perceived threat of those "against God" (or satanic as defined by those who place themselves on God's side). Because such an ethical framework causes more evil than good, we are in need of a new way of understanding what is satanic, what is Satan.

What if we begin to see the tragedies that Latino/as endure more than simply some type of punishment from God? What if, instead, our understanding of Satan was influenced by the concept of the "trickster" figure that is so prevalent within Hispanic culture? (Think of Elegguá, Quwi, Pepito, Juan Bobo, Don Cacahuate, Pedro Ordimales, or Cantinflas.) Learning to interpret Satan as the ultimate trickster, rather than the embodiment of absolute Evil, can lead to ethical praxes that are more liberative because they deal with the causes of oppressive structures in the physical world, rather than simply blaming the present reality on the metaphysical reality of evil or on the moral depravity of humanity.

Tricksters create situations that force the one being tested to look for new ways in which to deal with the discord that has entered their life. What society normalizes can mask oppressive structures that make resistance seem futile as both those who benefit from and those afflicted by those structures are lulled into complicity. Seeking new alternatives to the surrounding trials and tribulations can lead the one being tested to discover opportunities previously unrecognized. Likewise, it could raise the consciousness of the one benefitting from the status quo, leading them to repentance and to a more liberative course of action that can result in the former oppressors discovering their own salvation. Satan's role becomes a bit more complex than being simply Evil incarnate. The trickster's role can lead to good, as in the case of raising consciousness (think of the temptation of Jesús in the desert), but it can also lead to destruction.

Trials and tribulations can lead Hispanics to be of good cheer because they recognize that Jesús, who is with them, has overcome the world. Or they could be led toward greater misery and destruction because they refuse grace. If they believe the deception of Satan's tricks, rather than rise above it, they can face devastation. It does not depend on Satan, an implement used by God, but, rather, it depends on humans and the choices they make. The de-emphasizing of a binary system of either absolute Good or absolute Evil moves us away from the impossible task of maintaining an ethical framework where either we emulate God's pure goodness or we become wretched creatures under Satan's control.[11]

How many religious leaders, congregations, and movements attempt purity and self-righteousness only to ignore their darker side and, in so doing, fall victim to what they proposed to battle by persecuting others who fall short of their lofty and righteous expectations? When evil happens, it is either Satan's fault or the fault of those who follow Satan. Here then is the ethical concern: seeing Satan in other humans. To reduce individuals to a representative of evil justifies cruelties and atrocities to be committed by those engaged in the spiritual battle to save humans from Satan's corruption. No evil ever dreamed up by Satan or his demons can outdo the atrocities committed by good, decent people attempting to purge such evil forces from this world. Religion scholar David Frankfurter states it best: "Historically verifiable atrocities take place not in the ceremonies of some evil realm or as expressions of some ontological evil force, but rather in the course of *purging* evil and its alleged devotees from the world" (2006:224).

JESÚS: TEMPTED

Jesús was just baptized by Juan, signifying the start of his ministry. As the water poured upon his head, the Heavens opened and the Spirit of the living God descends upon him like a dove proclaiming God's pleasure with God's son. Immediately after this monumental event, Jesús is led to the wilderness for forty days to live among the animals and (according to the synoptic gospels) is tempted by Satan. During his time in the desert, Jesús fasted for forty days and forty nights. He was hungry, tired, weak. While in the wilderness, Jesucristo faced the same temptations that today's marginalized communities usually face—assimilation to the unwarranted possessions, privilege, and power of the dominant culture. For the disenfranchised, it is so tempting to be acquiescent to the prevailing power structures if it means a warm meal and a secure home. The despair brought by dispossession provides motivation for assimilation. For struggling Latina/os who are led by discriminative practices to reside in the wilderness for more than just forty days and nights, the temptation of possessions, privilege, and power becomes too prevailing a lure. Maybe, just maybe, if Hispanics stop being so ethnic and become more Euroamerican than the Euroamericans, the burden of survival might be lightened.

The first test Jesús faced was over possessions. Satan whispered in his ear, "If you are really God's child, then command that these stones become bread" (Mt. 4:2). For those who are hungry, eating bread is no sin, and in fact, if a means exists to provide bread for the hungry, then it is a sin if it is not employed. The medieval Parisian bishop Guillaume d'Auxerre reminds us, along with other church leaders and theologians living during the plagues and famine of the twelfth and thirteenth centuries, that it is not a sin to engage in "starvation theft" (Ferm 1986: 9). Unlike our present moral codes based on capitalist paradigms, the need to preserve life (human rights) trumps the need to protect possessions (private property rights). In this instance, Jesús' hunger was not a result of unjust economic struggles that sell the poor for a pair of slippers. Jesús' hunger was a result of devotion, a self-imposed fast. So the taking of unearned possessions, when proper means of acquisition existed, to satisfy the consequences of his actions (participating in a ritual fast) would have been problematic. Following Jean Valjean's example to feed hungry children is quite different from taking shortcuts if opportunities to make one's own bread exist. Regardless of the situation in which the hungry Hispanics find themselves, Jesús' response serves as a guiding principle for praxis: "We do not live by bread alone, but on every word that comes forth from God's mouth" (Mt. 4:4). The concern of any praxis that is self-beneficial is the danger of spiritually self-justifying actions. Although liberative praxis leads to the construction of theology, still it must not wander too far from the biblical principle of putting the needs of others first through solidarity with the least of these.

The second temptation faced by Jesucristo dealt with privilege. Taking Jesús to the highest pinnacle of the Temple, Satan whispered "If you are the son of God, throw yourself down." And then, quoting Psalm 91, he added, "God will command [God's] messengers concerning you, and they will lift you up in their hands, so that your foot will not strike against a stone" (4:6). Even Scripture is misquoted, as so often is done, to entice the marginalized. Unfortunately, those who usually suffer due to the undeserved and unearned privilege that flows to the dominant culture dream more of joining their ranks than dismantling the structures that privilege one group—any group—over others.

John Raines, the chair of my PhD committee, often said during class, "We dream upward, but blame downward." Low wages are not perceived as the direct consequence of the greed of CEOs whose own wages increased from forty-four times that of the average factory worker in 1975 to 325 times the average worker by 2010 (De La Torre 2014, 161–62). While CEO salaries increase and record profits are posted, workers are pressured to accept wage freezes (if not cuts), work part-time, and/or work with fewer employee benefits. Instead of looking upward toward the cause of the ever-increasing wage gap, we blame downward, specifically the undocumented Mexicans and Central Americans crossing our southern borders who come to take away our jobs. Hope of making it someday, of sharing in unearned privilege, serves as a deterrent from being critical of those who presently occupy that position. All too often, Hispanics desire to surmount the structures of oppression so they too can benefit at the expense of others, rather than dismantling said structures. While the politics of Jesús might lead to liberation, succumbing to Satan's enticements to use Scripture to justify one's right to privilege seems more attractive, especially when one has spent too many generations on the underside of Eurocentric privilege. The Latino/a quest to move upward and join the crowd with privilege, a difficult task in and of itself but made easier for those with light skin and an education, creates an inability for Latina/os to work together politically to dismantle oppressive structures.

The final temptation that came from Satan was power. Taking Jesucristo to a very high mountain and showing him all the governments of the world in their entire splendor, he whispered, "I will give all these [kingdoms] to you if you fall down and worship me" (4:9). Latina/os who experience disempowerment and disenfranchisement dream of having power one day. And of course, there is nothing wrong with having power in determining one's own destiny—itself a sign of liberation. But the power offered to Jesús was over others. It is the power enjoyed by the elite of the dominant culture and the power that leads many of us to work against the interest of other disenfranchised Latino/as. While Hispanics should greatly appreciate those progressive Euroamericans who are always willing, with their resources and their person, to stand in solidarity, Latino/as must take political ownership of their own process of liberation. As long as the dominant culture gets to define what is "justice," Hispanics will never achieve any form of liberation from oppressive structures but instead will individually seek their own privilege. Unfortunately, there are at times too many among us willing to do the dirty work of those wanting to protect the power and privilege of the dominant culture. I'm sure the priestly leaders were glad when one of Jesús' own came forward willing to betray him.

It is interesting to note that Satan's first appearance in the Gospel story is not as the personification of absolute evil, but as one who tricks, as one who as trickster tests Jesús. Jesús, like us, can yield to temptation provided by the trickster and undermine his entire life and ministry before it even begins, or he can trust God and remain faithful to his calling rather than taking the easy road to possessions, privilege, and power. Jesús falls not into temptation and, in so doing, thanks to Satan, learns something about himself and his mission. Only after Satan's testing does Jesús begin his public ministry with a clearer understanding of his mission. Likewise, Satan's testing can be useful in the lives of Hispanics, providing focus to our own purpose, but only if we resist, like Jesús, the temptation of unearned possessions, privilege, and power—that is, surmounting the oppressive social structures that exist, rather than dismantling them.

3

NOWHERE TO LAY HIS HEAD

When I try to remember my very first memory of life, I recall seeing my mother sitting on a stool crying her eyes out. "*¿Por qué Dios mío? ¿Por qué?*—Why my God? Why?" she mumbled to herself. I must have been about three or four years old. As I looked around the bare room that doubled as both our living room and bedroom, I noticed the cause of her anguish. The ceiling and walls were moving. It was an eerie spectacle, something out of some horror flick. As I focused closer at what was causing this phenomenon, it became obvious that the ceiling wasn't moving; but rather the hundreds, if not thousands, of roaches crawling along the ceiling had created this false illusion. There were so many roaches that it seemed as if the ceiling was an ocean whose waves lapped upon the bordering walls. Although I was quite young, this image was seared into my consciousness, and probably will be the last thing I recollect when I lay on my death bed as an old man.

Just as First World conditions exist among the elite in the Third World, Third World conditions exist in the First World in the form of barrios (as well as Black ghettos and American Indian reservations). Later in life, I would discover that in the early 1960s, we were living in Third World conditions on the eastside of New York City, around 53rd Street, an area close to Hell's Kitchen (way before it became a trendy neighborhood). Back then, these were rat- and roach-infested tenement buildings dating to the early twentieth century, located close to the Lincoln Tunnel. There was only one bathroom per tenement floor to be shared by all of the floor's inhabitants. The conditions were so unsanitary that it was safer to relieve myself in an old cracker tin can than to use the floor bathroom. Our neighbors were pimps, prostitutes, and drug addicts, being replaced by Hispanic families who, for whatever reason, found themselves in this cold arctic city, far from the tropical climates of our homelands.

All day long, my mother worked like a dog to clean the apartment. She was expecting guests that evening and, regardless of our poverty, wanted everything to look as decent and respectable as possible. However, when she stepped into the living room, all she saw, in spite of her efforts, were these vermin, taunting her, as if to say that no matter how hard she tried, she would always be a dirty, poor Latina. Eventually, we were able to move up into a ghetto, then a low-income neighborhood, and finally into a working-class, blue-collar neighborhood. Both of my parents held several jobs for decades just to rise to the economic level of poverty. And even though they, along with past generations of Hispanics, bought into the American dream, the economic structures have been, and continue to be, constructed to maintain Latino/a economic disenfranchisement. Before it was a popular term among Euroamericans, I was a latch-key kid. No matter how hard my parents tried to shield me from our poverty, they were unsuccessful. Street violence was so prevalent that to this day, on both my physical body and my metaphysical soul, I carry the stigmata of the mean streets.

Popular culture, specifically television, provided a reminder that I was different. All I had to do was compare my life with the so-called typical American family on the then popular television show *Leave It to Beaver* to know that something had to be wrong with my family and with me. The images on the small screen were not my experience or reality, so obviously my people and my family were falling short of the norm. How else could one explain our poverty and marginalization? Self-loathing and self–ethnic hatred easily developed as I tried to become White; for to become White, I erroneously believed, meant to stop being poor. But no matter how hard I tried, my poverty, my Hispanicness, my inability to master the English language all prevented me from assimilating. I would always be seen as a spic, no matter how much I tried to ape the dominant culture. This child of the barrios, of the underside of the American life, would always be "poor" no matter how many academic degrees or how much wealth I might eventually obtain.

JESÚS: CHOOSING POVERTY

Growing up in poverty induced great shame. Even as I attended college, and was a successful young businessman, I still felt shame concerning my humble beginnings. I lacked the social capital that comes with economic privilege that would lead me to feel at ease at public gatherings. Even as a full professor, as my colleagues name the Ivy League schools from which they received their academic degrees, it is somewhat embarrassing that my degree comes from a community college, because that is all I was able to afford; and even then, I had to work full time to put myself through school, taking seven years to complete a four-year degree. Those who are poor usually reflect upon their economic condition with shame. And yet, Jesús accepted poverty so that Latino/as (as well as all who are economically disenfranchised) could be rich. Though Jesús enjoyed the riches of Heaven, for our sake he became poor, so that we, through his poverty might become rich (2 Co. 8:9). Jesús could have been born to the rich house of Caesar; instead, Jesús was born into, lived, and died in poverty. Like a barn animal, on that first Christmas night, María (as we saw in an earlier chapter) was forced to give birth amid unsanitary conditions.

Throughout his ministry, Jesús lived in privation. He reminds us that "the foxes have holes, and the birds of the heavens have nests, but the Son of man has nowhere to lay his head" (Lk. 9:58). A homeless man, he was able to celebrate his last supper due to the generosity of strangers (Lk. 22:17–13). He wandered without money in his purse (Mt. 17:22–27; Lk. 20:20–26), relying on the charity of others (Lk. 8:1–3). As he was hanging on the cross, his only earthly possessions, his clothes and undergarment, were rationed out, through the casting of lots, to the executioners (Jn. 20:24). Totally naked, with nothing left to call his own, Jesús died. Because Jesús chose solidarity with the poor, I have a God who understands not just my privation, but the poverty of all who are excluded from the earth's abundance. The radicalness of Jesús' poverty is that he chooses to side with the poor, giving the Gospel message a political and economic edge. My childhood poverty ceases to be a thing of shame due to something defective within me, my family, or my ethnicity. I can begin to understand our poverty not as the failure of my parents, but as a product of a society designed to privilege one group over others. While not attempting to romanticize poverty (there is nothing romantic about not having enough food to eat), I can better deal with my disturbing memories (or present realities) because Jesús' poverty has enriched me, making me richer than those who live in luxury.

Our present capitalist economic structure remains the means by which a new color and ethnic line has been drawn. The poverty that I experienced growing up is, unfortunately, often the norm for Hispanics. The vast majority of the poor—those locked out of the economic benefits this country has to offer—are and will continuously be Latina/os. Rates of poverty, generally speaking, are higher and income levels are lower when Latino/as are compared to non-Hispanic Whites. Not surprisingly, 66 percent of Hispanics have total family incomes that fail to provide economic security (McMahon et al. 2011:1). In 2006, the U.S. Census Bureau reported that Hispanic males' median earnings for full-time, year-round work was $26,769 and for Hispanic females, $24,214—compared to a median income of $41,386 for all males and $31,858 for all females within the general U.S. population (U.S. Census Bureau, 2006:22–23). The 2008 Great Recession further aggravated these figures, as Latina/os bore the brunt, experiencing the largest poverty rate jump among all ethnic and racial groups, from 21.5 percent to 22.4 percent (Garoogian 2012:9). By 2010, 22.4 percent of Hispanics lived below the poverty line during the previous twelve months—compared to 13.8 percent of the total population (Ibid., 12). The percentage of Latina/os who lived in poverty in 2010 was 26.6 percent (compared to

27.4 percent for Blacks, 12.1 percent for Asians, and 9.9 percent for non-Hispanic Whites). Median household income for non-Hispanic Whites was $54,620 compared to Hispanics at $37,759 or Blacks at $32,068 (DeNavas-Walt et al. 2011:8, 17; Wessler 2009:8). Hispanics, along with most people of color, find themselves relegated to inner city poverty, segregated from the middle-class suburbs (at times, gated communities), making it difficult for them to break through barriers that foster and maintain their poverty.

Not since the years of robber barons has this nation seen such an intense concentration of wealth in the hands of so few individuals. The rich are getting richer and the poor are getting poorer, thanks mainly to massive tax cuts to the wealthiest of Americans, instigated by the Reagan Revolution. We should not be surprised that those disenfranchised, those who suffered the most in the transfer of wealth from the poor to the rich, are disproportionately of color, especially Hispanics. Within the U.S. labor force, Hispanics are overrepresented in low-wage jobs with low requirements for education and experience. They comprise 14 percent of employed adults, yet they represent 20.2 percent of employees in the service sector. According to Toussaint-Comeau's socioeconomic index score, which measures wages and human capital requirements (i.e., education), more than half of the Latino/a workforce is employed in the eight major occupation groups with the lowest socioeconomic index scores (Singley, 2009:7–9). Furthermore, according to the U.S. Department of Commerce, "about 38% of non-Hispanic Whites worked in managerial, professional, and related occupations. . . . Hispanics were less likely to work in these occupations, with about 18% in managerial, professional, and related occupations" (2007:16). No matter how one chooses to quantitatively measure who is disenfranchised and dispossessed, every academic research study points to ethnic (and racial) inequalities. Those who are most removed from the "White ideal" disproportionately occupy the most menial jobs and live in the most economically deprived neighborhoods. Both exclusion and exploitation contribute to the conditions prevalent in this nation's barrios.

The defenders of neoliberalism insist that the economic privilege they share, thanks in part to tax cuts for the top echelons of wealthiest Americans, will "trickle down" to the masses. After all, "a rising tide lifts all boats." And while such slogans are usually associated with the political "right," members of the traditional left provide no better alternatives. Liberals may express, with teary eyes, guilt over the plight of the marginalized, but all too often it is done from the comfort of financial and sociopolitical security, unaware of their own complicity with oppressive social structures, while arrogantly professing to understand the disenfranchised social location. Fortunately, Hispanics have a Jesús who knows what it means to be consigned to the economic margins of society, for Jesucristo was also counted among the poor.

JESÚS: REJECTING CAPITALIST PARADIGMS

To understand Jesús from the social location of the poor is to create a sacred space where the marginalized can grapple with their spiritual need to reconcile their God with their struggle for economic justice and human dignity. If Jesús is indeed counted among the least of these, then any reading of the biblical text through the eyes of middle- or upper-class privilege becomes highly problematic. Only the poor have a better chance of understanding the nuances of the Gospels because they share the existential economic space of those who first heard the Gospel. This becomes evident when we consider the parable of the vineyard owner (Mt. 20:1–10).

Early one morning, a certain factory (vineyard) owner sets out to hire additional laborers to build widgets in his plant. He drives his pickup truck to the local bodega where several laborers usually wait to be hired, negotiates a fair day's wage, and he sends them to his factory. Several hours later, mid-morning, he comes across some individuals standing around the parking lot of the *jon dipo* (Home Depot), so he employs them too and sends them to build widgets in his factory. At noon, he finds more unemployed laborers in the parking lot of a justice-based church that, as part of their ministry, provides facilities for day laborers waiting to be hired. Again, in the mid and late afternoon, he finds some more laborers who were unable to find employment all day, so the factory owner sends them to his plant.

When the workday came to an end, and it was time to pay the workers, the factory owner reversed the order and began to pay those who were hired last and worked only a few hours. He paid them the amount he originally agreed to pay those whom he first hired in the early morning. In fact, he paid everyone the same amount, a full day's wage. Some may have worked all day, some just a few hours, but everyone got the same amount of money (Mt. 20:1–16). Now honestly, is this fair? Shouldn't workers be paid according to the amount of time they invested in the job? Doesn't time equal money? Is Jesús advocating an unfair wage structure? Those who follow Jesus instead of Jesús are caught in a dilemma. How does one reconcile how our present capitalist economic system defines monetary fairness? To do so, the Bible must be spiritualized. The parable is therefore interpreted as God providing the gift of salvation (the denarius), with no regard to how much work is done by the individual, nor by how long one has labored for God. All who come to God are given the same portion of grace irrespective of when in their life journey they turned to God. One can choose to follow Jesus as a child, or like one of the thieves crucified next to him, moments before death. All get to be in Paradise. But for Hispanics accustomed to standing at designated street corners throughout major cities of this country, waiting and hoping for a *patron* to stop and offer a job (off the books to avoid employment taxes), the fairness of this parable resonates. For those who are relegated to the barrios, where unemployed or minimum-wage service jobs abound, the fairness of this parable provides a vision for a just society based, not on neoliberal ethical principles, but on the mercies of God. How many day laborers end up working all day only to be paid a fraction of their worth because they have no recourse? Many don't even have proper documentation. How many of these workers injure themselves at the job only to be dropped off at the closest hospital and left to fend for themselves?

To read this parable as a Latino/a, from the perspective of the poor, is to recognize that the factory owner—or any employer for that matter—has a moral responsibility toward the laborers, a responsibility that goes beyond what traditional capitalist thinking defines as just. Jesús, himself coming from poverty, was aware of the laborers' plight. He fully understood that poverty prevented those who were created in the image of God from participating in the abundant life he came to give. In his parable of the employer hiring workers, Jesús attempts to teach economic justice so that all can have life abundantly. It was not the laborers' fault that they failed to obtain employment for that day. They awoke in the early predawn, walked to the spot where potential employers came to find workers and waited. Whether or not they were chosen to work that day, they still needed a full day's wage to meet their basic needs: food, shelter, and clothing.

In the capitalist model, a point originally made by Karl Marx in the first chapter of his classic, *Capital*, the product produced (widgets) has a usage value (the value of using a widget until constant usage causes the product to lose its usage value) and an exchange value (the usage value when someone else is willing to exchange money for the widget that no longer holds a usage value for the original owner). Both of these values can be determined. However, what is the value of the product itself? The time required to produce the widget constitutes the value of the product. This is determined when the capitalist and the worker join forces to produce the widget. The employer has capital and thus need not engage in the tedious labor of producing widgets.[1] The worker lacks liquid capital; nevertheless, the only thing they do possess is the time needed to constitute a workforce. Thus, the only capital that the worker brings to the table is their capacity to work. The employer hires the worker's time in order to produce the widgets.

Once an agreement is reached between the employer and the worker, the value of the workforce must be determined. What is the value of the work, the capital the laborer brings to the arrangement? The value of the workforce is equivalent to what is required for laborers to live. Whatever is required for a laborer to live, food, clothes, and shelter, becomes the value of her or his labor to ensure that, the next day, the laborer returns to work. For the worker during the times of Jesús, a *denarius* was the amount needed to sustain life. But the widget is not sold simply to cover the cost of the worker, a denarius. It probably is sold for two denarius. So the worker's capital, his or her time and labor, produces enough to pay for what is required to sustain their own life for one more day (a denarius) and enough to produce a surplus value (an additional denarius) for the employer. In an eight-hour workday, the laborer works four hours to ensure enough to live and survive one more day, and four hours to create the surplus value. While both contribute to the production of widgets (the employer capital in the form of money and the worker capital in the form of labor), only the employer benefits from the surplus value. Thus, the worker who owns no other property but their labor becomes the slave of the employer, who can manipulate the laborers' wages to increase the surplus value.

Surplus value can be increased by reducing the value of the workforce to below what is required to sustain life for an additional day, below what is required to provide adequate food, clothing, and shelter. What if six hours, instead of four, were dedicated to increase the surplus value? Consider the causes of the widening income gap phenomenon within the United States. Generally today, no matter how hard laborers work, they often continue to slip into greater poverty. By the eve of the 2008 Great Recession, profits of corporations represented the largest share of the national income since 1942, while salaries and wages were at their lowest level since 1929. While CEO salaries increase and record profits are posted, workers are pressured to accept wage freezes (if not cuts), work part-time, and/or work with fewer employee benefits (i.e., health insurance). Two adults working fulltime at the 2011 federal minimum wage of $7.25 equals a before-tax yearly income of $30,160 which is insufficient to meet basic necessities. A family with two working parents and two young children need $67,920 a year (or about $16.33 an hour per worker) to cover basic expenses and save for retirement and emergencies (McMahon et al. 2011:1–12). In 1962, the top 1 percent had a net worth 125 times that of the median household. By 2010, that net worth shot up to 288 times. The top 1 percent saw their net worth increase from $9.599 million in 1962 to $16.439 million in 2010.[2] Meanwhile, 45 percent of Americans lived in households that lacked economic security, representing 39 percent of all adults and 55 percent of all children. This means one out of every four fulltime working-age adults has an annual income that falls below the economic security baseline (Ibid.:1).

Increasing the surplus value at the expense of workers' wages commodifies and objectifies the worker, denying laborers their humanity. What was once the capital of the workforce is transformed to an expense, a production cost needing to be reduced to the lowest possible denominator so that the employer's surplus value could increase for the highest possible gain. By 1985, the average CEO salary rose to seventy times that of the average worker; by 1990 it was one hundred times.[3] If workers' annual pay during the 1990s had grown at the same rate as CEOs', workers' annual earnings in 2000 would have been $120,491. Or if the minimum wage of $3.80 an hour had grown at the same rate as CEOs' earnings, the 2000 minimum wage would have been $25.50 an hour rather than $5.15.[4]

Between 2003 and 2007, the average chief-executive salary increased by 45 percent, compared with a measly 2.7 percent increase for the average worker (Ebert et al. 2008:7). A 2011 report published by the Institute for Policy Studies revealed that corporate leaders in 2008, when the Great Recession occurred, were earning 299 times as much as the average worker. By 2010, when many workers lost their jobs, were outsourced, or were forced to take pay cuts, the earnings of CEOs increased to 325 times the average worker (Anderson et al. 2011:3). By 2012, the top 200 chief executives took home an average pay of $15.1 million, a 16 percent jump since 2011. While increases of CEO wages have become tied to the decrease of workers' wages (understood as an expense), those CEOs who announced layoffs of 1,000 or more workers between January 1 and August 1, 2001, earned 80 percent higher compensation than CEOs of 365 top U.S. firms that did not announce layoffs (Anderson et al. 2001:6–7). Franz Hinkelammert reminds us that "the existence of the poor attests to the existence of a Godless society, whether one explicitly believes in God or not" (1997:27).

What Jesús teaches in the parable of the factory (vineyard) owner is that earning only half a denarius meant that several family members would not eat that day. Only an uncaring and unmerciful heart would declare it just that these laborers leave without being able to meet their basic needs because, through no fault of their own, they were unable to find a job. Reading the Bible from the margins, the lesson is that those who are economically privileged, like the factory owner, must remain responsible for those who are not. For those who live under an economic system that commodifies the workers' time, justice is defined as a set pay for a set number of hours worked. Yet Jesús here defines justice as ensuring that each worker obtains a living wage, regardless of the hours worked, so that all can share in the abundant life. It did not matter how many hours a laborer worked, what mattered was that at the end of the day, she or he took home a living wage so that the entire family could survive for another day. The workers' responsibility was to labor, and it was the employer's responsibility to ensure that the employee left with enough. What does this say about our present system, where if a person works fulltime at the minimum hourly wage, he or she will earn several thousand dollars below what the U.S. government has determined to be the poverty level? Or, what does it say about the rich who hoard their wealth while so many suffer poverty?

Jesucristo tells a parable concerning a certain wealthy man who had an abundant harvest. Asking himself what he should do, for he lacked the space to store his surplus crop, he decided to tear down his barns and replace them with larger facilities. He then rested easy, confident that he had stored plenty of grain to meet his needs for many years to come. "Eat, drink, and be merry" became his motto, for he has achieved the goal of the capitalist, to live off of his investments (Lk. 12:16–19). Our capitalist-based worldview has taught us to consider this wealthy man as a wise entrepreneur. He saw a need, designed a plan, and then executed it to protect his investment. Many churches today would probably want such a person to head their finance committee, relying on his business acumen to help the faith community grow their stock portfolio. And yet, Jesús calls this man a fool. For that man will die; then who will get what he has prepared for himself (Lk. 12:20–21)?

The vineyard owner is but one example that illustrates what Jesús expects from those who hold power over workers. While illustrating how no one knows the day or the hour when Heaven and earth would pass away, Jesús tells the story of the master of a certain household who undertakes a long journey, leaving behind two stewards in charge—one who was conscientious, the other who was self-absorbed. But time passed on and the master delayed in his return. The conscientious steward fulfilled his ethical obligations to both the master and fellow servants, even though the master tarried. The self-absorbed steward meanwhile beat those under the stewards' authority. Rather than providing fellow servants a fair and decent wage for work performed, the steward instead ate and drank what was stolen from the laborers. One simply needs to consider the growing income gap that disproportionately impacts Hispanics (and other people of color) to recognize that this parable is as relevant today as when it was first uttered by Jesús. Rather than sharing profits, the steward, like many of today's CEOs of multinational corporations, hoarded the earnings to indulge in the excesses of wealth, forgetting that all must one day face a day of reckoning. When the steward least expected it, the stewards' master, without warning, came home. Seeing how both stewards behaved, the master rewarded the conscientious one while condemning the oppressive one, casting off the latter to where there is "constant weeping and grinding of teeth" (Mt. 24:45–51).

The parable's aphorism for our present time is that laws and government regulations increasingly seek to legitimize the power and privilege of today's stewards of the world. Because they lord it over the disenfranchised majority, contributing to their pauperization, salvation becomes ever so elusive for oppressive stewards seeking the face of God. But like the unfaithful steward who had to one day face the seat of judgment, so too will today's titans of corporations one day stand to be judged. And like the unfaithful steward, they too will be cast out for crushing the bones of the oppressed.

JESÚS: REJECTS THE PIOUS CEO

The deceitfulness of wealth chokes the Good News of Jesús, making it unfruitful (Mt. 13:22). This is best illustrated in the story of the rich young ruler, who today could easily be a chief executive officer. One day, a certain CEO of a multinational corporation came to Jesús asking him, "Good teacher, what must I do to be saved, how can I obtain eternal life?" Jesús responded by reminding the CEO of God's commandments. Don't commit adultery, don't murder, don't steal, don't bear false witness, but do honor your mother and father. The CEO, unlike his comrades, was a pious CEO. Since he was a child, he had kept all of these commandments. Fortunately, Jesucristo did not provide the response commonly given in modern Christianity. He did not invite the young CEO to repent of his sins by asking that he accept Jesus into his life as a personal savior. No doubt, having a pious CEO as an active member of a congregation would indeed be a plum. With the CEO's tithes and gifts, the church could easily become financially secure. Heck, a whole new fellowship hall could be built. Few who minister for Jesus would even question the economic structures that made this pious CEO so rich. But rather than simply accepting the young man as a follower, Jesús, out of love for him, tells the young CEO to sell all and distribute the proceeds to the poor. Only then can he follow Jesús. But when the rich young man heard this, the price to pay was too high, so he left full of sadness. Looking at him, Jesús proclaimed how difficult it is for the rich to enter the reign of God (Lk. 18:18–23). A faith solely based on individual belief and disconnected from public responsibilities and actions allows the rich young rulers of our time to claim to be followers and disciples of Jesús without it costing them anything. Nevertheless, Jesús determines salvation by how the rich interact with the poor.

Jesús' pronouncement asks way too much, so to soften the blow, many ministers of Jesus today interpret the text to assure their middle- and upper-class congregants that Jesus really didn't mean to give away everything to the poor. Rather, Jesus was dealing with the specific sin of this particular person. It was his riches that held him back from following Jesus. For others, it might be their jobs, their hobbies, or even their families. Whatever it is that we do not want to give up, that stands in the way of following Jesus, is what we must be *willing* to offer up. And the emphasis is on the willing. We don't actually have to give anything up, just be willing to do so. Hence, Jesús' words are so watered down that his interaction with the rich CEO loses all potency. Anyone who claims power and privilege forfeits his or her claim to God's eschatological promise, just like the rich young ruler. God's reign is not promised to those who are oppressors or benefit from oppressive structures, no matter how "good" they may be or which commandments they have kept. Believing in Jesús is insufficient for obtaining salvation. Jesucristo forces the rich young man, as well as all who are rich today, to move beyond an abstract belief in Jesús to a material response to those who are hungry, thirsty, naked, alien, sick, and incarcerated. Even though the Gospel of Luke fails to show how the rich young man was responsible for the plight of the poor, or even if he enriched himself at their expense, because he is rich, he automatically becomes linked to their poverty. To ignore the cry of those who are marginalized is to deny Jesús' message, regardless of whether or not we confess our belief in Jesús and proclaim his name with our lips. The author of Luke must have known many would read this passage in such a way as to ignore Jesús' radical call. So in response, Luke gives us, in the very next chapter, the story of Zacchaeus.

JESÚS: ACCEPTS THE IMPIOUS CEO

Jesús saves oppressors. The rich young ruler asks Jesús what he must do to enter God's reign. Even though he professed to keeping all of God's commandments, Jesús declared he lacked one thing. He was to sell all his possessions, give the proceeds to the poor, and follow Jesús. Jesús challenged the rich in the hopes that they would find their own salvation through solidarity with the poor. And while the righteous rich young ruler did not, the despised tax collector Zacchaeus did. While Jesús was passing through Jericho, Zacchaeus, who was the chief tax collector, making him a very wealthy man, wanted a glimpse. Tax collectors of the Roman Empire during the time of Jesús were despised by the Jewish common folk. They were perceived as unsaved, unclean publicans because they interacted with the Gentile Roman overseers. The Roman colonizers typically farmed out territorial regions to wealthy natives, contracting with them to collect the taxes for the empire. These entrepreneurs, some of whom were Jewish, paid a stipulated amount in advance to the empire for the right to collect taxes. These publicans squeezed as much in taxes as possible from the people, enough to cover their initial investment and enough to turn a profit. And if the people refused to pay? The tax collectors would hire local thugs to physically collect the taxes. Not only were these tax collectors seen as unclean, they were also despised because of their collusion with the Romans. They were traitors to their compatriots, thieves with imperial muscle, where graft and corruption abounded. Jewish tax collectors were stigmatized in their time the way many today would stigmatize pimps. No self-respectable Jew would eat, let alone associate with a tax collector, the perceived scum of the earth.

But the outcasts of society are the very ones Jesús came to heal—be they the oppressed, or their oppressors. Referring to another tax collector who became his disciple and for whom one of the Gospels is named, Mateo, Jesús reminded those who question why he ate with tax collectors and sinners that "the heathy have no need for a doctor, rather, the sick do." What Jesús and those who follow him desire is mercy. To forgive is better than the offering of sacrifices (Mt. 9:9–13). In fact, we are told that if we go to worship, and while presenting a sacrifice at the altar recall that someone has a grudge against us, we are to leave the offering before the altar and go first and be reconciled. Afterward, we can return and offer our sacrifice (Mt. 5:23–24).

Jesús did not come to call the just, but sinners, and Zacchaeus was a chief sinner. Being a short man, he was unable to get a good view of Jesucristo so he ran ahead of the crowd and climbed a sycamore-fig tree. Although a popular children's song about Zacchaeus climbing the sycamore tree exists, few recall the significance of this event. For when Jesús came to the spot where Zacchaeus was, he looked up and told him that tonight he was staying at his house. The oppressive activities of Zacchaeus are not condoned by Jesús. Compassion, not condemnation is offered. By recognizing the tax collector's humanity, grace makes salvation possible. Everyone who hears Jesús, even Zacchaeus, is shocked, for Jesús was to dine at the home of a tax collector, society's outcast. It was unheard of. But Zacchaeus, probably for the first time in his life, regained his humanity by Jesús' unconditional acceptance of him.

While the people judged Jesús, muttering among themselves that he had gone to be the guest of a sinner, Zacchaeus took stock of his own life. The grace and loving compassion shown him by Jesús was immediately manifested in his actions toward the poor, for Zacchaeus decided—then and there—to give half of his possessions to the poor and , to repay fourfold those he had cheated. Jesús responds by proclaiming that on this day, salvation entered Zacchaeus' house! (Lk. 19:1–10) In effect, Jesús links the salvation of oppressors to the actions they take toward the oppressed. Salvation entered Zacchaeus' house when God's grace was manifested as actions toward the poor, when Zacchaeus died to the power and privilege that had supported his lifestyle. Zacchaeus, unlike the rich young ruler whom Luke depicts in the previous chapter, recognizes what Adam Clayton Powell Sr., the renowned and dynamic pastor of Abyssinian Baptist Church of Harlem, called "cheap grace." God's grace devoid of a praxis-based, justice-seeking response indicates a lack of salvation.

Praxis as the starting point for philosophical, theological, and theoretical reflection contradicts the most salient characteristic of Eurocentric thought: individualism. Under the rubrics where individualism is the epistemological starting point, praxis becomes the action of an autonomous subject upon her or his environment, which reduces praxis to manipulation. In the past, movements to bring about just societies have failed because individuals were objectified because the State, be it Marxist or capitalist, reduced the totality of human life to an individual unit that is manipulated so that the person as "it" can contribute toward the desired results of the State. Theologian Roberto Goizueta elaborates on this point when he states that "in a capitalist society, those unable or unwilling to contribute to economic growth and profitability will be marginalized; in a Marxist society, those unable or unwilling to contribute to the revolutionary transformation of society will be marginalized" (1995:108). Philosopher Enrique Dussel argues that praxis of liberation puts the status quo into question, for it is a metaphysical, transontological praxis that serves as the procreator of a new order (1990:63–64). Justice becomes the unachievable goal, an outward revolutionary action within the milieu of peripheral social formation, which signifies an inward decision, like that of Zacchaeus, that to follow Jesús leads to the subversion of the phenomenological order allowing the metaphysical genesis of Hispanic thought to become a reality.

Juan el bautista was among the first to make the connection between salvation and praxis. When he saw the Pharisees and Sadducees coming to him for baptisms, he exhorted them, "You brood of vipers! Who warned you to flee from the coming wrath? Produce fruit in keeping with repentance" (Mt. 3:7–8). Both Juan and Jesús understood that praxis (i.e., works) did not save individuals (except maybe for those to whom the praxis is geared), but, rather, praxis becomes the fruits consistent with conversation, similar to the way we recognize a tree by the fruit it produces. Hence his final admonishment to the Pharisees and Sadducees, "The ax is already at the root of the trees, and every tree that does not produce good fruit will be cut down and thrown into the fire" (Mt. 3:10).

If Jesús had simply accepted the rich young ruler or Zacchaeus without thier wrestling with the connection between their wealth and the poverty of others, the economic oppression of the disenfranchised would simply have continued. Cheap grace would simply have masked the underlying causes of the marginalized pain, suffering, and misery. When Reverend Adam Clayton Powell Sr. coined the term "cheap grace," it was a reference to white Christian America's tolerance of Jim Crow, lynching, and racism (Clingan 2002:4).[5] For Jesús (and us for that matter) to simply forgive without any expectation of justice-seeking praxis on the part of the oppressor shortcircuits any hope of establishing the reign of God. It encourages what Powell, (and later Bonhoeffer) called "cheap grace," costing the perpetrator nothing and maintaining the very societal structures responsible for oppression in the first place. Not challenging these structures allows oppressors to continue profiting while resting on the "blessed assurance that Jesus is mine." The religious, rich, young ruler sought cheap grace and walked away feeling sad when Jesús refused to indulge him. Zacchaeus, the despicable sinner, sought and found something more permanent. The politics of Jesus has created a trend where it has become "politically correct" for members of the dominant group to publically confess their past transgressions, receive public affirmation for humbling themselves, and thus with forgiveness in hand, move on. This often obviates any need to consider or analyze the reasons for the oppression—indeed, this may be the intention from the beginning. The focus then shifts from the one who has been transgressed against to the one who benefits from the transgression. Such a focus is not only insulting to the one who has been abused, but it is likely to inflict greater pain as this "cheap grace" replaces any hope of creating a truly just social order.

The followers of Jesus might wish to remind us that we are saved by grace lest anyone should boast (Ep. 2:8–9). But Latino/as (who along with most of the disenfranchised who are normatively on the short end of the "cheap grace" stick, accustomed to seeing their oppressors—be they slum lords, rogue police, or bias judges—going to church on Sundays and singing of Christ's mercies) understand that cheap grace costs them too much. They are crucified on the crosses of economic oppression so that today's rich young rulers can have life, and live abundantly. Echoing Juan el bautista, Jesús also reminds his listeners that "trees that fail to bear fruit are to be cut down and thrown into the fire" (Mt. 7:19).

Good trees do not bear bad fruit, nor do bad trees bear good fruit. Each tree is recognized by the fruit it bears. Thus, people do not pick figs from thorn bushes, nor grapes from briers (Lk. 6:43–44). Justice-seeking praxis, the good fruits hanging on the tree, become—as demonstrated by Zacchaeus and not the rich young ruler—the outward expression of an inward conversion. If there is no fruit on the tree, then an intellectual decision might have been made, even if no conversion to Jesús took place.

The quest for justice brings about salvation and liberation for the oppressed and their oppressors. From marginality, Jesús challenged the rich in the hopes that they would find their own salvation through solidarity with the poor. To commit one's life to Jesús is to commit one's life to those Jesús opted for. Such a commitment to the poor is not ideological (Marxist or Compassionate Conservatism) but an expression of faith. Some did find God's salvation, as in the case of Zacchaeus. For others, the path to Heaven became impossible to achieve, as in the case of the rich young ruler who, while pious and virtuous and even keeping every commandment, still walked away from salvation out of reluctance to share his wealth with the poor. The fate that awaits those who walk away from the politics of Jesús can be quite disturbing.

If Zacchaeus becomes a model on how the wealthy can discover their humanity, and in turn their salvation, then the rich man portrayed in one of Jesús' parables can serve as a cautionary tale for all who are rich and unaware of how their wealth is linked to poverty. Once upon a time, according to Jesús, there was a very wealthy nameless man accustomed to feasting on only the best. At the gate of his mansion lay Lázaro, covered with sores, dreaming of a future based on the scraps that fell from the rich man's table. From the start of the story, Jesús subverts the norm. Today we can name those within our country who are wealthy; after all, buildings and foundations are usually named after them. But who can name the homeless? Jesús reverses this norm by naming the so-called nobody, while ignoring the one whose name society knows. Jesús continues the parable, informing his hearers that on a particular day, both men died. Lázaro was carried by angels to the bosom of Abraham, while the prosperous man went to Hell to be tormented for all eternity. The rich man, seeing Lázaro in Abraham's bosom, pleaded for mercy. He begged to have a few drops of water placed on his tongue to cool the agony of the flames. But Abraham refused, for a great gulf separated Heaven from Hell.

It is crucial to realize that the rich man was not condemned because he was wealthy. Likewise, nowhere in the text does it state that the rich man's opulence was accumulated unjustly or that he was directly oppressing Lázaro. His judgment and condemnation were based on the fact that, for all his affluence, he failed to share his resources with those, like Lázaro, who lacked the basics for survival. God's judgment was not based on anything the rich man did or any belief system he confessed or any particular church he attended. He was condemned for failing to give to the very least of God's children. But what if we read the text from the perspective of Lázaro? We may discover that his own sin of omission impacts the eternal condemnation of the rich man. What if, instead of sitting by the gate dreaming about scraps, Lázaro had been proactive? What if Lázaro had organized with other homeless folk and demanded food, shelter, and clothes? What if Lázaro had confronted the rich man for his sin of greed and hoarding? What if the rich man, upon hearing Lázaro's demands, repents? Then salvation would have also come to the rich man, and he too could have found comfort in the bosom of Abraham.

The politics of Jesús forces Hispanics not simply to sit beneath the tables of those in power waiting for the scraps to fall from the table, but to organize for justice. To struggle for justice is the praxis to which followers of Jesús are called. Not just to share in the abundance that the earth has to offer, but through organizing, the poor can shame those with power and privilege toward salvation. Following Jesús becomes a political process that brings salvation, liberation, to our fellow Latina/o *hermanas y hermanos* but also to our oppressors, who are waiting to become our sisters and brothers.

JESÚS: REJECTING RELIGIOSITY

To read about Jesucristo, especially from a position of power and privilege, runs the risk of romanticizing the plight of the poor, even to the point of making the condition of those oppressed the models for the victims of racism, classism, and sexism. This phenomenon of romanticizing the poor can be illustrated by how the dominant culture has come to interpret the story of a poor widow who gives all that she has to the Temple. The story of the widow's mite is generally idealized by the dominant culture as an example of Christian behavior for those who are poor. In Mark 12:41–44 (repeated in Luke 21:1–4) we are told that on a certain day, Jesús sat opposite of the Temple's treasury, watching how the crowd cast copper coins into the offering chests, called "trumpets" because they were shaped like one, narrow at the mouth but wide at the bottom. Many who were wealthy cast many coins, probably in small denominations, into one of the trumpets to emphasize the clinking sound made by numerous coins hitting the offering chest, thus demonstrating to all their pious generosity. But there was one poor widow who came and cast only two lepta, the smallest available denomination. Having called his disciples close to him, Jesús comments, "Truly I say to you that this poor widow cast more than all those casting into the treasury. For all cast out of their abundance, but she out of her poverty, cast all, as much as she had, her whole livelihood."

The widow becomes a paragon for the dispossessed. Those who are poor are expected, if they wish to be considered faithful, to give to the church—even if it means that they go without. Missing from most interpretations generated from economically privileged spaces is how the widow's self-sacrifice is related to the self-indulgence of the religious leaders who profit from her religious commitment. When we consider this story from the space of class privilege, we ignore how the normative interpretation maintains societal power relationships detrimental to the poor. While Jesus might praise the widow's faithfulness, Jesús offers a more critical assessment. All too often we fail to read Mark's entire account, for immediately preceding the widow's offering, Jesucristo expresses outrage toward the religious leaders who devour the possessions of widows. Specifically, Jesús tells his disciples that the religious leaders are "devouring the houses of the widows under the pretense of praying at length" (Mk. 12:38–40). If we were to read Luke's account of the incident, we would discover that Jesús immediately concludes the story of the widow's offering with his prediction of the Temple's destruction. According to Luke, "Some were speaking about the Temple, that it was decorated with stones and gifts. He said, 'These things you see, days will come when one stone will not be left on a stone'"(21:5–6). Reading Mark and Luke together, we discover that Jesús is not praising the widow's offering as a paragon to be emulated by the poor; rather, he is denouncing a religious social structure that cons the widow out of what little she has. It is bad enough that the biblical text is misinterpreted to mask the sin of the religious leaders who fleece the poor of the little they have. What becomes worse is when the poor, like the widow, begin to interpret the text in such a way that they maintain the structures designed to oppress them.

The widow requires liberation from the unjust religious structures that rob her of the little she possesses and from her colonized mind. We see today many widows being fleeced by televangelists who solicit donations to their ministries as concrete acts of faith by the least among us, as well as the churches of the rich who through another capital campaign sell visions of building crystal cathedrals as monuments to the fame of religious leaders. These ferocious wolves in sheep's clothing devour the widow's mite. The widow requires justice more than charity. But to stand in solidarity with the widow can never become a way of centering one's own activism so as to be praised by others, for Jesús reminds us to be careful not to participate in justice in front of others so as to be seen by them (Mt. 6:1). Until justice eliminates the need for charity, we are to give to the needy in a way that our left hand knows not what our right hand is doing. Our giving is to be done in secret, to be seen only by our God (Mt. 6:3–4).

Yes we are to strive for justice, but in the meantime, we are to follow the example of Jesús, who met the physical, not just the spiritual needs of the people. It seems as if people were always flocking to Jesús, many hoping to hear the Good News he had to offer. But like most preachers, Jesús had a tendency to be a bit longwinded. The day would drag on and soon night would fall. The people would grow hungry. Hunger is a major problem, for it distracts from participating in the moment. For those who have known, and continue to know hunger, there is a recognition that empty stomachs prevent eager ears from hearing. There comes a point for those originally listening to Jesús, then, and for many of today's disenfranchised, when hunger pangs drown out any message of salvation and redemption, even when coming from the very mouth of Jesús. Jesucristo was not so otherworldly that he was not in touch with the everyday experiences of hunger suffered by his listeners. So he ordered the multitudes, which numbered five thousand, to recline in small groups on the green grass. Then, taking five loaves and two fish, he gazed upon the heavens and provided a blessing. Breaking the loaves and dividing the fish, he gave them to his disciples so that they might divide them among the people. Everyone ate and was satisfied. After the feast, they collected twelve baskets of scraps (Mk. 6:39–44).

Educator Paulo Freire recollected several occasions of poverty and hunger early in his life and how hunger severely impacted his ability to learn anything. Once during an interview, he recalled, "I tried to read and pay attention in the classroom, but I didn't understand anything because of my hunger. I wasn't dumb. It wasn't lack of interest. My social condition didn't allow me to have an education. Experience showed me once again the relationship between social class and knowledge" (Gadotti 1994:5). Compare Freire's understanding of the politics of Jesús as demonstrated in his act of feeding the hungry with that of the great nineteeth-century evangelist Dwight Moody's understanding of the politics of Jesus. In a sermon Moody delivered in 1876, he stated his belief: "If I had the Bible in one hand and a loaf in the other, the people always looked first at the loaf, and that was just contrary to the order laid down in the Gospel" (Pell 1900:473). For Moody, and many who have reconciled Jesus with capitalist paradigms, providing bread to the hungry contributes to the person's poverty. We do more harm when we feed the hungry. Charity contributes to the incapacitating of character, for when the poor receive handouts, they lose motivation to work. In effect, God only helps those who help themselves. According to Moody, "There is a good deal that we think is charity that is really doing a great deal of mischief; and people must not think, because we don't give them money to aid them in their poverty, that we don't love them. . . . [I]t is a good thing that people should suffer. If they get a good living without work, they will never work. We can never make anything of them" (1885:340).

To be hungry is to be a failure. It is a personal character flaw not associated in any way with economic social structures designed to benefit an elite segment of society. If this is true, then Hispanics, along with other communities of color who are disproportionately poor, must be morally inferior to Whites who have a substantially higher median wage. To be poor is to be morally deficient. This simplistic understanding of the causes of poverty ignores how political contributions buy lobbyists who in turn "influence" politicians to pass tax and corporate laws that benefit them at the expense of everyone else (poor Whites included). Regardless, Moody, along with many who follow Jesus today, believed that all that was needed to escape the clutches of poverty was a belief in Jesus coupled with industry and initiative. For example, Ron Sider, best known for his classic *Rich Christians in an Age of Hunger*, blames the hungry for their hunger. For Sider, who is considered to be among the evangelical Christian left (but in reality is barely right of center in Christian circles) believes there can be no social justice if there is no conversion to Jesus. "[T]he problem," he says, "lies deeper than mere social systems and is located finally in distorted human hearts, personal spiritual conversion is also essential for long-term societal improvement" (1999: 54). Not only must the hungry embrace Jesus, they must also embrace one of the causes for their hunger, neoliberalism. He concludes by observing: "The twentieth century has taught us that market economies are more efficient than socialist economies. They also strengthen freedom. A biblical view of persons and sin also leads to the conclusion that market economies offer a better framework than present alternatives" (1999:87).

The politics of Jesus, that attempts to recognize either the primary principle of capitalism (seek self-interest) or the primary principle of the gospel (place the needs of others first) is irreconcilable with the politics of Jesús. Sharing Good News with the hungry, without taking into account their hunger or the causes of their hunger, might be sufficient for followers of Jesus like Moody and Sider. But those who follow Jesús understand that sharing the Good News remains meaningless if stomachs remain empty. Latino/as striving for faithfulness to the Good News, as per the example provided by Jesús, recognize that when the hungry are fed, the thirsty given drink, the naked clothed, that is, when the basic necessities of life are met, then, and only then can the dispossessed hear and understand that there is Good News.

JESÚS: MISSION AND PURPOSE

Theologian María Pilar Aquino claims that the "knowledge and understanding of [Jesucristo] has to do with the historical experience of the struggle against oppression and for liberation" (1993:139–40). Therefore, not suffering deprivation caused by a lack of food, water, clothing, or housing should be central to Jesús' mission statement. Knowing Jesús' mission statement is crucial if we hope to better grasp Jesús' purpose. But what exactly is his mission statement? It depends on who is reading the text. We all impose upon the text what we perceive to be Jesús' mission, depending upon the lens we created to read the Gospels. We usually enter the Bible with certain assumptions about the text, depending on our biases and prejudices concerning God. If our perception is that of a wrathful God, then the entire text is colored to understand God as an extracting disciplinarian. If, at the other extreme, we read the Bible through the lens of a God intent on pleasing us, then we run the risk of cheapening grace. How then should the faith community read the Bible, still claiming its importance for their lives while rejecting those passages that either appear to call for death-dealing principles from a vengeful God or cheap grace where anything goes?

To avoid a misunderstanding of Jesucristo's mission due to a mis-reading of Scripture, the text should always be read within the marginalized body of faith, cognizant of the basic liberative purpose of the Gospel. I would argue that Jesús' mission statement can be found in John 10:10: "I came that they may have life, and have it abundantly." If this is indeed Jesús' mission statement, and if the politics of Jesús is based on faithfulness to Jesús' mission statement, then any biblical interpretation that prevents life from being lived abundantly by any segment of the population, or worse, that brings death, is thus anti-Gospel. Likewise, any structures or individuals, whether they are interpersonal or corporate, that bring death rather than abundant life are also anti-Gospel.

Experiencing life more abundantly is not limited to waiting for some eschatological future; the message of Jesús is for the here and now. This abundant life that Jesús claims to offer reveals for us a God of life, not a God of death. The gospel message of liberation stresses liberation from all forms of oppression: social, economic, political, racial, sexual, environmental, and religious. The politics of Jesús becomes the process of integrating the mission of Jesús with the sociopolitical everyday (*lo cotidiano*) in which the oppressed find themselves. When a reading of the Bible ignores how disenfranchised groups are denied access to opportunities, or when the Bible is read to rationalize the riches of the center while disregarding the plight of the poor, or when reading the Bible vindicates the relegation of women, queer folk, and racial and ethnic minorities to second-class status, then such interpretations cease to be biblically based. Only those interpretations that empower all elements of humanity, offering abundant life in the here and now, as opposed to just the hereafter, are biblically sound.

Knowing Jesús' mission statement informs Jesús' purpose, a purpose his disciples are called to emulate. But where in the Gospels is Jesús' purpose best articulated? For most followers of Jesus, specifically evangelicals, the purpose of Jesus can be summed up in John 3:16, "For God so loved the world, that he gave his only begotten Son, that whosoever believeth in him should not perish, but have everlasting life" (KJV).

Even at football games, most people have spied a placard with the simple message "John 3:16" written on it. But for liberative-seeking followers of Jesús, his purpose statement can be found in the first recorded sermon Jesús ever preached. Jesús was traveling and preaching in the synagogues when his travels brought him home, to Nazareth, where he was raised. As was the custom of the time, he entered the synagogue on the Sabbath where he stood up to read the holy texts. He was handed the book of the prophet Isaiah, and when he opened the book, he found where it was written: "The Spirit of the Lord is upon me, anointing me to preach Good News to the poor. I am sent to heal those who are broken, to preach freedom to the captives, sight to those who cannot see, liberation to the oppressed and to proclaim the acceptable year of the Lord" (Lk. 4:17–18). Upon reading these words, he sat down, as all of the eyes within the synagogue were fastened upon him. Then he began to tell them that on "this day is this Scripture fulfilled in your ears" (v. 21). His bold pronouncement led to a heated debate concerning Jesús' authority, after all, wasn't he from Nazareth? Many in the synagogue were filled with anger, and they rose to thrust him out of the city and do him bodily harm, but he passed through the midst of them and went on his way.

What is crucial about Jesús' purpose statement is the focus on human needs rather than ecclesiastical dogma. For followers of Jesucristo, God is found in the gathering of the "least of these," the same place Jesús resided during his earthly ministry. We are called to emulate Jesús' purpose statement by committing to struggle with and for the oppressed, as well as being able to learn about God from the oppressed. Crucial to following Jesús is the process of breaking the tie between the privileged powerful and Christendom so that the church, the coming together of believers, can occur. Latin American liberationist Pablo Richards argued that the church must live in solidarity with the poor incarnated among the oppressed. Its mission is to serve the world, a witness to God's will for life. The politics of Jesús makes clear that the church can never be neutral in the face of injustices. When the church stands in solidarity with the marginalized, it ceases being an extension of Christendom and instead becomes the church of the oppressed. Crucial to following Jesús is the process of breaking the tie between the privileged powerful and Christendom so that the church, the coming together of believers, can fulfill its mission to serve the world—a witness to God's will for life.

JESÚS: A RACIST? A SEXIST?

Does the purpose of Jesús include liberation for the oppressed, truly for all, especially the most marginalized among us? At first glance, it seems as if this is true; but if it is, then Jesús might have had to also learn this lesson. Our faith may tell us that anyone can come to Jesús, that the evangelistic message means no one is turned away. We are supposed to come just as we are, ill and diseased. All who seek healing are supposed to find salvation and liberation in the arms of Jesús, for his unconditional love accepts everyone—regardless of their race or ethnicity. Or does it? Matthew 15:21–28 recounts the story of a Canaanite woman who came to Jesús desperately seeking a healing for her daughter, only to be sent away and called a dog. How many times have Latina/os heard similar remarks? The Canaanites during Jesús' time were seen by Jews as a mixed race of inferior people, much in the same way that some Euroamericans view Hispanics today, specifically the undocumented. The Canaanites of old—like Latino/as of our time—were foreigners who simply did not belong. They were no better than "dogs." I am old enough to remember restaurant signs throughout the southwestern United States that would say, "No dogs, no Mexicans." For this reason, Jesús' response to the Canaanite woman is troublesome. When she appealed to Jesús to heal her sick child, Jesús, succumbing to the prevailing xenophobia of his day, responded by saying: "I was sent only to the lost sheep of the house of Israel. It is not good to take the bread of the children and throw it to the dogs."

No matter how much we may try to redeem the text, we cannot ignore the fact that Jesús called this woman of color a dog! We are forced to ask the uncomfortable question: Was Jesús a racist? In this story, Hispanics might find themselves relating more with the Canaanite woman than with Jesús. When states like Arizona passed laws that targeted Hispanics in the name of catching the undocumented (a template for subsequent legislation throughout the country that restricts or denies medical and other services to immigrants who lack documentation), Hispanics were reminded that they are the dogs of society. When politicians like congressman and former presidential candidate Tom Tancredo state that Hispanics are "coming to kill you, and you, and me, and my children and my grandchildren,"[6] Latino/as are reminded that they are the dogs of society. When Latina/os are more likely than the general population to lack basic health coverage, less likely to receive preventive medical examinations, and less likely to receive early prenatal care, they are reminded that they are the dogs of society. And when Latino/as are more likely to live with pollution, exposing them to greater health risks, they are reminded that they are the dogs of society. Jobs, educational opportunities, and social services are for "real" Americans. Instead of taking food away from the children of hardworking "Americans" to throw to the dogs, "they" should just go back to where they came from. Jesús' response was typical for a person acculturated to believe in the superiority of his or her particular ethnicity or race.

How can such abusive words proceed from the mouth of Jesús? In the fullness of Jesús' Divinity, he had to learn how to be fully human. His family and culture were responsible for teaching him how to walk, how to talk, and how to be potty trained. He also learned about the superiority of Judaism and the inferiority of non-Jews, in the very same way that today there are those within the dominant culture, from childhood, who are taught America is number one, superior to other nations and thus, "exceptional." For some, this superiority takes on a racial component where those of European descent are more advanced than those of Hispanic ancestry. While the minority of Euroamericans who insist on voicing their superiority can easily be dismissed as racist and thus ignored, there remains an unexamined majority that is complicit with social structures that—whether they like it or not—are racially and ethnically discriminatory for them. They may not go to the extreme, like

Jesús did, in refusing a medical healing to a woman of color while calling her a dog; nevertheless, the inherent ethnic discrimination in the medical establishment accomplishes the same goal. That Latino/as are today's dogs is evident in a quality of healthcare that ranges from poor to nonexistent.

Nevertheless, for Christians, the *imago Dei* (the image of God) finds its fullest expression in the personhood of Jesucristo as he turned many "rules" upside down. This is a truth that even Jesús, in his full humanity, had to learn. To deny this woman a healing and calling her a dog reveals the ethnic discrimination that his culture taught him. But Jesús, unlike so many within the dominant social structure of today, was willing to hear the words of this woman of color and learn from her. And thanks to her, Jesús' ministry was radically changed. The Canaanite woman responded by saying, "For even the dogs eat the crumbs that fall from the table of their masters." She was not willing to wait for the crumbs to fall from the master's table; but as biblical scholar Guardiola-Sáenz reminds us, she approached Jesús in a "spirit of protest and reclamation . . . determined to take the bread from the table of those who displaced her." She refused to stay under the table by insisting to sit at the table as an equal. She refused to be a humble dog begging for crumbs. Instead, she was "a dispossessed woman who has awakened from her position as oppressed and now is coming to confront the empire and demand her right to be treated as human" (2002b:94–95). Her remark and attitude shocked Jesús into realizing that faith was not contingent on a person's ethnicity. In fact, Jesús had to admit that this was a woman of great faith. This woman of color had to cross the "border" demarcated by Jesús' culture. It matters little if she belongs. It matters less if she has proper documentation. Her daughter was sick, and because of her humanity, she was entitled to a healing. She was more than the dog Jesús called her.

As we consider this story from the Hispanic perspective, we are left wondering if Jesús is here struggling with racism or with assimilation. If we recall that Jesús is a colonized man who is seen by his contemporaries as a *mestizo*, a half-breed, then maybe the cultural norm he is learning to overcome is not the racism of the pureblooded, but the strong desire of *mestizos*, then and now, to belong to the dominant culture by becoming whiter than the Whites. For some who are oppressed for being "darker," an attempt is made to prove that one really belongs to the dominant culture. Maybe Jesús' dismissal of this woman of color had less to do with the cultural racism taught to him by society and more to do with the desire to assimilate to those who were seen as purer. Regardless of the reason for Jesús' comment, his mission is changed due to this encounter. How do we know this? Up to this point, the Gospel message was exclusively for the Jews. In Matthew 10:5, Jesús sends his twelve disciples on their first missionary venture. He clearly instructs them, "Do not turn your steps into other nations, nor into Samaritan cities, rather go to the lost sheep of the house of Israel." Yet five chapters later, Jesús encounters the Canaanite woman who existed on the margins of his society. She challenged Jesús with the Good News that healing was not the exclusive property of one ethnic group. Instead, healing should be available to all who come. By the end of his ministry, when he gives the Great Commission, he commands his followers to go out to all nations, not just to the people of Israel.

It should be noted that not only was the Canaanite whom Jesús calls a dog a person of color, but she was also a woman. If we ask if Jesús was a racist, we should also ask if he was sexist. After all, he chose twelve men to follow him; or did he? The Gospel of Luke tells us that Jesús went to every city and village, preaching with the twelve disciples, along with certain women whom he healed of infirmities, among whom were María Magdalena, Juana the wife of Chuza, who was Herod's steward, Susana, and many others. These women ministered unto him of their substance (8:1–3). Why can't these women who also follow Jesús be considered disciples, especially when we consider that women in other situations were named as church leaders by Jesús.

Take for example the story of two sisters, Marta and María. During Jesús' travels, he came upon a certain village, where Marta received him into her house. She had a sister named María who chose to sit at the feet of Jesús to hear his words. But Marta was distracted with all the serving and said, "Lord, don't you care that my sister left me alone to serve? Tell her then to help me." Answering her Jesús said, "Marta, Marta, you are anxious and troubled about many things when there is need of only one, and María chose the good part, which shall not be taken from her" (Lk. 10:38–42). This text has usually been translated as Marta complaining of being overworked. We assume that she is overwhelmed with housework; however, the Greek word used in the text for serving is *diakonia*, a word usually translated as *deacon*. The work she is doing, and needs help in completing, is in relationship to her role as the deacon of this house-church. Unfortunately, her duties and responsibilities as deacon deprive her of the opportunity to "sit at Jesús' feet," as her sister María did.

María, on this day, chose "to sit at Jesús' feet," rather than help Marta with her duties as the house-church deacon. To "sit at Jesús' feet" does not mean that there were no chairs available so she was forced to sit on the floor; to sit at someone's feet was, and still is, a euphemism for a teacher-student relationship. It is the student who "sits at the feet" of the teacher, or in this setting, the rabbi. For example, we are told in Acts 22:3 that Pablo sat "at the feet of Gamaliel," meaning Pablo was a student of Gamaliel. During Jesús' time, women were forbidden to touch the Torah, let alone read or study it. Contrary to all social and religious regulations of the time, Luke is telling us that María was Jesús' student and disciple, just like the other twelve men sitting at his feet. In the Gospel of John, Marta and María are portrayed as well-known apostolic figures of the early church that were beloved by Christ (11:5). In the same way that Pedro confesses the messiahship of Jesús (Mt. 16:15–19), so too does Marta as a spokesperson for the early church (Jn. 11:27). And finally, through María's evangelism, many came to believe in Jesús (Jn. 11:45). This interpretation allows us to retell the story, debunking the patriarchy of Jesús' time, as well as our own. Rabbi Jesús was received in the home of one of his apostles named Marta, who also served as founder and deacon of the house-church in Bethany in which she proclaimed God's word. On this day, her sister María the evangelist sat at the feet of Jesús to study Torah. Marta asked the rabbi to have his student help with the duties required by the deacon, but the rabbi responded that studying Torah was just as important as serving.

We may never really know what occurred in this encounter. Maybe Jesús also learned sexism from his culture in the same way he learned racism until the encounter with the Canaanite woman. Nevertheless, reading Scripture through a liberative lens allows for biblical text that has historically been used to enforce the oppression of women to instead, after careful delineation, be read to unmask seeds of liberation that challenge patriarchy, regardless of original intention.

JESÚS: DISRUPTOR

Learning from the Canaanite woman allows Jesús to truly fulfill his purpose of standing in solidarity with the world's marginalized people. The poverty that Jesús willingly assumed so we could be enriched provides the opportunity to achieve a humanity that is denied due to socially oppressive structures. Unfortunately, many with economic privilege who follow Jesus assume that the road toward salvation is paved with claiming worthlessness before God. The Englishman John Newton's classic hymn, "Amazing Grace" (1779), reminds us that God's grace "saves a wretch like me." Before God we are but wretched worms. Newton may have been a wretch due to his occupation as slave ship captain, but not all engaged in stealing the humanity of others were deemed unworthy of Jesús' promised abundant life. Ironically, Newton's conversion to Christianity, and his eventual ordination to be a minister in the Church of England, was due to an encounter with God during a violent storm at sea rather than conviction for his slave-promoting activities. Even after his conversion, he continued to work and profit from the slave trade, only renouncing it some forty years after his conversion (Hochschild 2010:70–132).

For the exalted of the earth (i.e., Newton), who live a life of privilege due to advantages paid for by those who were made to believe in their nonpersonhood (i.e., his slave cargo), such emotions of self-derogation may prove to be a healthy step toward a spiritual path of healing. The danger occurs when religious leaders legitimize their own experiences of conversion, based solely on their own needs. Universalizing their salvation experience by imposing upon the earth's wretched a similar path that requires similar feelings and emotions to those of the earth's exalted is, to say the least, problematic. One salvation size does not fit all. An assumption is made that the sin of the exalted is also the sin requiring repentance from the world's wretched. Followers of Jesus, like Newton, might need to recognize the depths of their depravity before accepting amazing grace, but the disadvantaged recognize how the sin of oppression that benefits others already makes their conditions wretched. Those exalted who have historically written deep theological concepts and self-justifying ethical precepts have wrestled with the prideful sin of self-centeredness. But the marginalized have instead suffered from a lack of self-identity. Their colonized minds have centered the image and thoughts of the exalted—interpreting reality through the eyes of the so-called righteous followers of Jesus rather than the eyes of those whom society disposes of.

Those who are already humble need not hear more sermons advocating humility. Humbled by their own sins and the sins of the dominant culture, they need not be exhorted to become more lowly still, quite the contrary. Sermons emulating from economically privileged spaces preach to the marginalized self-denial, submission, and worthlessness, when instead the wretched should be hearing pride in self, liberation, and worth. Crushed by the sins of the dominant culture, they need not be prodded to become more subservient. For those who are invisible, salvation becomes their transformation from nonpersons to personhood. The salvific message of the gospel of Jesús, which the dispossessed of the world need to hear, is that they are precious and due dignity because they are created in the very image of God.

Jesucristo understood that part of his purpose was to disrupt the social economic order by humbling the proud and uplifting the lowly. As it is written in the Magnificat, "[God] pulled down the powerful from their thrones, and exalted the humble ones. He filled the hungry with good things, and the rich he sent away empty (Lk. 1:52–53). He will humble the exalted and exalt the humble (Mt. 23:12). The first will be last and the last will be first (Mt. 19:30)." It is the privileged who need to come to terms with their spiritual wretchedness. It is the wretched who need to come to terms with their infinite worth. Because those who are disposable suffer like Jesús—crucified on the crosses of racism, sexism, classism, ethnic discrimination, and heterosexism—they become co-heirs to the throne. As the apostle Pablo reminds us, "If we are children, then we are heirs—heirs with God and co-heirs with Christ. If indeed we share in Christ's sufferings, then we may also share in God's glory" (Ro. 8:17). With confidence, the wretched of the earth can walk into the presence of God.

As for the followers of Jesus who amassed fortunes upon the backs of the dispossessed, they are the ones who will be pulled down from their thrones and sent away empty-handed. The normative social order is disrupted as those who have nothing become the inheritors of God's reign. Looking at his disciples, Jesús turned to them and said "Blessed are the poor, for theirs is the reign of God. Blessed are those who are hungry, for they will be satisfied. . . . But woe to those who are rich, for they have already been comfortable. Woe to those who are well fed, for they will go hungry" (Lk. 6:20–21, 24–25). If those privileged in our present reality ever hope to participate in God's reign, they will need a letter of reference from the dispossessed and disenfranchised of today, who will hold the keys to the future.

4

PICK UP YOUR DAILY CROSS AND FOLLOW ME

One of the unexamined assumptions of the Christian faith is a theology that is based on *esperanza*, on hope. "All things works for the good of those who love God, and who has been called according to God's purpose" (Ro. 8:28). To hope in English is to expect, to await something good. In Spanish, the word *esperanza* is derived from the word *esperar*. To hope in Spanish, *esperar*, means (according to the Velázquez dictionary) to wait in apprehension of either good or evil. The usage of the Spanish word connotes a darker, more complex meaning that implies fear of what is awaited. To wait doesn't always imply a happy ending, especially if the waiting drags on for centuries as in the case of Hebrew slaves in Egypt or Latino/as residing in the belly of the Empire. I have no problem with a hope in God; I do however find it problematic to hope that all things will work out for the best. History and personal experience show that it seldom does. Good Christians with plenty of hope in God's protection die in horrible accidents, experience financial collapse, and lose all that is dear—just like non-Christians. Bad things do happen—and happen often—to good people. Claiming hope as protection from evil becomes somewhat naïve, especially if, as Hispanics, one is perceived to be a perpetual foreigner. Many Latina/os can relate to King David's pronouncement, "We are foreigners and strangers before the eyes of God, just as were all our ancestors. Our days on earth are like a shadow, without hope" (1 Ch. 29:15). With Job, and all who suffer unjustly, we are forced to cry out to an apparent silent Heaven, "Where then is my hope and who can perceive any hope for me?" (Jb. 17:15).

If hope is irreducible to the personal, can we instead speak of the eventual hope of the triumph of justice? Does not history lead toward ultimate salvation for humanity? I am not convinced, as was Martin Luther King Jr., that "the arc of the moral universe is long, but it bends towards justice" (1986:52). I fear that philosopher Walter Benjamin might have been closer in understanding historical progress (or lack thereof) when he quipped: "There is no document of civilization which is not at the same time a document of barbarism" (1968:256). What if how we create history and how we remember our past simply justifies the values and social power of those who get to write history, literally writing their privileged space into the national epic? What if there is no historical movement leading toward some secular ideal based on enlightenment and reason or some religious ideal based on some heavenly paradise? When Benjamin gazes upon the Paul Klee painting *Angelus Novus*, he sees "an angel looking as though he is about to move away from something he is fixedly contemplating. His eyes are staring, his mouth is open, his wings are spread." For Benjamin, who owned this print, "This is how one pictures the angel of history. His face is turned toward the past. Where we perceive a chain of events, he sees one single catastrophe which keeps piling wreckage upon wreckage and hurls it in front of his feet" (Ibid.:257). There is nothing inevitable about the passage of time, no teleology to history, nothing but a game of random chance. What we call history is chaos, with no rhyme or reason, mainly because the events are as unpredictable and contradictive as humans. One is hard pressed to notice any type of progressive dialectical march toward a better human existence.

Suspicion concerning historical narratives is based on the role Eurocentric thought chose for itself. Georg W. F. Hegel argued that "Europe is absolutely the Center and End of the [premodern] world" with the Mediterranean as the axis of Universal History (1955:210, 235).

Hegel creates an entire philosophical endeavor that rests on the presupposition of the superiority of the Europeans and the inferiority of non-Europeans. Northern Europe, specifically the "Germanic Spirit, is the Spirit of the New World, its end the realization of absolute truth, as the infinite self-determination of freedom, which has as its content its own absolute form" (1970:413). For Hegel, universal history is a necessary movement that originated in Asia and moved toward Europe, where it became the end product of civilization and development. Africa, Latin America, and Southern Europe (Spain) are removed from the movement of world history and situated, like Asia, in a state where "the inferiority of these individuals in all respects is manifest" (Ibid.:199–200, 243). Thus, Europe becomes the self-appointed missionary of civilization. The consequences of Hegel's thoughts relegate non–northern Europeans (including Latina/os) to a space where they are incapable of providing any contribution to the philosophical discourse. Their purpose is reduced to simply serving the philosophical center created by Hegel. This becomes evident in Hegel's declaration that against the absolute right that Europeans possess by virtue of being the bearer of the development of the world Spirit, the spirit of other peoples has no right (1969:430, sec 346–47). Philosopher Enrique Dussel points out that power, domination, and the center become identical (1990:6, 1993:65–76). Hegel's anti–northern European biases complicate any ideal of an objective historical movement guided by reason. Modernity has taught us that we, as a species, are moving toward utopia; rather, we claim capitalism (a rising tide will raise all ships) or communism (the eventual withering away of the state). Both share a salvation history. Hope exists that the future, thanks to God or science or human ingenuity, will be more forward thinking and more egalitarian, than the past.

But what if there is no salvation history? What if the premodern (history made by God) and modern (history made by the human subject) views are wrong? What if the historical dialectic that moves history in an upward spiral is but an optimistic construct forced on a very select history? For Benjamin, a storm is blowing from Paradise that has caught the Angelus Novus wings with such violence that the angel can no longer close his wings. "The storm irresistibly propels him into the future to which his back is turned, while the pile of debris before him grows skywards. This storm is what we call progress" (1968:257). Dark ages of ignorance follow spans of enlightenment, creating at times downward spirals, at other times upward spirals and yet at other times unrelated and unconnected events: in other words, a nonlinear disjointed, multidimensional passage of time? Michel Foucault argued that history does not exist, as per Hegel, as an internal and necessary unfolding dialectic flow moving in linear discourse; rather, what exists is a permanent historical discontinuation. History is not defined through triumphant metanarratives but instead is a kaleidoscope comprised of contradictory and complex untold stories and struggles of the very least among us who remain unnamed. History is full of stories of evil vanquishing good, brutality crushing peace. We presently live in a world that is not getting better for the global marginalized, rather, due to the widening wealth gap, getting worse. Billions are born into poverty and die of its consequences so that a privileged few can enjoy First World status. The marginalized offer up their lives as living sacrifices so that an elite can be saved and live well.

William Shakespeare's character Macbeth, in a moment of darkness, comes to grips with the arbitrariness of history. Macbeth states: "All our yesterdays have lighted fools. The way to dusty death. Out, out, brief candle! Life's but a walking shadow, a poor player that struts and frets his hour upon the stage and then is heard no more: it is a tale told by an idiot, full of sound and fury, signifying nothing."[1] History is but a tale, a story recited by an idiot, a fool full of epic struggles that, when all is said, signifies nothing. Or, as the author of Ecclesiastes reminds us: "Vanity of vanities," says the teacher. "Absolute futility. Everything is meaningless" (Ec. 1:1). If all this is true, what role then is played by religious hope? Is it the opiate Marx claims it to be?

Hope, as a product of salvation history (either metaphysical or material dialectic) can be optimistically believed if we accept that the arch of history does bend toward justice. But if the past and present are any guides, the existence of such an arch is a faith statement assumed without proof. But hope, as a statement of unfounded belief, serves an important middle-class purpose. All too often, hope becomes an excuse not to deal with the reality of injustice. I first began to develop a theology of hopelessness when I took a group of predominately White students to the squatter villages of Cuernavaca, Mexico, to learn from the poor. During our outing we spoke with many families living in horrific conditions. Bugs crawled along the walls of the shacks constructed of discarded wood, cardboard, and plasterboard. Empty plastic bags and trash littered the flimsy structures, hugging huts as if they were adornments. That evening, as we processed the day's activities, one student stated that in spite of the miserable conditions in which these people lived, she still saw "the hope in the eyes of the little girls." My immediate response was that these same little girls would more than likely be selling their bodies to put food on the table or trapped in abusive marriages attempting to survive classism and sexism, so I wasn't sure what kind of hope my student saw. Among the disenfranchised, the dispossessed, the least of the least, I discovered an ethos where hope is not apparent. Since that encounter, I have been wrestling with the realization that for many of the ultra-poor, hope seems to be mainly claimed by those with economic privilege as a means of distancing themselves from the unsolvable disenfranchisement most of the world's wretched are forced to face.

Theologian Roberto Goizueta, when describing Catholics (to which I would also add Protestants) states that "If, among Euro-Americans, nominal Catholics are referred to as 'Christmas and Easter Catholics,' their U.S. Hispanic counterparts are often called 'Ash Wednesday and Good Friday Catholics'" (1998:2–3). For Hispanics struggling to survive, the truth remains that destitution and death await the disenfranchised. The reality of reading our daily newspapers is that for far too many who are on the margins of society, there is no hope. In a very real sense, waiting leads to nothingness. But we who are familiar with and/or grew up in marginalization are used to this. The oppressed of the world occupy the space of Holy Saturday, the day after Friday's crucifixion, and the not yet Easter Sunday of resurrection. This is a space where some faint anticipation of Sunday's Good News is easily drowned out by the reality and consequences of Friday's violence and brutality. It is a space where hopelessness becomes the companion of used and abused people. The virtue and/or audacity of hope become a class privilege experienced by those protected from the realities of Friday or the opium that is used to numb that same reality until Sunday rolls around. Regardless of the optimism professed, the disenfranchised, their children, and their children's children will more than likely continue to live in an ever-expanding poverty. Sunday seems so far away. Waiting, *esperando*, becomes tiresome. The situation remains hopeless.

The hopelessness I advocate rejects quick and easy fixes that may temporarily soothe the conscious of the privileged but is no substitute for bringing about a more just social structure that is not based on the disenfranchisement of the world's abuse. But this hopelessness that I advocate is not disabling; rather, it is a methodology that propels toward praxis. All too often the advocacy of hope gets in the way of listening and learning from the oppressed. To sit in the reality of Saturday is to discover that the semblance of hope becomes an obstacle when it serves as a mechanism that maintains rather than challenges the prevailing social structures. But this is never an excuse to do nothing. It may be Saturday, but that's no justification to passively wait for Sunday. The disenfranchised have no option but to continue their struggle for justice regardless of the odds against them. They continue the struggle, if not for themselves, for their progeny. But how?

Definitely not by following the Jesus of the dominant culture that fails to consider their complicity with injustice. The Jesus informed by the dominant culture is problematic for those residing on the margins of society because it reinforces the prevailing social structures by refusing to question the power relationships that undergird the everyday. Harold Recinos points out that "a Jesus who only provides consolation for persons crushed by a historical reality capable and deserving of change merits no following from God's people. [Jesús'] suffering directs us to question the meaning of the histories of women, the poor, and all people in desperate need" (1997:49). If this is true, then what does Jesucristo offer? Maybe not so much comfort, but a strategy of survival, a praxis that might easily fall short of the mark. I advocate that followers of Jesús wishing to do liberative ethics must approach the task from a theology of hopelessness, where meaning and purpose is given to life in the struggle of implementing justice-based praxis.

Walter Benjamin claims that "[t]he Messiah comes not only as a redeemer, but he comes as the subduer of the Anti-Christs" (1968:255). History ceases to be a dialectical sequence of events, like the beads of a rosary, leading humanity to some utopian future. If we are to hope against all hope, then it will be in understanding what Benjamin called the present, the "time of the now which is shot through with chips of Messianic time. . . . For every second of time was the strait gate through which the Messiah might enter" (Ibid.:263–64). Messiahs don't show up once and for all. Instead, the presence of the Divine invades the here and now so that we are not alone in the midst of suffering due to oppression. Messianic solidarity with the oppressed in the midst of hopelessness might indeed be the only hope hoped for. Perhaps this is the sad paradox: that hope might be found after it is crucified and then may be resurrected in the shards of life. For this is the hopelessness that was described in Pablo's admonition to imitate father Abraham who "beyond all hope believed in hope" (Ro. 4:18).

JESÚS: THE BETRAYED

It becomes too easy for marginalized communities like Hispanics' to create neat dualisms between oppressors and oppressed. All that is White is oppressive while all that is Latino/a is victimized. Reality usually is more complex than simple right/wrong, good/evil, oppressed/oppressor dichotomies. Any serious exploration concerning the politics of Jesús requires a more nuanced understanding of how power operates. This is not to excuse oppressive social structures that benefit the dominant culture of the Roman Empire, or of the U.S. Empire, but it is to say that within the dominant culture there exist members who have taken great material and personal risk, not only to stand in solidarity with the oppressed, but to work ceaselessly to dismantle the very structures that privileges them. During the time of Jesús, examples are given of the Roman centurion who asked for the healing of his servant while recognizing his unworthiness, leading Jesús to compliment his faith, a faith no greater found in all of Israel (Mt. 8:5–13).

Just like there are those of the dominant culture who betray their own culture for the sake of justice for all, there exist those within marginalized communities who also betray their ethnic or racial communities in the hope of being rewarded by those in power via acceptance. During the time of Jesús, the person who best manifests this is Judas. No Latina/o (or Euroamerican for that matter) would ever name their son Judas, history's ultimate villain. Dante, in Canto XXXIV, places Judas, along with Brutus and Cassius, in the Ninth Circle—the deepest realm—of the Inferno. Dante notices that under his feet are the most evil of sinners, traitors of their benefactors, completely covered in ice. They are in contorted poses, several feet deep. In this darkly cold inner circle of Hell, Dante notices a giant Lucifer with three faces. In each of Satan's three mouths, Lucifer eternally chews a sinner. The center mouth holds Judas, the traitor of Jesús; in the mouths to the right and left are Brutus and Cassius, the traitors of Julius Caesar.

It is simple, if not cathartic, to demonize those who betray their benefactors. Unfortunately, Hispanics (as well as other racial and ethnic groups) have had a Judas or two in their lives. A fellow Latina or Latino to whom great love and kindness was shown, someone who was taken under one's wing in the desire of helping a fellow Hispanic succeed, someone to whom one served as a benefactor. We have opened doors for them, provided them with tremendous opportunities, fought battles for, and even lost friends and funds by choosing to stand up in their defense. Maybe our attempts to create a type of "good old boys" club based on Hispanic characteristics rather than ability is just as damning to both the benefactor and the one they hope to help succeed. And yet, out of nowhere, they have been sideswiped by betrayal, by having the person not only lie but publically do so in an attempt to destroy the benefactor's reputation, honor, and career. Yes, we can understand Dante's desire for vilifying the ingrates of the world, but I wonder if pity might be a more appropriate response.

One joy of living in Miami during the 1970s was crabbing. Many of us would go to the beach to hunt crabs, placing our prey in a bucket. Later at home, they would be prepared for dinner. However, on the way home the youngest had the responsibility of keeping an eye on the bucket, lest a crab escape. Yet surprisingly, none ever did. You see, every time a crab climbed to the top rim of the bucket, one of those below would pinch the would-be escapee's leg and drag it back down. In a way, Latino/as (and other oppressed groups) have historically behaved like the bucket of crabs, at times responsible for our own oppression. Just as Jesús was betrayed by one of his own, so too are Hispanics today betrayed by other Latina/os if it would help them succeed. I am among the first to recognize the complicity of well-meaning Euroamericans with institutionalized racism, but it is just as important for those of us from marginalized communities to move beyond the rhetoric of blame. It is easy to simply blame Euroamericans for being White and privileged. But we must also honestly gaze at our Hispanic community, cognizant that at times the knife protruding from our backs has the fingerprints of a Hispanic Judas. We must avoid the trap of romanticizing our *comunidad* so that we make it devoid of any faults, when the reality is that the oppressed at times can be as cunning as their oppressors if it would help one advance and succeed even at the cost of fellow Latino/as. To design a strategy for dealing with our disenfranchisement that solely relies on blaming our oppressors is insufficient for bringing about a justice-based community. Unfortunately, like the bucket of crabs, we are at times our own worst enemies.

Why are fellow crabs quick to play the role of Judas? Could it be that most crabs have overblown egos? Or worse, larger insecurities? Have the oppressed learned from oppressors that the way to succeed is to make sure no one else in the bucket achieves such heights; thus, they have to be brought back down? Hispanics are no different from a bucket of crabs when we choose to live up to the stereotypes imposed upon us by the media and the dominant culture, feeling that in order to "belong" to our marginalized group we must exhibit counterproductive activities to avoid the accusation of being "too White." Are we a bucket of crabs when we are more concerned with protecting our "turf," our fragile egos, or our "recognized" status within the disenfranchised community than with protecting the rights of our people as a whole? Are we a bucket of crabs when we allow the dominant culture to choose for us our leaders and spokespersons, individuals indebted to those who placed them in power, thus making them overly cautious about making any waves or demanding justice for our people? Are we a bucket of crabs when those who have achieved some measure of success refuse to reinvest their talents and resources in others who are disenfranchised, striving to raise both consciousness and the quality of life of those marginalized? Are we a bucket of crabs when our self-appointed leaders refuse to become involved in supporting those who are working to establish justice because they will neither receive the credit, nor be spotlighted? Are we a bucket of crabs when we would rather sit in climate-controlled committee rooms talking about leadership rather than working selflessly within the community to bring about change?

While we should greatly appreciate those progressive Euroamericans who are always willing, with their resources and their person, to stand in solidarity with us, we should be greatly disillusioned when our own people refuse to take ownership of our own process of liberation. As long as we allow the dominant culture to define "justice" for us, we will never achieve any form of liberation from oppressive structures. Unfortunately, there are at times too many Judases among us willing to do the dirty work of those wanting to protect the power and privilege of the dominant culture. The priestly leaders were glad when one of Jesús' own came forward to spew all types of lies and allegations against his benefactor. Also, I'm sure the Romans were quick to believe these same lies and allegations when brought to them from those who they oppressed. Yes, those closest to us can do the greatest harm. But what can be learned from the politics of Jesús so that we can proceed? Should we stop being benefactors? Stop fighting for justice? Become a recluse?

We are called to unconditionally continue to love deeply and to humbly walk on the path of justice. We will be hurt, and our enemies might very well believe the lies, and, based on false accusations, call for our crucifixion; but they do not judge us. Rather, we stand with confidence before the throne of justice. As per Judas—let there be compassion. After all, when Jesús said that he was going to be betrayed that night, did not all of the disciples wonder if it was them (Mt. 26:20–22)? You see, any one of us can easily betray our own benefactor, for in reality, we are all stuck in the bucket of oppression. No—Judas should not be vilified (not to excuse the horrible betrayal) but he is to be pitied.

JESÚS: THE FORSAKEN SUFFERER

That great modern theologian, Woody Allen, in his film *Husbands and Wives* (1992), plays the role of Gabe Roth. As Gabe watches television, a scientist quotes Einstein's famous quip, "God doesn't play dice with the universe." Gabe turns off the television set and walks away saying, "No he doesn't play with dice. He plays hide and seek." All too often, the forsaken have a God who is more interested in playing hide and seek than providing explanations for so much of the world's sufferings. This makes engagements in the politics of Jesús a hopeless task, whose road usually leads to crucifixion. And yet, most of us have become accustomed to the muscular Jesus of empire that reeks with triumphalism. "Onward, Christian soldiers! Marching as to war, with the cross of Jesus going on before. Christ, the royal Master, leads against the foe; forward into battle, see his banners go. At the sign of triumph Satan's host doth flee; on, then, Christian soldiers, on to victory."[2] The Jesús Latina/os read about in their Bibles, on the other hand, is one who in the moment of despair cries out unashamedly, *"Eli, Eli, lama sabachthani?"*—My God, my God, why have thou forsaken me? (Ps. 22:1; Mt. 27:46). Faithfulness to the cause of justice usually does not lead us to glorious victory but, more often than not, to betrayal, abandonment, and hopelessness. Ever since the U.S. Empire, motivated by the jingoism of Manifest Destiny, moved the borders to encompass us (i.e., in the Mexican-American War and the Spanish-American War), countless nameless Hispanics have lost their lives or livelihoods for refusing to remain submissive to a dominated culture whose power and privilege were derived through the crucifixion of Latina/os. Yes, the virtuous do suffer and usually suffer terribly, and sadly enough, their suffering is lost in the pages of history. And while such suffering might be bearable if God's presence was known, Jesucristo cried out to a deaf God—a God who, for all practical purposes, was absent.

It is easy to be emboldened in the safety of our houses of worship when contemplating engagement in the politics of Jesús, strengthened by past testimonies of yesteryear's bearers of the faith. But such reassurances prove insufficient when facing jeering crowds who sneer: "You relied on God, then let God save you! You say God is your friend, then let God rescue you!" (Ps. 22:8). In the randomness of life's vicissitudes, in the hopelessness caused by oppressive structures, in the solitude of a silent God, those who place their trust in the Almighty can still be like drained water and like those whose bones are all disjointed. A once courageous heart melts like wax as the tongue fastens itself to a dry palate (Ps. 22:14). Simplistic religious rhetoric that provides uncomplicated and unsophisticated answers to the tragedy of the human experience is insulting of those who suffer and makes a mockery of those struggling to believe in a God who is silent in the face of oppression. All things do not work for good for those called by God's name. We should remember Job. A more faithful servant of God did not exist. And yet, on a dare from Satan, who proposed Job would curse and reject God if God visited calamity on him rather than blessings, God took away his wealth, slaughtered his children, and afflicted his health. When Job looks to the heavens for an answer, he receives a troubling response from God: because I am God and I do whatever I want. Besides, who are you, mere human, to even question me?

Today, the world's disenfranchised cry out from the crosses upon which they hang asking, like Jesucristo, why has God forsaken them. Or, like Job they sit in the dust contemplating why their life is full of misery and misfortune, only to hear from God, "Tough!" Turning to God for the answers is problematic because we assume doctrinal answers that fail to materialize for so many who claim to be believers. So if we don't look to God for complex answers to the messiness of life, why bother with Jesús? If we want answers, knowing that God is either silent or provides unhelpful explanations, why don't we just look to ourselves for answers? Although we are capable of deducting the causes of oppression, although we are capable of conceptualizing how oppression is institutionalized so as to privilege the few, although we are capable of hypothesizing upon the intersectionality of different oppressive social structures, still, we can find in Jesús an individual who chose solidarity with our suffering and, thus through his example, provides a body of action to emulate. Jesús' importance is less for the philosophizing, theologizing, or theorizing about why people are oppressed; rather, Jesús provides us with praxis-based survival strategies whose purpose is to bring about salvation/liberation via a more just social order. We seek not answers that lead us to correct doctrines as to why we suffer. We seek correct actions, correct praxis to employ, fully aware of the injustice that may signal our demise.

Those who engage in the politics of Jesús, fighting in the cause of justice, seeking a more liberative community, usually are the ones who end up crucified. In the midst of suffering for choosing to engage in the politics of Jesús we demand to know why God is so inattentive, where God is hiding, why God does not give a damn. Maybe the problem is that we have become too accustomed to seeing God as some type of magician whose sole purpose is to wave his magic wand and solve our problems. Maybe the answer to our queries is that God is in the same place where God was while God's beloved child was being lynched on a Roman tree. Maybe God doesn't provide us with satisfactory answers but, rather, sustains us during the unanswerable questions. Maybe because Jesús was also forsaken, he is more present in the midst of our own forsakenness. When we are faithful to the cause of liberation, surely we do not deserve all the terror that befalls us, specifically the agony of the cross; and yet, Jesucristo demonstrates how to remain faithful in the presence of a silent God. The cross exists not for us to figure out why it is there but, rather, to show us how our undeserved sufferings, our rejection by those privileged by society, and our death become the suffering, rejection, and death of God. As unfair and unjust are the consequences for Hispanics struggling for common dignity, which are taken for granted by the dominant culture, we can still have faith in God, even when this God appears absent, because through Jesús, God intimately knows our pain since God experienced our pain, creating solidarity with all who continue to be crucified today on the crosses of ethnic discrimination so that the privileged few can continue to have abundant life at the expense of poor, marginalized Latina/os.

The author of the epistle of Peter reminds us: "Beloved, do not be surprised at the fiery ordeal that is taking place among you, as if something strange was happening to you" (1 P 4:12). First, Peter reminds the reader that Jesús suffered; therefore, we should not be surprised when those who engage in the politics of Jesús also suffer. It is inevitable. Many Latino/as suffer not for their wrongdoings, but for doing what is right, hoping against all hope that in spite of God's silence, God's glory will be revealed. In an ironic twist, to be reviled by this world for engaging in the politics of Jesús is to be considered a blessing. First, Peter attempts to provide comfort and reassurance for those who face, or will be facing, persecution due to their commitment to the politics of Jesús. For most Euroamericans who study the biblical text and who usually place an emphasis on correct doctrine, the cause for the hostility faced by the early church is usually understood to be the Christian tenets in which the early church believed. Yet Empire, then and now, seldom cares what the masses actually believe, as long as allegiances to the ruling elites remain uncompromised. The early churches were persecuted not for what they believed but for what they did. To engage in the politics of Jesús is threatening. The hostility provoked by the early church, or any other church that radically lives out the Gospel message of liberation, should not be surprising. Those whom society benefits employ whatever means necessary to protect, maintain, and expand their power and privilege. The threat to the Empire was not that this group of Christians believed Jesús preached love or that he rose from the dead. The threat was that Jesús, not Caesar, was Lord. If this is true, then the question facing today's Eurocentric churches is why Christians do not experience hostility. And if we are honest with ourselves, why do those in power care less that our Latino/a churches gather regularly? Could it be that today's churches are irrelevant because they traded the Gospel message of liberation for conformity and complicity with Empire? If today's churches were to place less emphasis on orthodoxy (correct doctrine) and more on orthopraxis (correct action), would their efforts to bring about justice provoke persecution?

JESÚS: THE PURPOSE OF THE CROSS

Crosses are the electric chairs of the past, the means by which the civil authorities punished transgressors of the law. If Rome had had the means of electrocution as opposed to crucifixion, I wonder if today's Christians would be walking around wearing miniature golden electric chairs around their necks. Because we "resignified" the cross to point toward a religious tradition as opposed to a means of state-sponsored capital punishment, we lost the original purpose of the cross, to kill enemies of the state. All executions eliminate those who do not "fit" in with how those in power define civilized society. And while today's U.S. capital punishment system is usually geared toward those who have engaged in acts where someone lost their life (i.e., murder),[3] we cannot ignore the fact that the poor and those who are of color are disproportionately imprisoned and executed.[4] Ethicist María Teresa Dávila reminds us that

> all crucifixions take place under the law . . . are presented as having
> given "to each their due," an essential element of many modern
> conceptions of justice. . . . To say that justice occurs "under the law"
> blinds us to the ways entire systems historically protect privilege and
> its abuse. And to say that justice is achieved when everyone is given
> what is their due "under the law" can, in itself, be a form of institu-
> tionalized violence.[5]

The Jesús of the Gospel narratives, and the Jesús sitting today on death row share a similar circumstance; both are executed under the law that, in spite of its obvious flaws, contradictions, and biases, is presented as fair. But there is a reason we do not talk about a "court of justice," but instead use the term, "court of law"; we as a society follow laws, not seek justice. And because laws have historically and consistently been written to the detriment of Hispanics (and other marginalized communities), we are left wondering if the purpose of the cross, like the purpose of all executions, is to reinforce control over darker bodies to demonstrate what awaits those on the margins of power and privilege who dare to rebel against the current social structures. The punishments meted out by courts of laws, laws designed to the detriment of the disenfranchised, are more for the benefit of others from disadvantaged communities to serve as warning that if they too step out of place, then they can expect similar punishment (revenge).

Executions repulse. For philosopher Miguel de Unamuno, the bloody Jesús nailed to a wooden cross repels, if not sickens, all who fail to understand the cult of suffering attached to him (1968a:273–76). Surely a more civilized and less gory process can be designed by the Creator of the universe to redeem the world. Yet the bloody tortured body of Jesús humanizes him by depicting the dehumanization of Jesús' suffering. This process crystallizes the Jesús who suffered freely, not as the single basic causality of God, but as the causality of a world that also suffers—a suffering and violence spilled over into the Divine. As religion scholar Sixto García points out, "The broken humanity of [Jesús] stands as a sacrament of the brokenness of the body of the Hispanic communities" (1992:94). Today's crucified Hispanics also suffer, seemingly abandoned by God. Any presence of God is not as a transcendent power over or against injustice; rather, God is present from within a self-negated Jesús whose own power of love surrenders his life to the political injustices of his day. His crucifixion becomes a scandal, signifying failure and powerlessness. The powerful and privileged are not hung from trees; only Latino/as in the southwestern United States (Blacks in the South) have the historical memory of being lynched.

"Anyone hung on a tree is cursed by God" (Dt. 21:23) the Scriptures remind us. Crosses are places of violence, littered with broken lives and bodies. Those who are disenfranchised, those who are marginalized are the ones who can be abused, persecuted, and oppressed. To be crucified means nakedness, vulnerability, loss of control over bodily functions, and excruciating pain. Only the outcasts face this Roman form of execution, reserved for those who refuse to acknowledge the Caesars of history. Even religious leaders of the time were quick to proclaim that they had no king but Caesar (Jn. 19:15). There is nothing glorious or wonderful about an instrument of death, especially when presented as some old wooden cross. It is ironic that today's wearing of a gold cross has become a fashion statement that masks the horror of failure and execution. What the cross truly signals is how Jesucristo's ministry was botched. For God in-flesh to be lynched becomes a shameful disgrace that questions God's omnipotence; it questions all that Jesús claimed.

These concerns have led theology to wrestle with the question of why Jesús had to die. In response, many Euroamericans who follow Jesus rush to resignify the cross as a sign of hope, as a salvific symbol, not pausing long enough to dwell on the tragedy of the moment, on the hopelessness, on the failure, on the powerlessness of the moment. For them, there is redemption in Jesus' sufferings—there is atonement. The cross becomes a necessity for a salvation that leads toward a life of bliss in some hereafter. Yet for most Hispanics seeking a life in the here and now, there is nothing redemptive about suffering. This theology of atonement was not always the norm. Anselm of Canterbury (1033?–1109) created this theology, reasoning that the cross was necessary to satisfy God's anger, to serve, specifically, as a substitute for us. Before an angry God who requires blood atonements, sinful humans could not redeem themselves. Only a sinless God-as-human-being could gratify God's thirst for vengeance, make restitution, and restore creation. In other words, in order to satisfy God's vanity, God's only begotten son must be humiliated, tortured, and brutally killed, rather than the true object of God's wrath—us humans. God is placated by filicide. The problem with Anselm's constructed theology of atonement is that it casts God as the ultimate abuser, the ultimate oppressor who finds satisfaction through the domination, humiliation, and pain of God's child. Such a theology of atonement becomes difficult to reconcile with the concept of a "loving Father."

Furthermore, the theology of substitution has historically provided justification for so much of the global violence done in the name of Jesus. If Jesus took my place, that is, if it was I who deserved the cruel and unusual punishment of crucifixion, then all humans who reject what Jesus has done for them deserve a similar fate. We are reminded that "whosoever believes in him will not be condemned, but whosoever refuses to believe already stands condemned because they do not believe in the name of God's one and only begotten Son. . . . Whosoever believes in the Son has eternal life, but whosoever rejects the Son will not see life, for the wrath of God will be upon them" (Jn. 3:18, 36). I am spared because I am a Christian. But those who reject Jesus, be they Jews, Muslims, Atheists, so-called witches, and so on, continue to deserve such horrific violence for their wanton rejection of the one true God. We who are Christians become the instruments by which God's violence is visited upon infidels, returning the viciousness they executed upon Jesus during his crucifixion. Violence against nonbelievers becomes justified because they basically ask for it by refusing to allow Jesus "to take their place."

Maybe the question with which theology should wrestle is not why Jesús had to die, but what we do with the fact that the political and religious authorities killed him. If the tortured Jesus on a cross before a silent, and seemingly uncaring God is replicated throughout history, as illustrated in numerous massacres of the innocent, uncountable carnage, and savage butchery, then should not the quest for today's crucified be to resignify the Jesus of the dominant Christian culture that is now the crucifier of the world's disenfranchised? Could Primo Levy, a holocaust survivor, be right when he states that there is no God, only Auschwitz? If only Auschwitz exists, then the ethical and moral call for humans (regardless of faith tradition or lack thereof) is to become the incarnated word that stands in solidarity with those who justifiably conclude that God cannot exist after all the Christian-led Auchwitzes of history. If crucifixion, rather than the goodness of humans, is the historical norm, a norm in which Christians (as well as believers from other faith traditions) willingly participate to protect their perverted definition of the good, then does not a substitution theological theory of a God who employs crucifixion to satisfy God's vanity only aid and abet all the crucifixions that have brought so much of human life to a brutal and torturous end?

For Hispanics, and others from marginalized communities, the importance of the cross is not its redemptive powers, for all aspects of Jesús' life are redemptive. Crucifixion should never glorify unjust suffering, for there is absolutely nothing redemptive about crushing the disenfranchised so that a small privileged elite that benefits from their suffering can have life, and life abundantly. Nor should the cross become a paragon to be visited upon those who refuse to allow Jesus to be their substitute against a God who is angry because of our infidelity. The importance of Jesús' crucifixion is that this is the historical moment when Jesús chose solidarity with the world's marginalized, even unto death. He invites his disciples to put their hands in his wounds (Jn. 20:27). To touch the wound of Jesús is to touch the wound of God caused by the wounds suffered by all who are crucified. Jesucristo becomes one with the crucified people of his time, as well as with all who are crucified today on the crosses of sexism, racism, ethnic discrimination, classism, and heterosexism that secure the power and privilege of the few. Jesús takes up his cross as the definitive act of solidarity. For us to pick up our cross, deny ourselves—that is deny our status and station—then follow and die with Jesús so that we can also live with him means that we, too, must find solidarity with the world's crucified people. For what good is it to gain all the wealth, privilege, and power of the world, yet forfeit our soul, our very humanity (Mk. 8:34–37)? Jesús' solidarity with the world's so-called losers and failures leads us to become one with the God of the oppressed.

Although Jesús' death is no more redemptive than any other aspect of his life, it is an action he undertook so that divinity could learn, through solidarity with the oppressed, what it means to be among the wretched of the world. Through Jesús, God learns what it means to suffer under unjust religious and political structures. The cross is meaningless except for fidelity to the mission of Jesús. His condemnation to death is the ultimate consequence faced by many Hispanics who struggle against unjust oppressive structures. All too often, Jesús' crucifixion is spiritualized, ignoring that this moment in history was both a political and religious act. But Jesús carries the stigmata of oppression upon his feet, hands, and side; thus, God can learn dispossession, discrimination, destitution, disinheritance, and disenfranchisement. Those who suffer under oppression have a God who personally understands their suffering due to the incarnation. Because Jesús suffered oppression on the cross, a divine political commitment to stand against injustices exists, a stance believers are called to emulate.

The paradox of the cross is that in spite of what it symbolizes, there is resurrection. The tragedy known as the cross, the symbol of failure and shame, is transformed to glory and power through Jesús' solidarity with all who are, and continue to be, crucified. This transformation is not brought about because of anything salvific found in the instrument of violence and death. It is brought about because Jesucristo went to the cross to hang with the oppressed. And it was through this act of solidarity that the church of the oppressed was born. Death is resurrected as one body composed of the crucified that has Jesús for its head. The cross can never be reduced to an individual satisfaction of sin nor Jesús to some personal savior. Yet we should not be surprised that a hyper-individualistic culture would reduce sin and salvation to the personal. For many Euroamerican followers of Jesus, sin is an action, or omission, committed by an individual who now stands guilty before God. This individual action (or lack thereof) creates alienation between the individual and God. Sin becomes universal, with sin being defined by those in power. The sin of those privileged by the prevailing social structures becomes normative for all humans, ignoring that power relationships mean different groups are tempted in different ways. For example, what is considered a sin for a White male with economic class (i.e., pride) may be a needed virtue for a poor Black Latina woman who has been told all her life that she is a worthless nobody. The act needing remedy, in this Eurocentric theological view, is the sin committed by the individual, and the act providing the remedy is Jesus' death on the cross.

Yet Latina/os understand that sin always manifests itself socially, through laws and regulations that permit the few to live in privilege and the many to live in want. Laws, customs, traditions, moral regulations, and so-called common sense are constructed by society to normalize and legitimize the prevailing power structures. By making sin a private matter, little is done to challenge or change structural sin. Those benefiting from how society is structured may recognize that sin may have been individually committed but ignore that, because we are communal creatures, it affects other humans. For many within the dominant culture, a failure to recognize complicity with structural sin exists. Sympathy concerning the plight of oppressed Hispanics is meaningless if those whom society benefits remain ignorant of how structural sin maintains and sustains poverty, violence, and oppression within the nation's barrios. Even if individuals repent of their biases, society will continue implementing oppression in their stead. Complicity to structural sins, regardless of the beliefs and practices of the individual, makes everyone a sinner who benefits by how society is structured, for all sins have individual and communal dimensions.

Hispanics' understanding of sin and salvation as more communal recognizes that all sins have a social context. While not minimizing the importance of living a moral life as an individual, Latino/as also recognize that sin is not limited to the personal. Sin also exists within the social structures of society. The consequences of oppression and violence can be caused by the acts of an individual, as well as by the normal and legitimate policies, laws, and moral regulations of the social order. These structural sins exist in the economic policies, the cultural traditions, and the legal codes of the society. To simply concentrate on personal piety ignores how sin, in the form of social structures, is designed to privilege a minority group at the expense of those disenfran chised by the social order. Hence, all sins, as relational, not only create alienation between the individual and God but also between the individual and his or her neighbor, the individual and her or his community, and the individual and God's creation. Recognizing the social dimension of sin leads to an understanding of sin, not from the perspective of the sinner, but from the perspective of the one sinned against.

Structural sin cannot be redeemed by individual atonement. Atonement ceases to be limited to Jesús' death on the cross. His life and resurrection are just as salvific. For Jesús, salvation from sin can never be reduced to the individual, but must encompass the community. Individual repentance of sin may be welcomed, but remains insufficient as long as structural sins remain. Individual repentance is insufficient because it fails to change or challenge the status quo. The society as a whole requires redemption, a moving away from structural sins toward a more just society. Hispanics are not the only ones negatively affected by structural sins. Those who benefit from the status quo are also negatively impacted and thus in need of salvation. Members of the dominant culture must live up to a false construction of superiority that justifies why they are privileged by the social structures. This false construction requires a complicity with structural sins that usually results in a loss of one's humanity. Not only are those oppressed by structural sin in need of salvation from oppression, those benefiting from structural sins are also in need of salvation—of regaining their humanity. The danger of reducing sin and atonement simply to the personal masks the causes and consequences of structural sin and the need of both the privileged and the disenfranchised for salvation.

JESÚS: CALLING MANY, BUT CHOOSING FEW

To most Hispanics, the historical Jesús is the Jesús of faith, not because the Bible tells us so, but because Jesús himself was a person of faith who lived as a witness to that faith (Boff 1978:12–15). The importance of Jesús lies in his liberating ability to call both individuals and communities to conversion, turning away from oppressive sinful structures toward personal and communal salvation and liberation. It is for this reason that Latina/os center Christian thought on Jesús, so we can launch out toward the path of reconciliation in the midst of an oppressive and repressive world.

Jesús voices an eschatological admonishment on what is expected from those who would follow him. There can be no faith, in fact no salvation, without justice-based actions, not because such actions cause salvation, but rather because they are their manifestation. To participate in ethical actions, enduring to the end is to seek justice. For the marginalized, the ultimate goal of any ethical act is the establishment of a more just society. Yet justice has become a worn out, rhetorical expression used as an abstract and detached battle cry. Every political action initiated by those in power, no matter how self-serving, is construed as just. The maintenance of an economic system that produces poverty is heralded as being based on the just principle of *suum cuique tribuere* (to each what is due). We dispatch the U.S. military to protect "our" natural resources located on the lands of others by framing a moral justification of securing or protecting our freedoms and way of life. The most unjust acts are portrayed as just by those with the power and privilege to impose their worldview on the rest of society. The beliefs, ideologies, and sentiments held in common by those with power and privilege provide the moral norms codified in shaping laws, customs, and traditions. Consequently, the primary function of society becomes the reaffirmation, protection, and perpetuation of the dominant culture's collective or common conscience.

Amid the vicissitudes of life and the hopelessness of vanquishing oppressive social structures, followers of Jesús are given God's peace. This is not a peace that magically makes the trials and tribulations disappear; rather, this is a peace embedded in a messianic vision of a God that prepares a banquet for all people, where everyone, regardless of race, ethnicity, class, gender, ability, or gender preference is welcomed to feast on the finest wines and richest foods. This is a messianic vision that serves as a paragon for how we are to relate with each other, especially within the church. On that day, we await mourning to end, death to be vanquished, and every tear ever shed over the world's injustices to be wiped away by the very hand of God. For now, it becomes the role of the church to serve as comforter for the afflicted. A hopeless hope in a messianic future will not be in vain, for liberation comes from God's outstretched arm as demonstrated through the praxis of those who claim to adhere to the politics of Jesús.

However, while all are invited to this banquet, then and now, not everyone will choose to come. God's reign, according to Jesucristo's parable in Matthew 22:1–14, is like a ruler who prepared a feast for his son's wedding. He sent his servants to the home of those who were invited to the banquet to inform them that all has been prepared and to please come, but they refused, providing flimsy excuses. Likewise, many today have disregarded or disparaged God's gracious invitation to join the divine feast. Unfortunately, many churches today block admission to God's communion table, often refusing to welcome immigrants and minorities. Assuming the invited misunderstood, the ruler sent more servants who informed the people that the oxen and fattened cattle had been butchered and everything was ready; but they ignored the messengers, being more preoccupied with their own business affairs. Some even took to mistreating and even killing the ruler's messengers. So the ruler sent his servants to the crossroads and byways to invite everyone, both the deserving and unworthy, to the banquet. The house was filled with guests, but not everyone chose to be "changed" by the invitation. One individual did not even bother to put on the proper attire. This individual, like some of us, trusted his old rags, his former self, and refused to be renewed by the invitation to liberation. Salvation, understood as liberation, is for everyone—oppressed and oppressor, slave and slaveholder, subjugated and subjugator. But while many are called, few are chosen. Jesús warns his followers to enter through the narrow gate, for wide is the gate and broad the road that leads to ruin, and many are those who enter in this fashion. But small is the gate and narrow the road that leads to life and few find it (Mt. 7:13–14). Those who oppress, enslave, and subjugate are on the broad road that passes through the wide gate, hence preventing them from experiencing salvation or liberation due to their complicity with social structures that brings misery to the vast majority of humanity, regardless as to whatever commitment made to Jesus or whatever sinner's prayer recited.

In fact, many of those who profit on the backs of the world's wretched call themselves Christians and believe they are so, due to some cultural upbringing or some intellectual (or emotional) decision to follow Jesus. But for Jesús, not everyone who calls him Lord will enter God's reign. On the ultimate day when all must give an account, many will say, "did we not prophesy in the name of Christ, or cast out demons in Christ's name, or even perform miracles through Christ?" We know these are Christians because only those claiming to be Christians would call Jesús "Lord" or would prophesy, cast out demons, and perform miracles in Jesús' name. But Jesús will respond, "away from me you evildoers, for I never knew you. Only those who do the will of God will see the glories of his reign" (Mt. 7:21–23). And what is the will of God? What does the Lord require? Simply stated: To act with justice, to love mercy, and to walk humbly with one's God (Mic. 6:8).

Personal piety and clean living becomes, all too often, the mark of Jesus followers, the ethical practices derived from reading the biblical text with dominant eyes. When Christianity is reduced to personal piety, individual conversion, and philanthropic service, the Empire is seldom held accountable to the moral principles of the Gospel. Personal piety short-circuits the justice-based politics of Jesús. He may praise the religious leaders of his time for being meticulous in their personal piety, calculating the tithe on minuscule spices—mint, dill, and cumin. Yet he condemns them for neglecting the more important aspects of the law—justice, mercy, and forgiveness (Mt. 23:23). The politics of Jesus, as understood by many within the dominant culture obsessed with the cultural wars fueled by personal piety, seldom explores the church's complicity with the empire that denies the vast global majority justice, mercy, and forgiveness. Few religious leaders or churches question neoliberalism or unrestrained free market capitalist economics as foundational in the production of values. Instead, several view themselves as God's chosen people called by the Almighty to witness their version of a capitalist-based Christianity throughout the world. The imposition of this pro-capitalist Christianity can only be accomplished if the United States remains a militarily and morally strong nation—itself a religious imperative. Rather than challenging the empire, some powerful religious leaders instead proclaim the virtues of the Empire and unwittingly cloak its military missions abroad, as well as its racist domestic policies. Ironically, the religious apologists of the Empire fail to remember that Jesús was also persecuted by the empire of his time, Rome, in cooperation with his contemporary religious leaders who cried out during Jesús' trial, "We have no king except Caesar" (Jn. 19:15).

It would appear that today's religious leaders' support for Empire joins the religious leaders of old in proclaiming the supremacy of the earthly state. And while religious establishments have historically been co-opted by states to advance the states' interests, what is new about the present day manifestation of this equation is how the pro-Empire religious establishments have fused the pro-capitalist undergirding of empire with Christianity.

We are not saved by the Bible but by the justice-based praxis rooted in the reading of the Bible, a reading made ours when done from a Latina/o perspective. Such a reading requires us to turn away from Eurocentric theological triumphalism and to search within our own community for our understanding of who Christ is.

JESÚS: WELCOMING THE INDECENT

For the ruler to invite everyone, including the outcasts to the banquet table is considered inappropriate. How can we expect the refined to dine with philistines? It is one thing to dine with the uncouth; it is quite another thing to include their voices or perspectives. To seriously do theological and ethical analysis from the social location of the outcast, specifically the sexual outcast, is usually considered indecorous if not indecent. It is precisely this indecency that theologian Marcella Althaus-Reed calls for as she seeks a theology that can challenge oppressive social structures. Those most likely to be considered indecent are usually poor women of color. Constructing acceptable theological perspectives of sexuality often ignores the complex set of sexual regulations and gender expectations placed on women. To counter this imposed "decency," she calls for the doing of theology with one's panties off. In other words, she calls for a move beyond what has been constructed as proper behavior, which in reality masks oppressive relationships. The "indecent theology" that she advocates is a perverse and subversive theology that starts with people's experiences without censorship. It is a theology that tells people to come as they are, by first coming out of the closets that constrain and domesticate them (2000:1–9).

In a similar way, I argue for an indecent approach to justice-based praxis. The global success of neoliberalism makes any real hope of liberation from oppressive global economic systems unrealistic. The politics of the Euroamerican Jesus will not save Hispanics, mainly because we remain complicit with the very neoliberal colonial venture that oppresses the world's marginalized, ignoring or providing justification for the prevailing structures of oppression that remain detrimental to Latino/as. If the Eurocentric politics of Jesus fails to address oppressive structures, then Hispanics must construct the politics of Jesús for their communities, rooted in the Latina/o social context. Those who benefit from the power and privilege accorded by the dominant culture are incapable of fashioning an objective political ethics because their standing within society is protected by the prevailing social structures. If the foundation for the politics of Jesús lies within our cultural context, then I turn to my mother for inspiration as to how this politics is to be constructed.

Mirta—may she rest in peace—was an illiterate country girl from the hills of Santa Clara, Cuba, who was sold as a preteen to a family in the city to work as their domestic maid, where she faced physical and sexual abuse. It was the only way her poverty-ridden family could provide food for themselves. Mirta, a santéra, taught me the ways of the *orishas*, specifically the ways of my *orí*, my head, *Ellegúa*—the trickster.[6] Mirta's faith forged the trickster's ethics needed if one wanted to survive the mean streets of New York City. It is Mirta's life experiences, and the life experiences of all the Mirtas of the world, that have become the foundation of the ethical thoughts of Mirta's child. I even name this paradigm after the loving and gentle phrase I can still hear *mi mamí*— my mother—constantly say to me: *"Coño Miguelito, no jodas mas!"* This becomes my Caribbean habitus, and it is from her words of wisdom that I advocate what I have come to call an ethics *para joder* (De La Torre 2013b:11). An ethics *para joder* attempts to situate an effective response within the consequences of colonialism, the oppression of normative social structures, and the pain of the domesticated Hispanic. Coining a term to describe an ethical practice already occurring among the marginalized implies that this methodology of *jordiendo* already exists; but as an organic intellectual, I simply am reflecting upon this existing praxis for the purpose of theorizing and theologizing.

To *joder* is a Spanish verb, a word one would never use in polite conversation. Although it is not the literal translation of a certain four-letter word beginning with the letter *F*, it is still considered somewhat vulgar because it basically means, "to screw with." Note: it does not mean to screw—but to screw with, an important difference in semantics. The word connotes an individual who purposely is a pain in the rear end, who purposely is causing trouble, who constantly disrupts the established norm, who shouts from the mountaintop what most prefer to be kept silent, who audaciously refuses to stay in his or her place. I have been taken somewhat aback by some who have objected to the use of profanity in describing this ethical political paradigm. But in all reality, what is truly profane is not the word that is used; rather, it is the oppressive death-dealing conditions under which Hispanics are forced to live. An ethics *para joder* is an ethics that "screws" with the prevailing power structures.

Those who are among the disenfranchised, who stand before the vastness of neoliberalism that offers little hope for radical change in their lifetimes, have few ethical alternatives. Regardless of the good intentions of those who are privileged by society, or the praxis they employ to paternalistically save and rescue Hispanics, the devastating consequences of Empire will worsen as the few get wealthier and the many sink deeper into poverty. The dominant culture, including progressive ethicists, may be willing to offer charity and to stand in solidarity, but few are willing or able to take a role in dismantling the very global structures designed to privilege them at the expense of the majority of the world's inhabitants (De La Torre 2010:92). When those who are disenfranchised start to *joder*, it literally creates political instability. An ethics that upsets the prevailing social order designed to maintain Empire is an ethics that arises from those on the margins of society who are disillusioned and frustrated with normative Eurocentric values and virtues. While the majority of all Euroamerican ethicists insist on social order, marginalized communities must call for social disorder, a process achieved by *jodiendo*. Perhaps, it might lead some within the dominant culture to share in the hopelessness of overcoming the global forces of neoliberalism. If so, it may be the only way that progress is made. A liberative ethics *para joder* can be frightening to those who are accustomed to their power and privilege because hopelessness signals a lack of control. Because those who benefit from the present social structures insist on control, sharing the plight of being vulnerable to forces beyond control will demonstrate how hope falls short (Ibid.:94).

To *joder* means refusing to play by the rules established by those who provide a space for orderly dissent that pacifies the need to vent for the marginalized, but it is designed not to change the power relationships within the existing social structures. If the goal of the politics of Jesús is to bring about change, then it is crucial to go beyond the rules created by the dominant culture, to move beyond what is expected, to push beyond their universalized experiences.[7] In a very real sense, Jesús is a holy *joderon* (a holy screwer). Usually when we think of Jesus, images of a peace loving, gentle pacifist come to mind, at least they did to the mind of Howard Yoder. Ignored is Jesús the troublemaker, the bringer of conflict, the disrupter of unity. This is a violent Jesús who makes a whip and forcefully drives out the moneychangers in the Temple, overturning their tables (Jn. 3:15). This is a strategic Jesús who prepares his disciples for what is to come. He instructs them that before, when he sent them out without a money belt, bag, or sandals, they lacked nothing. But now, they are to bring their money belt and bag, and if they lack a sword, they are to "sell their cloak and purchase one" (Lk. 22:35–36). Jesús the so-called pacifist is instructing his followers to buy a sword? It would be like today instructing the purchase of a gun. This is a realistic Jesús who warns his disciples that he did not come to bring peace to earth, but division (Lk. 12:51). He did not come to bring peace to earth, but rather a sword. He has come to turn a son against his father, a daughter against her mother, and a daughter-in-law against her mother-in-law. Even a person's enemy will end up being a member of one's own household (Mt. 10:34–36). On the night he was betrayed and arrested, Pedro impulsively drew the sword he had, and struck Malchus, the high priest's slave, cutting off his ear (Jn. 18:10). Jesús responds to this act of violence by stating "All those who take the sword shall perish by the sword" (Mt. 26:52).

Jesús may be speaking to Pedro, but to whom is he directing his comment? After all, it was Jesús who told his disciples to sell their cloak and buy a sword. In fact, some of the disciples were already armed, for they boasted, "Look Lord, we already have two swords. That's enough!" (Lk. 22:38). If Jesús' comments are directed to his disciples, then he is contradicting his earlier instructions. No, he was not speaking for the benefit of his disciples, but for those aligned with the colonizer who came to arrest him. Those who are the muscle of the colonizer, picking up the sword to defend the empire, will along with the empire perish with the sword. We may argue that Jesús abhors violence, but it would be simplistic to argue that he was a pacifist. He calls his disciples to become the recipients of violence, calling them to radical solidarity with a bloody cross. Violence can never be accepted as a necessary evil as per some revolutionaries, nor rejected as antithetical to Jesus as per pacifists. After all, Jesús prophesies about the violence of the Day of Judgment.

History demonstrates the futility of simply denouncing unjust social structures, for those whom the structures privilege will never willingly abdicate what they consider to be their birthright. Not all violence is the same. The violence employed by the marginalized to overcome oppression is in reality self-defense to the oppressor's violent employment of terror to maintain their subjugation. Unconditional love for the very least among us might lead a person, in an unselfish act, to stand in solidarity with the oppressed in their battle for self-preservation. Protecting a "nonperson" might invite a violent confrontation, as the oppressor, feeling backed into a corner, fights tooth and nail to maintain the status quo. To make a preferential option of love for the oppressed means harming the oppressor, who has a vested interest in insisting on the use of nonviolence, as the only ethically acceptable methodology, by those who she or he oppresses. The conflict and disruption that comes with following Jesús, whose consequence at times is violence, illustrates the need for an ethical praxis for colonized people that lack the physical or military power to confront or overcome the colonizer. Because the usage of violence all too often becomes the oppressor's excuse to unleash greater violent retaliation, a need to be as wise as serpents but gentle as doves is required. How does one create ethical acts that disrupt structures that support and maintain oppression?

I suggest the need to *joder*, even though the call to *joder*, the call to disrupt the social structures that privileges an elite minority segment of society, might very well bring the unwanted consequence of the sword. Subscribing to this indecent ethics *para joder* recognizes that the prevailing social order exists to legitimize and normalize the privileges of the few at the expense of many. *Joderones* are tricksters who lie so that truth can be revealed. When they lie, cheat, joke, and deceive, they unmask deeper truths obscured by the dominant culture's moralists. These means employed by *joderones* in the struggle for liberation may not be considered moral by the dominant culture; nevertheless, such tricksters are ethical, operating in a realm that moves beyond good and evil, beyond what society defines as being right or wrong.

Joderones are consummate survivors that serve as exemplars for the disenfranchised in need of surviving the reality colonialism constructed for them. By disrupting the empire's equilibrium to create compromising situations for those in power, the *joderon* reveals their weaknesses, exposes what they prefer to remain hidden, and removes their artificial masks of superiority. Disrupted established norms create new situations that provide the marginalized fresh ways of approaching oppression.

The biblical text is full of *joderones*, whether it be Abraham tricking the Egyptian Pharaoh and King Abimelech of Gerar into believing that his wife was his sister, resulting in financial gain (Gn. 12:10–20, 20:1–18), his son Isaac attempting to pull off the same charade with King Abimelech of Gerar (Gn. 26:1–14), or his grandson Jacob who tricked his older brother Esau out of their father's blessings (Gn. 27:145). But even the *joderones* can get tricked, as in the case of Laban, Jacob's father-in-law, who tricks Jacob out of seven years of labor and the woman he wants to marry by switching brides on the wedding night (Gn. 29:15–30). During Egyptian captivity, the Hebrew midwives Shiphrah and Puah deceived the Pharaoh to save the lives of the Hebrew babies (Ex 1:15–21). The Hebrews are then tricked by an elaborate scheme perpetrated by the Gibeonites to enter into a treaty of nonaggression (Jo. 9:3–20). In the book of Judges there is Ehud, who tricks Eglon the King of Moab into a secluded room so that he could kill him and free his people from tyranny (Jg. 3:12–30). Jael also frees her people by providing Sisera deadly hospitality (Jg. 4:17–22), and there is Samson, who through his riddles tries to achieve personal gain only to eventually be tricked himself by his wife Delilah (Jg. 14; 16). Then you have King David, who feigns madness before the King Achish of Gath to preserve his life (1 Sa. 21:11–14). And there is his son, King Solomon, who tricks the two women fighting over the baby to discover who is being truthful by suggesting he would cut the baby in half (1 K. 3:16–28). These tricksters, these *joderones*, these screwers with the established order, engaged in deception to achieve personal gain (Jacob), survival (David), and salvation of their people (Shiphrah, Puah, Jael, and Ehud) and to discover truth (Solomon).

These holy *joderones* provide a moral justification for the employment of deception as a means of self-preservation for those who face overwhelming odds against surviving. Although a thorough examination of the biblical text for purposes of uncovering the many manifestations of *joderones* and their importance to the development of the Judeo-Christian faith is a worthy project that can serve as a corrective for the prevailing Eurocentric confusion of ethics with personal piety, such an endeavor is beyond the scope of this book. For our purposes, we need to focus on just one *joderon*, Jesús, the colonized man. Jesús the liberator screws with the established political and religious authorities by subverting the legitimacy they constructed, a running theme throughout this book. For this, he pays the ultimate price of crucifixion, accused of being a heretic. Jesucristo *el joderon*, screws with those who established themselves as the political and religious leaders of the people and from their lofty positions screw the very people they are entrusted to represent, support, and protect. By employing an ethics *para joder*, Jesús literally screwed up their plans for oppressing the people. Cleansing the Temple becomes a liberative praxis that literally overturns the established tables (Mt. 21:12–13). Those today wishing to be imitators of Christ by following his politics are called to do likewise, to *joder* (De La Torre 2010:114–15).

To *joder* is not a praxis that the disenfranchised engage in out of vengeance or spite. To *joder* is an act of love toward oppressors, designed to force them to live up to their rhetoric in the hope that confronting their complicity with oppressive structures might lead them toward their own salvation. Oppressors are also victims of the structures that are designed to privilege them yet rob them of what it means to be human. Jesús rejects what has been the norm, to love your neighbor and hate your enemy. Instead, he commands his followers to love and pray for those who oppress and persecute. After all, God causes the sun to rise on the evil and good, and sends rain to the just and unjust (Mt. 5:43–45). The wheat and weeds grow together, even though on the day of the harvest, the weeds will be bundled together and burned, while the wheat will be brought into the barn (Mt. 13:30). To *joder* is a survival strategy based on love, designed to liberate the abused from death-dealing social structures that deny them their humanity, and to liberate the abusers whose own humanity is lost through their complicity with these same structures.

JESÚS: ACCEPTS US JUST AS WE ARE

I was living in Miami, Florida, when Pope John Paul II made a papal visit in 1987, delighting the city's large Hispanic community. I remember (although some claim this is an urban legend) a local Euroamerican entrepreneur who decided to capitalize on the event by making commemorative t-shirts. He designed thousands of shirts that were supposed to read "I saw the Pope" in Spanish. Unfortunately, he never bothered to check this sentence with those who actually knew the language. Rather than using the masculine definitive article "el," the shirt maker used the feminine definitive article "la." Hence the shirts instead read, "I saw the Potato." Euroamerican churches that follow the politics of Jesus often repeat the shirt maker's mishap. Although attempting to reach out to the Hispanics of their community, a lot gets lost in the translation. In an age of political correctness, many predominate Anglo churches are scrambling to erase centuries of exclusion by now appearing to be multicultural, making diversity the church buzzword of our time. Three hundred-year-old German hymns are quickly translated into Spanish and flashed on the overhead screen. Sermons are preached instructing Euroamericans why it is their Christian duty to reach out to their less fortunate Latino/as with the Gospel message of salvation. Attempts are made to appear culturally sensitive by offering Taco Tuesdays at the congregational fellowship meal.

I do not question the sincerity of those Euroamerican churches that wish to see their congregations better reflect the diversity of humanity. Still, for many, their approach attempts to include Latino/as without necessarily changing the cultural milieu of the congregation. All too often, when the predominately White, middle-class congregation wrestles with issues of inclusiveness, they unwillingly revert to a multicultural facade for the sake of political correctness. All are welcomed, as long as the church power structures that privilege the predominant Euroamerican congregation remain intact. The underlying meaning of politically correct congregations is that Hispanics can join, as long as they first convert to Euroamericanism, and respond appreciatively to whichever way their culture gets "translated." Latina/os who wish to participate in the dominant culture's churches must assimilate by putting away their Jesús for Jesus.

One of the first challenges faced by the early church dealt with the inclusion of non-Jews. Must these Gentiles first convert to Judaism before they can become Christians? More specifically, do they first need to be circumcised before becoming a follower of Jesús? Pablo and Bernabé were staying in Antioch when some church leaders came down from Judea and began teaching that "unless you are circumcised, according to the custom taught by Moses, you cannot be saved." Their teachings led to a sharp dispute and debate between them and the mission of Pablo and Bernabé (Ac. 15: 1–2). Even the most faithful can reveal the prejudices lurking in their hearts for Pedro, too, refused to eat with the Gentiles. This is the same Pedro who faced criticism for visiting the home of the Gentile Cornelius, a Roman centurion (Ac. 10–11). Yet, some time later while in Antioch, when certain men of Jerusalem arrived to insist that Gentiles must first be circumcised before being saved, Pedro withheld eating with the uncircumcised (Ga. 2:11–14). The controversy was eventually settled in Jerusalem in favor of the Gentiles. They could become Christians without first having to become Jews.

Nevertheless, the circumcision controversy still exists today. The debate no longer centers on cutting off one's foreskin. Instead what Hispanics are often called to do is cut off their identity, their culture, the symbols by which they perceive the Divine. In many cases, Latina/os (as well as all other people of color) must first become Euroamerican before becoming Christians. They must adopt Euroamerican theology, hermeneutics, philosophy, liturgy, politics, and most importantly, church structures. They must prove their Christianity by describing their faith in the cultural symbols of the dominant culture. To insist on believing through one's own Latino/a symbols only proves (like the uncircumcised Gentiles of old) that they are not really believers. Unfortunately, the Jesus presented to these uncircumcised Latina/os is wrapped within Euroamerican cultural structures. Christian theology assumes the superiority of Euroamerican paradigms and methodologies, even when they directly contradict Latino/a culture and identity. Any understanding of faith based on the individualistic characteristic of Euroamericans will be destined to fail among a people who place greater emphasis on the communal. Latino/as are insisting in perceiving the Divine through their own Hispanic eyes. To do otherwise becomes blasphemous. But what about the pressure to assimilate to the dominant culture? Pablo's rather earthy rebuttal is worth noting. He tells those Gentiles being hounded to become circumcised so that they may be saved not to be concerned. Specifically, he writes, "I wish that the ones causing you to doubt would castrate themselves" (Ga. 5:12).

JESÚS: THE CALL OF GOOD NEWS

Not only Gentiles, but all of creation is to be evangelized with good news. But what followers of Jesús have considered to be good news, has historically been received as a political club that forces "the uncircumcised" into submission. "Go into all the world, and proclaim the good news to the whole creation" (Mk. 16:15). Known as the Great Commission, this verse is probably more responsible than any other biblical verse for most of the blood that has historically been shed over religious, racial, ethnic, and cultural differences. For many, the verse has been interpreted to mean that disciples have an obligation to proclaim the Good News to all of humanity. And while this is beneficial, how the Good News has been interpreted has been deadly. For many Christians throughout history, the Good News has been understood as a choice between Jesus and Hell. Not to choose Jesus was to be condemned to Hell. More exactly, not to believe in Jesus the same way the church dictates meant that the "uncircumcised heathens" were worthy of Hell, and the church was responsible in their elimination from this life lest they lead others astray. Think of the European religious wars, the Inquisition, the genocide in the so-called New World, the religious justification of slavery, or the religious impulse of colonization.

But what if the Good News had nothing to do with believing in Jesus the way the church states one should believe? What if the Good News has to do with being Jesús? For those who are disenfranchised, Luke 4:18–19 is the Good News that should be proclaimed not through words, but through actions. The words of the first sermon Jesús ever preached, in effect, the thesis statement of his ministry, resonates with the poor for whom the Good News is given; the broken in need of healing; the captives who require liberation; the ones refusing to see who necessitates consciousness-raising; the wounded who want freedom from their chains; and everyone else who hopes for the year of Jubilee, biblically understood as the "year of redistributing wealth to create economic justice."

Rather than proclaiming a good news that liberates the oppressed, the Great Commission has been reduced, specifically among evangelicals, to a simple acknowledgment that Jesus is sufficient for salvation. Salvation is obtained through right beliefs, right doctrines, orthodoxy. Yet even demons believe. Santiago, the brother of Jesús, challenges the believer. "So, you believe that there is only one God, fine; but the demons also believe, and tremble. You fool; don't you know that faith without works is dead?" (Jm. 2:19–20). Demons and Christians prospering from power and privilege believe. The emphasis can never rest on belief, rather, on what actions are committed.

Pablo preached good news. "Remember that Jesucristo, from the seed of David, was raised from the dead. This is my good news; for which I have suffered; even placed in chains like a criminal. But the word of God cannot be chained" (2 Ti. 2:8–9). However, the good news that Pablo preached continues to be lost whenever the missionary venture is transformed into enriching the conquering nations. Evangelism has come to mean converting people into thinking what we think and believing the doctrines we believe. Those who refuse to accept our brand of Christianity are branded infidels, enemies of the true faith, thereby justifying their destruction. At times, in the missionary's attempt to protect the truth, great evil in inflicted upon the indigenous population. The zeal to propagate the good news of Jesus becomes fused and confused with profiting at the expense of those whom we hoped to evangelize. An old African proverb best captures this phenomenon: "When the missionaries came, they had the Bible and we had the land. When we opened our eyes after praying, we had the Bible and they had the land."

Yet Pablo had a very different understanding of the good news. To be a Christian is for those who are in power to share the plight of those labeled subservient. Solidarity with the oppressed can lead to being "chained like a criminal;" nevertheless, the acts for justice committed in the name of the good news can never be chained. To die with Jesús is to live with Jesús. The good news of liberation proclaimed by Jesús becomes a message of liberation from all forms of human oppression, such as social, economic, political, racial, sexual, environmental, and religious. This call to full humanity, not just for the oppressed but also for their oppressors, is indeed good news that should not be restricted to Christians. Those of other faiths, or of no faith whatsoever, can also use this good news. The Great Commission is not to convert the other to believe what I believe, but to raise the consciousness of those who have believed the lie of their worthlessness with the good news of their personhood. For those of us who claim Christianity, believing becomes the process of integrating faith with the sociopolitical everyday in which the oppressed find themselves.

JESÚS: WHAT TRINITY MEANS

Religion scholar Harold Recinos reminds us that from the barrio "of concrete misery resulting from economic and political injustice, the questions that are posed to faith require answers that inspire social behavior that changes real conditions of life" (1997:39). An example of how our politics reflects the call of Jesús to "change real conditions" by sharing what we do have with those who have nothing can be found in the Gospel of Luke. "If anyone has two cloaks, they must share with the one who has none; and the one with something to eat should do the same" (3:11). Consider the fact that seldom does one see overweight individuals in economically stressed countries. In fact, indigenous medicine is usually sold, whose properties are supposed to help people gain weight. And here is the global irony: while most of the world seeks calories, we in the United States pay not to eat! In 2010, Americans spent $60.9 billion to lose weight. But for many of the world's inhabitants, the vast majority of the day is spent finding the next meal. Today's world agriculture produces 17 percent more calories per person than it did in the 1970s, despite population increases. This rise in calories is enough to provide every person in the world with enough food to live. If indeed the earth provides enough to sustain all life residing upon it, why then do so many go hungry? The answer is not a lack of resources but, rather, an unjust distribution system. World hunger can be reduced if humans learn how to live in harmony with nature. Shortages occur when humans attempt to impose their will upon the fair and natural distribution of nature's resources according to the needs of the people. The natural distribution of the earth's resources is disrupted by the few who control the majority of food and water resources for personal gain and funnel the world's food resources to the industrial north, specifically the United States.

If everyone on earth ate like Americans, current food supplies would only be able to feed 2.5 billion people, or about half of the world's population. However, if we all ate a subsistence diet, getting the calories we need, current annual food production could feed six billion people. Juan el baptista instructs us that if we possess two cloaks and our neighbor has none, then I should give from my abundance to the one who lacks. If I consume 5,000 daily calories and my neighbor consumes none, then shouldn't I reduce my intake to about 2,500 daily calories (2,000 is what is needed) to make it possible for those who receive none to get something? This radical act of sharing can be found in the essence of the Trinity. The concept of Trinity has fascinated Christian thinkers since the start of Christian thought. Was Jesús divine or human? If divine, how does it reconcile with the concept of monotheism? What about the Holy Spirit? Are there really three Gods? It is interesting to note that the writers of the Gospels don't seem to care. Theologian Luis Pedraja observes: "The writers of the New Testament do not concern themselves so much with questions about the person of [Jesús]—that is, his divine nature or substance. Instead, they are concerned with [Jesús'] deeds, proclamations, miracles, and salvific actions" (1999:95). The doctoral "truth" that emerged from the early discourse occurring centuries later with the established church was the concept of Trinity. There is only one God, but this one God is three: Father, Son, and Holy Ghost. Although the concept sounds incongruent (1=3), it is a doctrine accepted by faith, even though throughout history tomes have been written trying to explain this contradictory concept of trinity.

It is not our goal here to enter the conversation by attempting to provide an explanation for the doctrine. In fact, Hispanic Christians seldom spend much ink trying to resolve this mystery. However, triune God does provide Latino/as with an economic pattern to be emulated. Unfortunately, when most Christians think of the Trinity, they automatically impose a hierarchical relation that first privileges the Father, then the Son, and finally, trailing in third place, the Holy Spirit. This imposed hierarchy contradicts Christian doctrine that considers each person of the Trinity to fully participate equally in divinity, sharing God's power and nature, while maintaining their distinct functions. There is supposed to exist no hierarchy within the concept of Trinity, for God's nature is to share. God moves beyond simply offering a relationship with humanity by inviting all to share divinity and power with God and each other, or as Pablo would promise, to become "co-heirs with Christ" (Ro. 8:17).

Pedraja explores the consequences of an "economic" Trinity to be emulated. The Trinity as model reveals how we are to live with each other and in God's image that calls us to engage in a life of sharing. Trinity reveals a God who exists by sharing both divinity and power. This sharing, this communal nature was witnessed by the early church, exemplified in the Book of Acts. If God does not hoard power, then neither should we. If the essence of the Divine is in sharing, then we are called to politically live in a similar fashion (2004:56). Implementing the "economic" Trinity model significantly impacts how followers of Jesús attempting to establish a just distribution of power should do economics and politics. The "economic" Trinity calls not only for the dismantling of social structures that maintain economic injustices but also calls for all powers to be shared, destroying structures of dominance and oppression that foster marginalization. Those hoarding power and privilege can never become part of the body of Jesús whose very essence, as part of the Trinity, is to share. For those of the dominant culture to sit next to the disenfranchised at church in an attempt to create a politically correct multicultural worship experience, yet retain their power and privilege within society Monday through Saturday, contradicts the basic intent of Christian fellowship based on the model of Trinity.

If the Trinity model represents radical sharing, then the bond that holds three in one is love. When the religious leaders attempted to trap Jesús by asking him to name the greatest commandment, Jesús responded: "You shall love the Lord your God with all your heart, your soul, and your mind. This is the first and great commandment; the second is like it: you shall love your neighbor as yourself. In these two commandments all the Laws and the Prophets hang" (Mt. 22:37–40). For Jesús, these two commandments are interconnected through love and cannot be separated. To be faithful to one requires obedience to both. Simply stated, one cannot love God while hating one's neighbor, a point made by the disciple Juan, who wrote, "Anyone stating to be in the light, yet hating [another] is still in darkness. The one loving [the other] rests in the light, and no offense is in them" (1 Jn. 2:9–10). If salvation is manifested as love for both our God and our neighbor, and if a tree is known by its fruit, then those who dominate or oppress others fall short because they "do not love their neighbors [specifically their neighbors of color or a lower socio-economic class] as themselves." Domination by members of a Euroamerican culture has created a history marked by the genocide of Native Americans, the enslavement of Africans, and dispossession of Hispanics throughout the Western Hemisphere. And this history thrives today in a global political strategy that continues to ensure the economic privilege of one nation at the expense of the "Two-Thirds World" nations whose raw material and cheap labor are exploited for capital gain.

Jesús calls us to *comunidad* whenever the faith community gathers to celebrate the Eucharist. During that last supper, Jesús asks that we repeat the sharing of bread and wine "in remembrance of me" (Lk. 22:19). Theological questions concerning transubstantiation[8] are less important than the purpose of celebrating the Eucharist, the creation of a sharing *comunidad*. Although it would be easy to simply translate the Spanish word *comunidad* into the English word *community*, it should be noted that for Hispanics, the emphasis is based on the Latin word *communis*, which connotes "common sharing." As social scientist Rafael Luévano reminds us, *comunidad* refers to a religious sharing that embodies the history and culture and considers the vibrant spirituality of Hispanics. *Comunidad* becomes a spiritual experience rooted in a grass-roots faith journey lived out day by day (*lo cotidiano*): walking with the others in all the joys and sorrows of daily life, becoming a moving blend of both the spiritual and cultural expressions of the Latino/a's inclination for communal sharing. One family's tragedy becomes the *comunidad*'s collective tragedy, and one family's success becomes the joy of the *comunidad* (2009:142–43). When Jesús was crucified, the Trinity suffered, sharing in the pain of one. Likewise, the suffering of any part of the *comunidad*'s body not only becomes the suffering of the whole, but is a suffering shared by Jesús, who is one with the *comunidad*. Trinity becomes an invitation into *comunidad* with our God and with Hispanics.

JESÚS: AN ALTAR CALL

Love is the bond of the Trinity and the bond that makes us one with the Divine. In effect, God's essence, God's purpose, and God's call is love, or as the apostle Juan reminds us, "Whoever does not love, knows not God—for God is love" (1 Jn. 4:8). If this is true, that God is love, then the only absolute that can be claimed with any certainty is love. Maybe ethicist Joseph Fletcher was right when he claimed that love should therefore be the prime motive behind every ethical decision taken (1966:57). We are told to love one another as we are loved by Jesús so that everyone will know we are followers of Jesucristo by the love we demonstrate (Jn. 13:34–35). This love offered by Jesús is a self-giving love best captured by the Greek word *agape* that connotes the concept of unconditional love, best demonstrated through the offering of forgiveness for his murderers while he was hanging from the instrument of his death (Lk. 23:34). But is the biblical concept of unconditional love realistic? All too often, those in power define love as either paternalistic or as "tough" love, thus masking their self-interest, making their will predominant. The basic flaw of relying solely on love as defined by the dominant culture is one of trust. Can they be trusted to act in love? If the past history and current affairs of how people of color have been treated in the United States by its social structures is to serve us as a guide in answering this question, then the answer is obviously no. When we define love from the centers of power and privilege, the focus is usually on how to love the disenfranchised. But love can never be one way (i.e., love from the privileged toward the marginalized) lest it reduce the marginalized to an object used for those in power to express their paternalistic charity.

Love must be mutual. To love the marginalized is to serve them and receive in return God's love through them. In this way, those who are privileged and powerful find their salvation by discovering God in the lives of the least of these. Thus, God's love can be experienced, a love manifested in the establishment of just relationships that can lead toward just social structures. Only then can community be established and hope created for a just social order. Unfortunately for so many from the U.S. church of Jesus, they remain similar to the church of Laodicea. The apostle Juan, while exiled on the island of Patmos, writes a letter to the Christians of this church, accusing them of being neither cold nor hot. Because they are lukewarm, God plans to vomit them out. But the church of Laodicea says to itself "I am rich, I have made a fortune, and have everything I want" (Rv. 3:15–17). Like many churches today that have merged the politics of Jesus with a neoliberal economic order,

there exists an acceptance of the false doctrine of prosperity theology—
a theology that advocates a God who wants to see God's followers
wealthy and healthy. If we lack wealth, all we need to do is name and
claim it in the name of Jesus. Yet God says they fail to realize just how
wretchedly and pitiably poor they have become. They may have physical wealth, but in fact they live in spiritual poverty. Nevertheless, in the
midst of their wealth, God sends Laodicea and today's churches a messenger with an invitation. "Look," says the Lord, "I am standing at the
door, knocking. If one of you hears me calling and opens the door, I will
come in to share their meal" (Rv. 3:20).

Unfortunately, too many churches have failed to recognize the one
knocking on the door, confusing the doorknocker with someone hand-
ing out blessings. Not long ago, I saw a mime of the stereotypical blue-
eyed Jesus with reddish blond hair knocking on an old wooden door
(http://imgur.com/gallery/i8yV7sN). The caption read: "Knock,
Knock, . . . Who's there? *It's Jesus, let me in.* Why? *I have to save you.*
From what? *From what I'm going to do to you if you don't let me in.*"
For centuries, a Christian invitation has been given to accept Jesus—or
else. Those who accept get to enjoy eternal bliss in Heaven, those who
refuse, burn for all eternity in Hell. No doubt, this is a very strange
understanding of Divine love, resembling more extortion. Rather than
understanding that the invitation of the one knocking at the door is to
live a praxis-filled life of service that leads both Laodicea and today's
churches to a fulfilled life now, we have resignified this passage to be
about some promised afterlife devoid of praxis, except to accept Jesus as
Lord and personal Savior. But scaring people into Heaven is, at the very
least, problematic. Let's consider for a moment the words of John Lennon's song. "Imagine there's no heaven; It's easy if you try; No hell
below us; Above us only sky; Imagine all the people living for today."[9]
What if there is no Heaven, no resurrection, only this life. If so, here is
the real question those who choose to follow Jesús must answer: Would
you still accept his radical revolutionary call to praxis? Do you follow the
justice-based teachings of Jesús only because of some promise of Heav-
en? If so, then like the one who places their hand on the plow and looks

back, you are not worthy of God's reign (Lk. 9:62). To be a disciple means loving so deeply the other that one is willing to forfeit any hope for eternity. Take Moses and Pablo as examples.

Moses, while standing before the living God, cried out, "But now, if you will forgive [Israel's] sin—but if not, then blot me out of the book you have written" (Ex. 32:32). He would rather lose having his name written in God's book of life than see Israel not receive God's forgiveness. For Moses, getting to Heaven wasn't the reason he followed God. Maybe it was because he approached God, not as an individual (a common Eurocentric characteristic), but as part of a community. If we understand salvation as liberation from sin—sins committed by the individual, and just as important, committed to the individual by others through social structures, then reducing salvation to some personal choice, disconnected from the community, becomes a foreign biblical concept. Moses was not alone in this communal understanding of salvation; neither was Pablo of the New Testament. Pablo was willing to be condemned and cut off from Christ if it would help his Jewish compatriots find salvation (Rm. 9:2). Both of these men were willing to be cut off from God for the sake of the liberation of their community. Moses and Pablo refused to exchange the quest for transforming society as an expression of their love for their neighbor for some privatized faith that assured them of individual immortality. They understood the depths of the words of Jesús when he said, "A person can have no greater love than to lay down one's life for one's friends" (Jn. 15:13).

Personally, I don't know (and I really don't care) if there actually is an afterlife. If there is, great, icing on the cake. The choice to respond to the one knocking on my door is not based on some reward in the hereafter; it is based on the meaning and purpose it gives to my life in the here and now. The Jesús who did not come to be served, but to serve (Mt. 20:28) through the ultimate act of solidarity with the least of these, demonstrated by picking up a cross and following them to crucifixion, becomes a model to emulate. The reward of giving my life meaning and purpose in the chaos and absurdity of history and the hopelessness of life caused by global oppressive structures is more than anyone could ask. If indeed there is no resurrection, then I can rest in peace knowing that a life well lived in service was a life not lived in vain. So then, who really is this one called the Lord standing at the door of Laodicea and today's churches asking to be let in? Is it not enough to insist that the Jesus of the dominant culture needs to be rejected?

Throughout this book, we have envisioned a Jesús that is incarnated in the everyday. Whatever Jesucristo means to Latina/os, he is understood within the sociohistorical and ecopolitical context of the Hispanic community of faith that responds to the biblical message and mandate of the Good News of the Gospel. We find in our *biblía* a Jesús that tells us that whatever we do to the very least of these, we do unto him. Jesús knocks on the door wearing a disguise, coming in the form of the one who is hungry, thirsty, naked, the undocumented alien, the infirm and/or the incarcerated. The knock on the door is not an invitation to receive a free gift of eternal bliss; it is an invitation to pick up one's cross and follow Jesús in his call to serve and be in solidarity with the marginalized. By accepting the invitation of the one knocking on our door, Laodicea and today's churches find their own salvation. The very least among us, who is Jesús in the here and now, welcome their oppressors to join them in the economic model of Trinity bonded by love. The question that is left to consider is if the followers of Jesus will discover their salvation by joining disenfranchised Hispanics in implementing the politics of Jesús.

NOTES

FOREWORD

1. It should be noted that the author did all biblical translations (unless otherwise noted) from the original Greek or Hebrew.

2. Latin American liberationist thinkers have taught us to reflect on auto-biographical elements to avoid creating lifeless theoretical concepts. The methodological inclusion of one's story powerfully connects theory with reality, producing a "Feet-on-the-Ground-Theology" as per Clodovis Boff (1987). Of course, the danger of including one's story is falling into the fallacy of an exaggerated individualism, as in a conversion testimony. While it is not my intention to write my memoirs, I find it important to situate myself within the quest for a Jesus that resonates with the Hispanic community. I recognize the risk that some within the dominant culture will dismiss such an inclusion as unscholarly.

INTRODUCTION

1. Neoliberalism is a relatively new economic term coined in the late 1990s to describe the social and moral implications of the free-trade policies of global capitalism (liberalism) since the collapse of the Eastern Bloc ("neo," meaning new or recent). Neoliberalism signifies the increasing disparity in global wealth, creating a parasitic relationship where the poor of the world sacrifice

their humanity to serve the needs, wants, and desires of a privileged few. The few are provided with the right to determine what will be produced, who (nation-state or group of individuals) will produce it, under what conditions production will take place, what will be paid for the finished product, what the profits will amount to, and who will benefit from the profits. Neoliberalism justifies the transfer of most of the world's wealth, in the form of raw materials, natural resources, and cheap labor, through unfair trade agreements, to an economically privileged elite.

2. Lynnley Browning, "U.S. Income Gap Widening, Study Says," *New York Times*, September 25, 2003; Carmen DeNavas-Walt, Bernadette D. Proctor, and Jessica C. Smith, *Income, Poverty, and Health Insurance Coverage in the United States: 2010* (Washington, DC: U.S. Census Bureau, September, 2011): 5; and Binyamin Appelbaum, "For U.S. Families, Net Worth Falls to 1990s Levels," *New York Times*, June 12, 2012.

3. U.S. Census Bureau, Department of Commerce (http://www.census. gov/hhes/www/poverty/about/overview/).

4. Sanjeev Gupta, Michael Keen et al. *Fiscal Policy and Income Inequality* (Washington, DC: International Monetary Fund, 2014): 9.

5. Facundo Alvaredo, Anthony B. Atkinson, Thomas Piketty, and Emmanuel Saez, "The Top 1 Percent in International and Historical Perspective," *Journal of Economic Perspectives* Vol. 27, No. 3 (Summer 2013): 5.

6. "Inequality Highest for 20 Years—Save the Children," *British Broadcasting Corporation*, October 31, 2012.

7. "[A human is] more likely to prevail if [she or he] can interest their self-love in [his or her] favor, and show them that it is their own advantage to do for [her or him] what [she or he] requires of them. . . . It is not from the benevolence of the butcher, the brewer, or the baker that we expect our dinner, but from their regard to their own self-interest. We address ourselves not to their humanity but to their self-love, and never talk to them of our own necessities, but of their advantages" (Smith 1776:22).

8. Look not merely to your own self-interests, but also for the interests of others (Ph. 2:4); Do not seek your own good, but that of your other (1 Co. 10:24); For I seek not my own good but the good of others, so that they may be saved (1 Co. 10:33).

9. The usage of terms like *Euroamerican* and *Hispanic*, which at times is tied to terms like *oppressor* and *oppressed*, or *dominant culture* and *the marginalized* might mistakenly lead the reader to assume that neat dichotomies exist

between an ethnic group that benefits from oppressive structures (whites) and those who do not (people of color). The reality, obviously, is a bit more complex. There are many poor whites (especially post-2008 Great Recession) who are marginalized and many wealthy Latino/as who benefit from the current structures. The usage of terms like *oppressor* and *disenfranchised* are symbols that point to those within an elite class (predominately white) who benefit from the way society is structured at the expense of the many (predominately of color). Because these descriptors fall short as to who benefits and who does not from the present social structures, it is quite possible for Hispanics to assimilate to the dominant culture (derogatively known as coconuts); thus they will be included in the term *Euroamerican*, which signifies Western, European capitalist thought. These Hispanics are Euroamerican, not due to genetics, but from a decision to identify with and assimilate to the dominant culture. Likewise, there exist Euroamericans who, following Jesús' lead, found solidarity with the oppressed of the world, casting their lot with them. They will be referred to by the term *Hispanic*. Hence, identity is fluid, not captured by the rigidity of the ethnicity under which one is born.

10. Recognition exists that the Jesús of conquistadores and caudillos is just as oppressive and satanic as the Jesus of Empire. Nevertheless, the Jesús signified throughout this book is the Jesús of disenfranchised Latina/os, those relegated to the underside of U.S. power and privilege. The Jesús we are seeking is the Jesús of the marginalized Hispanic, not the economically privileged Latina/o.

11. This section is an expanded update based on an article I previously wrote (2013a: 131–42).

1. FOR UNTO YOU IS BORN THIS DAY A LIBERATOR

1. The normative practice of racial profiling on the New Jersey Turnpike became headline news in the late 1990s when then State Police Chief Carl A. Williams stated that it would be naive to believe that race was not an issue in crimes involving drugs and that traffickers of marijuana and cocaine are most likely to be members of minority groups. See Robert D. McFadden, "Whitman Dismisses State Police Chief for Race Remarks," *New York Times*, March 1, 1999. According to a 2009 study conducted by the Pew Center, Latino/as are

two to three times more likely than Euroamericans to experience unjustifiable stops, insulting language, excessive force, or corrupt activities when dealing with the police (López and Light 2009:1–4).

2. There is no question that the Hispanic body has a high probability of being confined to a physical prison. According to the U.S. Department of Justice, Latino male bodies have an imprisonment rate that is 2.7 times higher than Euroamericans (African American males are 6.7 times higher). Latina female bodies' imprisonment rate is 1.6 times higher (African American women are 2.8 times higher). These trends have remained constant throughout the first decade of the twenty-first century (Guerino, Harrison, and Sabol 2011: 1, 7, 26–29).

3. Those wishing to reconcile this contradiction in the biblical text have designed several theories to explain the differing genealogies. Among the most popular is that Matthew's genealogy follows the lineage of Joseph, while Luke's is that of Mary, the mother of Jesus.

4. This century-old custom, introduced to what today is known as the southwestern United States, is credited to an Augustinian missionary called Fray Diego de Soria, who expanded a traditional *novena*, a prayer said over nine successive days (Hughes 1996:12).

5. I, and several of my fellow companions, were detained for hours by the Border Patrol for providing medical attention and a place to rest in our camp to several immigrants who lost their way in the desert and were dying from exposure.

6. I use the term "inhuman" here, and in other places, realizing how problematic the usage of this word is. In describing atrocities that cause human anguish, suffering, misery, and death, the usage of "inhuman" signifies that these atrocities are not the norm, moving beyond what is considered humane. The term *inhuman*, in the long run, relieves us from responsibility for complicity with praxis that leads to such atrocities. But in fact, rather than stating that these atrocities are inhuman, we might be more accurate in stating that they are very human, for the normative conflict and struggle to impose the will to power over others has always left atrocities in its wake.

7. A pejorative term, "anchor baby" signifies a child born within the United States to undocumented immigrant parents. Because the child is an American citizen, as per the Fourteenth Amendment of the Constitution, it is presumed that the child will later facilitate the immigration and eventual citizenship of relatives.

8. Latin for "the Roman peace."

9. John L. O'Sullivan is credited with coining the term "Manifest Destiny" in his 1839 newspaper essay, "The Great Nation of Futurity." By synthesizing a romanticized ideal of nationalism with the economic ideology of unlimited progress, O'Sullivan ushered in a national myth that impacted American politics from 1840 to the early 1900s. Anglo-Saxons were believed to be destined by God to settle the entire North American continent; called to develop its natural resources and spreading liberty, democracy, and Protestantism. Besides justifying westward expansionism, Manifest Destiny's racial overtones influenced the conquest and removal of indigenous people from their lands. Today Manifest Destiny is understood to be the ideology behind U.S. colonialism and imperialism.

10. During the twentieth century, throughout the Caribbean basin, either U.S. military incursions (*italicized*) or covert/indirect operations (**bold**) occurred in the following countries so as to bring about regime change or protect the status quo: Cuba, *1906*, *1912*, *1917*, *1933*, **1960**, **1961**; Costa Rica, **1948**; Dominican Republic, **1904**, *1916–24*, **1930**, **1963**, *1965*; El Salvador, **1932**, **1944**, **1960**, **1980**, **1984**; Granada, *1983*; Guatemala, **1921**, **1954**, *1960*, **1963**, **1966**; Haiti, **1915**, *1994*; Honduras, *1905*, *1907*, **1911**, **1943**, **1980**; Mexico, *1905*, *1914*, *1917*; Nicaragua, **1909**, *1910*, *1912*, *1926*, **1934**, **1981**, **1983**, **1984**; Panama, *1908*, *1918*, *1925*, **1941**, **1981**, *1989*.

11. Gunboat diplomacy, like big stick diplomacy, refers to the U.S. pursuit of foreign policy objectives through the display of military might, specifically through the use of naval power in the Caribbean basin. This normative twentieth-century U.S. international policy constituted a direct threat of violence and warfare toward any nation that would choose to pursue its own sovereign destiny by refusing to agree to the terms imposed by the superior imperial force.

12. The difference in time for impurity depending on the gender of the child born is, to say the least, highly problematic, revealing another example of how sexism is inherent within the biblical text. A discussion can also ensue as to why the natural body function of a woman's menstrual cycle would be considered unclean to begin with, unless it is a further attempt to shame the woman's body.

13. Caiaphas, according to the Gospels, was the high priest who organized the plot to crucify Jesús.

2. CAN ANYTHING GOOD COME FROM NAZARETH

1. July 2, 2009—http://www.glennbeck.com/content/articles/article/198/28262/.

2. October 17, 2008—http://voices.washingtonpost.com/44/2008/10/palin-clarifies-her-pro-americ.html.

3. March 17, 2000—http://abcnews.go.com/GMA/story?id=125282.

4. It is not my attempt to fall into the trap of advocating some type of rural romanticism where a neat dichotomy is created between the "pure" Jews living in Jerusalem and the more "mixed" Jews living in Galilee. Surely, sociopolitical construction of societies existing during the time of Jesús was more complex, a complexity that remains beyond the scope of this book to explore in all its nuances. Suffice it to say that Jesús comes from the periphery of the center of Yahweh worship and the financial/political center of the region. This understanding where Jesús comes from, as witnessed in the comments he received that are recorded in the Gospels, is an understanding with which today's Latina/os can relate.

5. For the latest unemployment rates, updated monthly, see http://www.bls.gov/news.release/empsit.nr0.htm.

6. b. Sanhedrin, 94b.

7. Even if María conceived while still a virgin, the birthing process would have certainly ruptured her hymen. And while the state of the hymen fails to conclusively indicate virginity, conceiving other children does not. We are told that Jesús, son of María, had several brothers (not cousins), Santiago, Josés, Judas, and Simón, along with several unnamed sisters (Mk. 6:3). Even if we accept the miracle of the Immaculate Conception, María, due to conceiving other children, could not have remained a virgin. And yet, insisting on María's perpetual virginity only contributes to shaming women's sexuality as being less than the so-called purity of virginity, thus raising the questions: Is the veneration of María contingent on her sexuality? On abstaining from the pleasures of the body? Are these anti-body views more the influences of the flesh-spirit divide present in Neo-Platonic thought and the Stoic philosophical proclivity of devaluing the body—both trends that were prevalent during the creation of Christian theology that, nonetheless, remains foreign to the Hebrew Bible?

8. For example: Eccles. X:8; Ecl. Proph. III:10; Panar. LXXVIII:7, 5.

9. It should be noted that the usage of the word "thou" in the King James Bible reflects a time when Old English also had an informal pronoun for the word "you," that was also used when referring to God; however, with the passage of time, a reverse popular meaning was attached to "thou," as it began to signify a more formal, reverent understanding of "you."

10. A Spanish idiom for humanity's existentialism.

11. It should be noted that my usage of *Satan* neither confirms nor denies some actual being by said name. See my coauthored book *The Quest for the Historical Satan* (2011). *Satan* is used here to signify the ambiguity of moral certainties.

3. NOWHERE TO LAY HIS HEAD

1. One might ask how the employer achieved liquid capital. Marx, in chapter 24 of *Capital*, would argue that the accumulation of wealth was a direct result of the colonial venture. It should not be surprising that the British industrial revolution was launched in the same cities that the ships engaged in the slave trade sailed from. The industrial center exists due to the pillaging of the colonized margins.

2. Tami Luhby, "The Wealthy Are 288 Times Richer than You," *CNN Money*, September 11, 2012.

3. David Leonhardt, "The Imperial Chief Executive Is Suddenly in the Cross Hairs," *New York Times*, June 24, 2002.

4. Gretchen Morgenson, "Explaining (or Not) Why the Boss Is Paid So Much," *New York Times*, January 25, 2004.

5. Dietrich Bonhoeffer, who is usually associated with the term "cheap grace," learned this ethical principle from Clayton Powell while attending his church during his student days at Union Theological Seminary.

6. Dan McLean, "Immigration's Tancredo's Top Topic," *New Hampshire Sunday News*, June 12, 2005.

4. PICK UP YOUR DAILY CROSS AND FOLLOW ME

1. William Shakespeare, *The Tragedy of Macbeth*, Scene 5, 1606(?).

2. Christian Hymn "Onward Christian Soldiers"; text by Sabine Baring-Gould (1865), music by Arthur S. Sullivan (1871).

3. While most murders within the United States are intra-racial (the murderer and victim are of the same race), of the 1,283 prisoners executed from 1976 through 2012, 42 cases (of the 724 Whites executed) or 5.8 percent were of a White defendant killing a victim of color, while 332 (of the 559 people of color executed) or 57.6 percent were of defendants of color executed for killing White victims (Death Penalty Information Center 2012:1–2).

4. At the close of the twentieth century, the United States incarcerated more than two million of its citizens, of which 70 percent were people of color. The first ten years of the new millennium reveals that much has not changed. According to statisticians with the U.S. Department of Justice, 67.8 percent of the 2010 prison population was non-White. Black non-Hispanic males and Latino males had respectively an imprisonment rate of 6.7 and 2.7 times higher than Euroamerican men, while Black non-Hispanic and Latina females' imprisonment rate was respectively 2.8 and 1.6 times that of Euroamerican women. These trends have remained consistent throughout the first decade of the millennium (Guerino, Harrison, and Sabol 2011:1, 7, 26–29).

5. http://www.politicaltheology.com/blog/political-theology-or-social-ethics-under-the-law-m-t-davila/.

6. Santería is an Afro-Cuban religion, which many, not just Cubans, follow and practice. The *orishas* are quasi-deities to whom all of humanity belongs as children. These *orishas* watch over each human head. The *orisha* of my head (*orí*) is *Ellegúa*, known as the *trickster*. The trickster figure becomes an important component of the ethics that I propose. For a better understanding of *Santería*, see my award-winning book *Santería: The Beliefs and Rituals of a Growing Religion in America* (2004).

7. The *ethics para joder*, which I advocate, that arises from the underside of society is an ethics which: 1) disrupts the social order and equilibrium; 2) employs the cultural Hispanic symbol of the trickster in the formation of praxis; 3) looks toward the biblical text for narratives of figures who played the role of trickster; 4) moves beyond the Civil Rights' concept of civil disobedience toward the Sanctuary Movement's concept of civil initiative; and 5) roots itself in the pastoral, which is linked to a communal, not individualistic, ethos of the marginalized. Space prevents a thorough exploration of all of these components; nevertheless, a full elucidation of these components can be found in De La Torre, *Latina/o Social Ethics*, 2010: chapter 4.

8. Transubstantiation denotes the theological discussion that focuses on the conversion of the bread and wine's substance to that of the substance of Christ's body and blood, respectively.

9. John Lennon, "Imagine," Chappell Music, 1971.

BIBLIOGRAPHY

Acevedo-Garcia, Dolores, and Lisa M. Bates. "Latino Health Paradoxes: Empirical Evidence, Explanations, Future Research, and Implications." In *Latinas/os in the United States: Changing the Face of América*. Ed. by Havidán Rodríguez, Rogelio Sáenz, and Cecilia Menjívar. New York: Springer, 2008.

Althaus-Reid, Marcella. *Indecent Theology: Theological Perversions in Sex, Gender and Politics*. London: Routledge, 2000.

Anderson, Sarah, John Cavanagh, Chris Hartman, and Betsy Leondar-Wright. *Executive Excess 2001: Layoffs—Tax Rebates—The Gender Gap*. Washington, DC: Institute for Policy Studies and United for a Fair Economy, 2001.

Anderson, Sarah, Chuck Collins, Scott Klinger, and Sam Pizzigati. *Executive Excess 2011: The Massive CEO Rewards for Tax Dodging*. Washington, DC: Institute for Policy Studies, 2011.

Anzaldua, Gloria. *Borderlands—La Frontera: The New Mestiza*. San Francisco: Aunt Lute Book Company, 1987.

Aquino, María Pilar. *Our Cry for Life: Feminist Theology from Latin America*. Maryknoll, NY: Orbis Books, 1993.

Bellah, Robert N., et al. *Habits of the Heart: Individualism and Commitment in American Life*. New York: Harper and Row, 1985.

Benjamin, Walter. "Thesis on the Philosophy of History." In *Illuminations*. Ed. by Hannah Arendt. Trans. by Harry Zohn. New York: Schocken Books, 1968 [1940].

Bhabha, Homi K. *The Location of Culture*. New York: Routledge, 1994.

Boff, Clodovis. *Feet-on-the-Ground-Theology: A Brazilian Journey*. Trans. by Phillip Berryman. Maryknoll, NY: Orbis Books, 1987.

Boff, Leonardo. *Jesus Christ Liberator: A Critical Christology for Our Time*. Trans. by Patrick Hughes. Maryknoll, NY: Orbis Books, 1978.

Bourdieu, Pierre. *Language and Symbolic Power*. Ed. by John B. Thompson. Trans. by Gino Raymond and Matthew Adamson. Cambridge, MA: Polity Press, 1991.

Burge, Gary M., Lynn H. Cohick, and Gene l. Green. *The New Testament in Antiquity: A Survey of the New Testament within Its Cultural Context*. Grand Rapids, MI: Zondervan, 2009.

Center for Labor Studies, *Left Behind in America: The Nation's Dropout Crises*. Boston: Department of Economics of Northeastern University, 2009.

Chaney, Bradford, and Laurie Lewis. *Public School Principles Report on Their School Facilities: Fall 2005*. Washington, DC: National Center for Educational Statistics—U.S. Department of Education, 2007.

Clingan, Ralph Garlin. *Against Cheap Grace in a World Come of Age: A Study in the Hermeneutics of Adam Clayton Powell, 1865–1953, in His Intellectual Context*. New York: Peter Lang, 2002.

Cone, James H. *A Black Theology of Liberation*. Maryknoll, NY: Orbis Books, 2010 [1970].

Costas, Orlando. *Liberating News*. Grand Rapids, MI: Eerdmans Press, 1989.

Death Penalty Information Center. *National Statistics on the Death Penalty and Race*. Washington, DC: Death Penalty Information Center, April, 2012.

De La Torre, Miguel A. *Reading the Bible from the Margins*. Maryknoll, NY: Orbis Books, 2002.

———. *Santería: The Beliefs and Rituals of a Growing Religion in America*. Grand Rapids, MI: Wm. B. Eerdmans Publishing, 2004.

———. *Trails of Hope and Terror: Testimonies on Immigration*. Maryknoll, NY: Orbis Books, 2009a.

———. "Constructing a Cuban-Centric Christ." In *Jesus in the Hispanic Community: Images of Christ from Theology to Popular Religion*. Ed. by Harold J. Recinos and Hugo Magallanes. Louisville: Westminster John Knox Press, 2009b.

———. *Latina/o Social Ethics: Moving Beyond Eurocentric Moral Thinking*. Waco, TX: Baylor University Press, 2010.

———. "A Thick Jesús." *Perspectives in Religious Studies*, Vol. 40, No. 2 (Summer, 2013a): 131–42.

———. "Doing Latina/o Ethics from the Margins of Empire: Liberating the Colonized Mind." *Journal of the Society of Christian Ethics*, Vol. 33, No. 1 (2013b): 3–20.

———. *Doing Christian Ethics from the Margins*, 2nd edition. Maryknoll, NY: Orbis Books, 2014.

De La Torre, Miguel A. and Albert Hernández. *The Quest for the Historical Satan*. Minneapolis: Fortress Press, 2011.

DeNavas-Walt, Carmen, Bernadette D. Proctor, and Jessica C. Smith. *Income, Poverty, and Health Insurance Coverage in the United States: 2010*. Washington, DC: U.S. Census Bureau, 2011.

de Saussure, Ferdinand. *Course in General Linguistics*. Ed. by Charles Bally and Albert Sechehaye. Trans. by Wade Baskin. New York: Philosophical Library, 1959.

de Unamuno, Miguel. "Arbitrary Reflections upon Europeanization." *Essays and Soliloquies*. Trans. by John Ernest Crawford Flitch. New York: Alfred A. Knopf, 1925.

———. "Unamuno y Ortega y Gasset: dialogo entre dos españoles." *Cuadernos de la Cátedra Miguel De Unamuno*. Ed. by Emilio Salcedo. Salamanca, 1956.

———. *La agonía del cristianismo, Obras Completas, Vol VII*. Ed. by Manuel García Blanco. Madrid: Escelicer, 1967.

———, *El Cristo español. Obras Completas, Vol II*. Ed. by Manuel García Blanco. Madrid: Escelicer, 1968a.

———. *Sobre la europeización. Obras Completas, Vol III*. Ed. by Manuel García Blanco. Madrid: Escelicer, 1968b.

Díaz, Miguel H. "God." *Hispanic American Religious Cultures*, Vol. 2. Ed. by Miguel A. De La Torre. Santa Barbara, CA: ABC-CLIO, 2009.

Dussel, Enrique. *Philosophy of Liberation*. Trans. by Aquilina Martinez and Christine Mor-kovsky. Maryknoll: Orbis Books, 1990.

———. "Eurocentrism and Modernity: Introduction to the Frankfurt Lectures." *Boundary 2* Vol. 20, No. 3 (1993): 65–76.

Ebert, Franz Christian, Raymond Torres, and Konstantinos Papadakis. *Executive Compensation: Trends and Policy Issues*. Geneva: International Institute for Labor Studies, 2008.

Elizondo, Virgilio. *Galilean Journey: The Mexican-American Promise*. Maryknoll, NY: Orbis Books, 1983.

Espey, Jessica, Alison Holder, Nuria Molina, and Alex Cobham. *Born Equal: How Reducing Inequality Can Give Our Children a Better Future*. London: Save the Children, 2012.

Ferm, Deanne William. *Third World Liberation Theologies: An Introductory Survey*. Maryknoll, NY: Orbis Books, 1986.

Fernández, Eduardo C. "Liturgy and Worship." *Hispanic American Religious Cultures*, Vol. 2. Ed. by Miguel A. De La Torre. Santa Barbara, CA: ABC-CLIO, 2009.

Fletcher, Joseph. *Situation Ethics: The New Morality*. Louisville: Westminster John Knox Press, 1966.

Food and Agriculture Organization (FAO) of the United Nations. *The State of Food Insecurity in the World, 2012*. Rome, Italy: Food and Agriculture Organization of the United Nations, 2012.

Foucault, Michel. *Madness and Civilization: A History of Insanity in the Age of Reason*. Trans. by Richard Howard. New York: Vintage Books, 1965.

———. *The History of Sexuality*, Vol 1. Trans. by Robert Hurley. New York: Vintage Books, 1978.

———. *The Foucault Reader*. Ed. by Paul Rabinow. New York: Pantheon Books, 1984.

———. *Discipline and Punish: The Birth of the Prison*. Trans. by Alan Sheridan. New York: Vintage Books, 1995.

Frankfurter, David. *Evil Incarnate: Rumors of Demonic Conspiracy and Ritual Abuse in History*. Princeton: Princeton University Press, 2006.

Gadotti, Moacir. *Reading Paulo Freire: His Life and Works*. Trans. by John Milton. New York: State University of New York, 1994.

García, Sixto. "United States Hispanic and Mainstream Trinitarian Theologies." *Frontiers of Hispanic Theology in the United States*. Ed. by Allan Figueroa Deck. Maryknoll, NY: Orbis Books, 1992.

Garoogian, David. *The Hispanic Databook*, 3rd edition. Amenia, NY: Grey House Publishing, 2012.

Goizueta, Roberto S. *Caminemos con jesús: Toward a Hispanic/Latino Theology of Accompaniment*. Maryknoll, NY: Orbis Books, 1995.

———. "A Matter of Life and Death: Theological Anthropology Between Calvary and Galilee." *CTSA Proceedings* Vol. 53 (1998): 1–20.

González, Justo L. *Mañana: Christian Theology from a Hispanic Perspective*. Nashville: Abingdon Press, 1990.

———. *Santa Biblia: The Bible through Hispanic Eyes*. Nashville: Abingdon Press, 1996.

Gray, Rockwell. *The Imperative of Modernity: An Intellectual Biography of José Ortega y Gasset*. Berkeley: University of California Press, 1989.

Guardiola-Sáenz, Leticia. "Border-Crossing and Its Redemptive Power in John 7:53–8:11: A Cultural Reading of Jesus and the *Accused*." In *John and Postcolonialism: Travel, Space, and Power*. Ed. by Musa W. Dube and Jeffrey L. Staley. Sheffield, UK: Sheffield Academic Press, 2002a.

————."Reading from Ourselves: Identity and Hermeneutics among Mexican-American Feminists." In *A Reader in Latina Feminist Theology: Religion and Justice*. Ed. by María Pilar Aquino, Daisy L. Machado, and Jeanette Rodríguez. Austin, TX: University of Texas Press, 2002b.

Guerino, Paul, Paige M. Harrison, and William J. Sabol. *Prisoners in 2010*. Washington, DC: U.S. Department of Justice, Bureau of Justice Statistics, December 2011.

Hauerwas, Stanley. "The Gesture of a Truthful Story." *Theology Today*, Vol. 42, No. 2 (July 1985): 181–89.

————. *After Christendom? How the Church Is to Behave if Freedom, Justice, and a Christian Nation Are Bad Ideas*. Nashville: Abingdon Press, 1991.

————. *Wilderness Wanderings: Probing Twentieth-Century Theology and Philosophy*. Boulder, CO: Westview Press, 1997.

Hegel, G. W. F. *Sämtliche Werke*. Ed. by J. Hoffmeister. Hamburg: F. Meiner, 1955.

————. *Encyklopädie der philosophischen Wissenschaften: im Grundrisse*. Ed. by F. Nicolin and O. Pöggler. Hamburg: F. Meiner, 1969.

————. *Werke*, Vol 12. Frankfurt: Suhrkamp, 1970.

Hinkelammert, Franz J. *Cultura de la Esperanza y Sociedad sin Exclusión*. San José, Costa Rica: Departamento Ecuménico de Investigaciones, 1995.

————. "Liberation Theology in the Economic and Social Context of Latin America." In *Liberation Theologies, Postmodernity, and the Americas*. Ed. by David Batstone, Eduardo Mendieta, Lois Ann Lorentzen, and Dwight N. Hopkins. London: Routledge, 1997.

Hochschild, Adam. *Bury the Chains: The British Struggle to Abolish Slavery*. London: Pan Books, 2010.

Hughes, Ellen. *Christmas in the American Southwest*. Chicago: World Book, 1996.

Isasi-Díaz, Ada María. "Identificate con Nosotras: A Mujerista Christological Understanding." In *Jesus in the Hispanic Community: Images of Christ from Theology to Popular Religion*. Ed. by Harold J. Recinos and Hugo Magallanes. Louisville: Westminster John Knox Press, 2009.

————. *En la Lucha/In the Struggle: Elaborating a Mujerista Theology*. Minneapols: Fortress Press, 1993.

Jeremias, Joachim. *Jerusalem in the Time of Jesus: An Investigation into Economic and Social Conditions during the New Testament Period*. Philadelphia: Fortress Press, 1969.

Kessel, Edward L. "A Proposed Biological Interpretation of the Virgin Birth." *Journal of the American Scientific Affiliation* (September, 1983): 129–36.

King, Martin Luther, Jr. *A Testament of Hope: The Essential Writings and Speeches of Martin Luther King*. New York: HaperCollins, 1986.

Klor de Alva, J. Jorge. "Spiritual Conflict and Accommodation in New Spain: Toward a Typology of Aztec Response to Christianity." In *The Inca and Aztec States, 1400–1800: Anthropology and History*. Ed. by George A. Collier, I. Rosaldo Renato and D. Wirth John. New York: Academic Press, 1982.

López, Mark Hugo, and Michael Light. *A Rising Share: Hispanics and Federal Crime*. Washington, DC: Pew Research Center, February 2009.

Luévano, Rafael. "Comunidad." In *Hispanic American Religious Cultures*, Vol. 1. Ed. by Miguel A. De La Torre. Santa Barbara, CA: ABC-CLIO, 2009.

MacMullen, Ramsay. *Roman Social Relations: 50 B.C. to A.D. 284*. New Haven, CT: Yale University Press, 1974.

Magallanes, Hugo. "'Who Do You Say I Am,' Jesús or Jesse?: A Reflection on Christology and Christian Identity." In *Jesus in the Hispanic Community: Images of Christ from*

Theology to Popular Religion. Ed. by Harold J. Recinos and Hugo Magallanes. Louisville: Westminster John Knox Press, 2009.

Maldonado Pérez, Zaida. "Exploring Latino/a Titles for Christ." *Jesus in the Hispanic Community: Images of Christ from Theology to Popular Religion*. Ed. by Harold J. Recinos and Hugo Magallanes. Louisville: Westminster John Knox Press, 2009.

Martell-Otero, Loida I. "Encuentro con el Jesús Sato." In *Jesus in the Hispanic Community: Images of Christ from Theology to Popular Religion*. Ed. by Harold J. Recinos and Hugo Magallanes. Louisville: Westminster John Knox Press, 2009.

McMahon, Shawn, Yunju Nam, and Yung Soo Lee. *The Basic Economic Security Tables for the United States*. Washington, DC: Wider Opportunities for Women, 2011.

Moody, Dwight Lyman. *The Gospel Awaking*. Chicago: Fairbanks and Palmer Publishing, 1885 [1877].

Orfield, Gary. *Reviving the Goal of an Integrated Society: A 21st Century Challenge*. Los Angeles: The Regents of the University of California, 2009.

Ortega y Gasset, José. *Ensimismamiento y alteracíon. Meditación de la técnica*. Buenos Aires: Espasa-Calpe, 1939.

———. *Esquema de las crisis, y otros ensayos*. Madrid: Revista de Occisente, 1942.

Ortiz, Fernando. "La cubanidad y los negros." *Estudio Afrocubanos* 3 (1939): 3–15.

———. *Los factores humanos de la cubanidad*. La Habana: *Revista Bimestre Cubana*, XLV, 1940.

Pedraja, Luis G. *Jesus Is My Uncle: Christology from a Hispanic Perspective*. Nashville: Abingdon Press, 1999.

———. "Trinity." In *Handbook of U.S. Theologies of Liberation*. Ed. by Miguel A. De La Torre. St. Louis: Chalice Press, 2004.

Pell, Edward Leigh. *Dwight L. Moody: His Life, His Work, His Words*. New York: Cornell University Library, 1900.

Pérez Firmat, Gustavo. *Life on the Hyphen: The Cuban-American Way*. Austin: University of Texas Press, 1995.

Pineda, Ana María. "Hospitality." In *Practicing Our Faith: A Way of Life for a Searching People*. Ed. by Dorothy C. Bass. San Francisco: Jossey-Bass, 1997.

Recinos, Harold J. *Who Comes in the Name of the Lord?: Jesus at the Margins*. Nashville: Abingdon Press, 1997.

Rosado, Caleb. "The Church, the City, and the Compassionate Christ." In *Voces: Voices from the Hispanic Church*. Ed. by Justo L. González. Nashville: Abingdon Press, 1992.

Said, Edward W. *Culture and Imperialism*. New York: Vintage Books, 1994.

Sider, Ronald J. *Just Generosity: A New Vision for Overcoming Poverty in America*. Grand Rapids, MI: Baker Books, 1999.

Singley, Catherine. *Fractures in the Foundation: The Latino Worker's Experience in an Era of Declining Job Quality*. Washington, DC: The National Council of La Raza, 2009.

Smith, Adam. *The Wealth of Nations*. Oxford, UK: Bantam Classics, 2003 (1776).

Tinker, Tink. "American Indian Traditions." In *Handbook of U.S. Theologies of Liberation*. Ed. by Miguel A. De La Torre. St. Louis: Chalice Press, 2004.

Turner, Margery Austin, et al. *Housing Discrimination against Racial and Ethnic Minorities, 2012*. Washington DC: U.S. Department of Housing and Urban Development, 2013.

United Nations Development Programme (UNDP). *The Real Wealth of Nations: Pathways to Human Development*. New York: Palgrave Macmillan, 2010.

United States Census Bureau. "Ethnicity and Ancestry Statistics Branch Population Division." *U.S. Hispanic Population: 2006-Population Size and Composition*. Washington, DC: U.S. Census Bureau, 2006.

United States Department of Commerce, Economics and Statistics Administration. *The American Community—Hispanics: 2004-American Community Survey Reports*. Washington, DC: U.S. Census Bureau, 2007.

Valentín, Benjamín. "Who Do We Say He Was and Is?" In *In Our Own Voices: Latino/a Renditions of Theology*. Ed. by Benjamín Valentín. Maryknoll, NY: Orbis Books, 2010.

Verhey, Allen. *Remembering Jesus: Christian Community, Scripture, and the Moral Life*. Grand Rapids, MI: W. B. Eerdmans, 2002.

Wessler, Seth. *Race and Recession*. New York: Applied Research Center, 2009.

Wiener, Ross, and Eli Pristoop. "How States Shortchange the Districts That Need the Most Help," *The Funding Gaps, 2006*. Washington, DC: The Education Trust, 2006.

INDEX

ABOUT THE AUTHOR

Miguel A. De La Torre is professor of Social Ethics and Latino/a Studies at the Iliff School of Theology. He is author or editor of numerous books, including *Santeria: The Beliefs and Rituals of a Growing Religion in America* (ForeWord Magazine Book of the Year finalist), *Hispanic American Religious Cultures* (CHOICE Outstanding Academic Award), and *Reading the Bible from the Margins* (Catholic Press Association First Place for Educational Books). He has produced or been featured in a number of documentaries, including *Trails of Hope and Terror* based on his book by the same name. He has been interviewed in media, ranging from CNN and Al-Jazeera America to *Time* and *The Denver Post*. Nationally known for his work on social ethics, he has served as the president of the Society of Christian Ethics, on the editorial board of the *Journal of the American Academy of Religion*, and executive officer of the Society of Race, Ethnicity, and Religion.

CPSIA information can be obtained at www.ICGtesting.com
Printed in the USA
BVOW02s1533010615

402461BV00002B/4/P

9 781442 250369